Fat and Queer

of related interest

Trans Love
An Anthology of Transgender and Non-Binary Voices
Edited by Freiya Benson
ISBN 978 1 78592 432 3
eISBN 978 1 78450 804 3

Queer Sex
A Trans and Non-Binary Guide to Intimacy,
Pleasure and Relationships
Juno Roche
ISBN 978 1 78592 406 4
eISBN 978 1 78450 770 1

Non-Binary Lives
An Anthology of Intersecting Identities
Edited by Jos Twist, Ben Vincent, Meg-John Barker and Kat Gupta
ISBN 978 1 78775 339 6
eISBN 978 1 78775 340 2

Trans Power
Own Your Gender
Juno Roche
ISBN 978 1 78775 019 7
eISBN 978 1 78775 020 3

Fat and Queer

An Anthology of
Queer and Trans Bodies and Lives

Edited by
Bruce Owens Grimm
Miguel M. Morales
Tiff Joshua TJ Ferentini

Jessica Kingsley Publishers
London and Philadelphia

First published in Great Britain in 2021 by Jessica Kingsley Publishers
An Hachette Company

1

Copyright © Jessica Kingsley Publishers 2021
Foreword copyright © Roy G. Guzmán 2021

"Dropping Fictions and Gaining Visibility" by Bruce Owens
Grimm originally published by *The Rumpus*.
"The Trash Heap Has Spoken" by Carmen Maria Machado originally published by *Guernica*.
"Lessons Learned and Unlearned" by Edward Kelsey Moore
originally published by Minnesota Public Radio.
"The Gender Nonconformity of My Fatness" by Caleb Luna
originally published by *The Body Is Not An Apology*.
"About My Breasts, Since You Asked" by Sherre Vernon originally
published by *The South Broadway Ghost Society*.
"You're Too Fat to be Androgynous" by Nicole Oquendo originally published by *Nat. Brut*.

Front cover image source: iStockphoto®

A CIP catalogue record for this title is available from the
British Library and the Library of Congress

ISBN 978 1 78775 506 2
eISBN 978 1 78775 507 9

Printed and bound in the United States by West Publishing Corp

Jessica Kingsley Publishers' policy is to use papers that are natural, renewable and recyclable
products and made from wood grown in sustainable forests. The logging and manufacturing
processes are expected to conform to the environmental regulations of the country of origin.

Jessica Kingsley Publishers
Carmelite House
50 Victoria Embankment
London EC4Y 0DZ
www.jkp.com

This book is dedicated to the fat and queer
and fat and trans community, to our elders whose work led us to this
moment, and to our youth who inspire us to keep moving forward.

Contents

Foreword

Roy G. Guzmán

I was raised by two proud fat women, two sisters who were the constant recipients of double entendres such as "Your face is beautiful, but your body makes you look older," or "You're too pretty to be fat," or (the inverse, as a conundrum) "If you're that fat, how can you also attract men?" Back in Honduras, where my mother and aunt were raised, no one could protect them from verbal attacks save my grandfather, who focused instead on their beauty, their intelligence, and their self-reliance.

An early memory I have (I must have been six or seven) involves a phone call to our home. At the time—and that is still the case for many Hondurans—a household with a phone was a rarity. The phone rang and its ring became an occasion for children to run and answer it. Luckily for me, before the birth of my aunt's son, I was the only child in my household. I picked up the phone. It was a call for my aunt. She took the phone from me and sat down. She was in the middle of what seemed like a professional conversation when my mother pulled the curtain that separated the living room from one of our two bedrooms.

She stood there, with a towel rolled from her chest down, like an actor about to take the stage. I was shocked. My aunt covered her smile with her hand, holding back laughter. My mother proceeded to kneel, then started to catwalk towards my aunt, exaggerating her movements, provoking more laughter. Her arms jiggled. Her hips swung left and right. At this point, my aunt had to tell the person on the phone that an emergency had come up, and dropped the handset on the base. Her laughter became mixed with tears. I joined her, loudly, recklessly, as my mom struck more poses, her fat body the portal of strong familial bonds.

Years later, I'm obese, according to my doctor's reading of her scale. Newer stretch marks have blossomed on my sides and around my belly since my last doctor's appointment. She says that's a sign I must do something about my weight. My mother, whose legs are gripped by varicose veins, echoes this sentiment. When her health was in jeopardy, she was left with no other choice but to opt for a gastric sleeve. She worries about me. But my weight, as she has recently found out, is intimately connected to my queerness, my rebellious spirit, my adulthood, my traumas, and my freedom.

Fat queer people experience multidimensional forms of discrimination, not to mention those who identify as BIPOC (black, indigenous, and people of color). *Fat and Queer: An Anthology of Queer and Trans Bodies and Lives* is a testament to the feeling "guilty for existing in a world that didn't want me," to "exist[ing] as a contradiction," to the "never manag[ing] to starve myself into heterosexuality." The contributors of this anthology explore two historical forms of othering—fatness and queerness—but they complicate each category, adding energy to their relationship, and offering readers ways to (re) claim their bodies and, arguably, their queer sanities. "I am not fat solely," one contributor remarks, and that sentiment, besides summoning Zaddy Whitman, is one that pulsates throughout this collection. Fatness is measured against transness, gender expectations are measured against sexual violence, binders are measured against one's truth, and a fat nude body is measured against surveilled desires. These are bodies "too big / to be held /at once." These are radical bodies and radical odes to those radical bodies. They can no longer stay in the closet. Instead, they are nothing short of acts of witness for how the human body continues to be an, if not the, ultimate threshold between the now and what the world can be.

Introductions

Bruce Owens Grimm

I came out as fat five years ago. I enjoy being fat. I actively work to be fat, to be fatter. Why? I have no idea. Yet, thanks to diet culture and its intense focus on thinness, I kept this desire a secret for most of my life. I'm no stranger to secrets. I came out as gay after being in a heterosexual marriage for nine years. The closet door would peek open from time to time, but I never stepped out of it. Until I did.

After my divorce, after coming out as gay, many people asked me: how did you know you were gay? My answer: I just knew. This is true. There is no burden of proof necessary to confirm queerness. However, I came out of the queer closet only to find myself in the fat closet. It is impossible to separate my queerness from my fatness. I'm attracted, when I'm attracted, to fat men. At first, I thought I only wanted to look like them, not necessarily be with them. Turned out it was both. Turns out there is a whole community of gay men who also want to be fat—gainers. However, the insidiousness of fatphobia means that the gaining community maintains a strict policy of secrecy.

I understand. There's the terror that friends or family are going to find out that you enjoy your fat body. The worst. The shame.

Secrecy wears me out.

I grew tired of pretending that I had gained 100 pounds by accident rather than desire. So, five years ago, as my fingers shook, I sent an email to Arielle Greenberg pitching the idea of an essay about gaining for her (K)ink series at *The Rumpus*. It frightened me to write the essay, but her warmth, kindness, and guidance made it possible. This makes it sound easy. It wasn't. How would readers, the writing community, my friends react to me coming out as gainer? Would I be outcast? My career over? No and no.

This book only exists because Arielle and *The Rumpus* gave my gaining essay, "Dropping Fictions and Gaining Visibility," space. This book exists because readers connected with it. We need more fat and queer voices. The voices featured here celebrate the intersection of fatness and queerness. This is not a book focused only on gaining, although those voices are represented. The fat and queer experience is as varied as any other.

That's one reason why I'm so glad Miguel M. Morales and Tiff Joshua TJ Ferentini agreed to join me on the journey of editing this book. A multitude of voices needed to be represented on both sides of the page. Most importantly, for me, they brought a sense of family to the project. As RuPaul said to Roxxxy Andrews on season five of *RuPaul's Drag Race*, we as queer people get to choose our family. This is certainly true for me. I'm very happy that Miguel and Tiff are part of my chosen family. That sense of family now extends to the writers presented here. We all struggle. But when we stand together, we are strong. We're here. We're queer. We're fat.

Miguel M. Morales

When Bruce Owens Grimm invited me to co-edit this anthology, when we allowed ourselves to dream of what it could be, I knew I wanted to create a space where our contributors and readers could stand equally in their fatness and their queerness/trans experience. There are few places, in the real world or in the literary world, where we can occupy those spaces fully.

I especially wanted to hold space within this anthology for fat and queer and fat and trans BIPOC to stand in their shades of melanin, their ethnicities, their immigration status, and their other intersectional identities. We're often forced to leave at least one of our identities at the door for the comfort of others or for the "good of the cause."

I allowed myself to dream that a poem or a piece of prose could provide respite for fat and queer and fat and trans BIPOC. They can experience a moment to feel fully present in these pages, to breathe freely, to exist unrestrained in their scarred, stretched, and shaded skin.

It is unfortunate that when we began pulling this anthology together we found ourselves confronting a global pandemic and the racist and systematic killing of black and brown people. We mourn the loss and injuries of all those affected. We also know that contributing to an anthology was not at the top of the list for many of our fat and queer and fat and trans community members as they battled these two deadly infections.

Yet even with those two circumstances present, could there be more marginalized voices in this text? Absolutely. We hope all publication editors keep this in mind while they accept submissions, as they solicit work, as they bring on board other decision-making voices. Make room. Pull up.

We also read submissions from strong fat and queer and fat and trans voices that we wanted to include in these pages but couldn't. For this anthology to celebrate fat and queer and fat and trans bodies and lives, we needed writers to express fatness and queerness/trans experience in these pages. Our extended submission process introduced us to writers we will follow with eagerness as they further develop their craft, as they explore their relationship to their fat and queer/trans bodies. They will help shape this emerging genre.

We also learned it wasn't enough to create a space for fat and queer and fat and trans voices, we had to foster them. We met with writers in person and, when the pandemic hit, we met online. We held virtual write in sessions. We offered writing prompts. We shared example pieces. We shared snacks. We fully engaged our social media to talk with and signal boost other fat and queer and fat and trans voices. We quickly learned our editing process couldn't be just about structure or voice. We knew in some cases we were working with people who'd never written about their fatness. There was insecurity and doubt, there were even some tears, but there was also bravery, generosity, and freedom. I celebrate every piece in this anthology, every writer who submitted work, whether it found a home in these pages or will find it elsewhere.

When Tiff joined Bruce and me as an editor, I also allowed

myself to expand my dream for this anthology—that it would inspire more people to tell their fat and queer and fat and trans stories because it certainly had done that for us. Thank you for this opportunity and for this gift you now hold.

Tiff Joshua TJ Ferentini

The Venn diagram of folks who are fat and folks who are queer doesn't always intersect, but one thing the two groups have in common is the notion of being *the other*. If you are fat, you are always told to conform to the normal: the thin, the "healthy." Your body is on display for all to see, whether they have your consent or not; your own skin "outing you."

The same can be said for being queer: when queer people come out, they might be asked, when did they realize they were different, when did they realize they weren't straight? (After all, after calling infant sons "ladies' men" and telling young fathers that they'll have to watch out for the boys when their little girls grow older, how could this happen?!)

For those whose queerness is defined only by their sexuality, the struggle may be a more internal one; but for those existing along the gender nonbinary or transgender spectrum, the same sentiment of feeling as if you are on display for the rest of the world to see can also apply. Each crack in your voice, change in your mannerisms, cut of your hair, and change of your clothes is put under a microscope. Because, whether you want to be or not, you're being put into a box, your gender identity and expression on display for all to see—or *choose not* to see.

The sentiment is all the stronger for folks who are both fat *and* queer.

It's as if being thin, heterosexual, and cisgender is the norm, and if we stray away from that, there must be a reason *why*: that we're not eating healthy enough, exercising enough; that we're too young or simply just confused.

There's no way we can love ourselves the way we are.

We surely must wish that we were thinner, straighter.

Wish that we were not the other...

...is this what the world *wants* us to think, the narrative the world *wants* us to tell: of suffering, of sadness, of self-hate.

But that isn't the case at all.

The stories, poems, and essays in this anthology celebrate fat, queer, and trans bodies and lives like never before. They are stories that capture every adversity, every question, every struggle, ultimately morphing into narratives of acceptance, recognition, love, and pride. This anthology creates the space for these stories to be told—a space that wouldn't exist without these voices being brave enough to tell their own stories.

As a person who struggled with not only their fatness, but their identity, from a young age, I wish I had come across these kinds of stories when I couldn't find the words within myself, at a time when I didn't realize what I needed was to find stories of longing, of love, and acceptance: about fatness, about queerness, about transness.

And celebrating, rather than living in shame of, that.

I cannot thank Bruce and Miguel enough for inviting me to join them along this journey as part of the *Fat and Queer* editorial team and for bringing this collection to life, and for the amazing writers I had the opportunity and honor of discovering, reading, and working alongside with throughout the editorial process. Without them confronting their raw, real, and sometimes painful truth, this anthology would not exist—not only in the here and now, but for future generations of fat, queer voices.

The stories, essays, and poetry collected in the following pages come in all different shapes and sizes, but they are all connected by the same common thread: that they are unapologetically, shamelessly, uniquely themselves, and are unafraid to proudly take up the space to say:

We do love ourselves the way we are—in our fatness, our queerness, and our trans glory.

We don't wish to be thinner; or if we do, it's on our own terms; for ourselves.

We are the other, and we are goddamn proud of it.

Incantation
"a prayer for us"

Provvidenza Catalano

bless our fat bodies, they were the first ones to give us comfort

bless our queerness for showing us that love doesn't need to fit within culture's deceitful machination

bless our transness and its defiance giving no definition to the shapes of our bodies, but rather

asking the question of what do we want and need

bless us and the legend that we will become leaving them with the question

did they really exist?

"Fat Queer Freaks"

Hannah Propp

After only a few minutes of me nervously fidgeting by myself, Volare enters the cafe. We arranged to arrive a few minutes early. Her full figure seems to defy gravity, and she saunters through the cafe on impossible shoes (she never cared for sensible footwear). Today, it's black velour ankle boots with a gold stiletto heel and pointed toe.

"Cielo!" She says my name in her specific way, with her specific smile. There's a lengthening of the *e*, a deepening of her left dimple, that feels reserved for me and makes me feel 14 again.

The sway in her wide hips and round belly carries her gracefully around the spindly tables. Her long, black dress has a hem that curves up to a point in the middle of her thick, dimpled thigh. *Fat Femme*, the baroque script tattooed there reads. She smiles at me through her sheet of brown, wavy, shoulder-length hair. She radiates fullness and confidence, as if she's in on a secret that the rest of the world can only guess at.

My jeans, flannel, and band t-shirt suddenly seem ridiculous, as I completely forget the hours I spent deliberating about whether to wear a button-down and tie just this morning. I feel smaller in her presence, but in a good way. I rarely get to feel small, after years of being told I'm too big.

We settle in at the table, joking about the spindly chairs under our fat asses. With her, it feels like an honor to share this joke. Volare makes being fat feel like something superior.

We order cappuccinos, and immediately begin to strategize.

"I think she told, that's the thing," Volare says. "What other reason could she possibly have to ask to meet us after all these years?"

"Or maybe she just wants to catch up, like she said," I offer.

"Cielo, stop being so naive. You remember how Terre was; I don't think some questionable loyalty to us would stop her from telling."

"You really think she'd do that?" I ask, doubting the thing that I've been assuring myself of for months since Terre messaged us. Before then, we'd both lost touch with Terre over the ten years since we all graduated high school together.

"Yes," Volare states, without hesitation.

I look at her eyes; one a quiet, deep green, and one an impossible, fluorescent turquoise. My thoughts race back to 14 years ago on July 22, when everything changed for me and Volare, and when Terre left herself behind.

❀ ❀ ❀

We were the kind of kids in high school who were cool enough to know where we could get some weed, but not cool enough that we had friends—besides each other—to smoke it with.

It was a Friday night. We had got the aforementioned drugs, and Volare had stolen exactly one six-pack of wine coolers from her gas station job that she had for, perhaps, a total of three weeks that summer. The brevity of her employment likely had everything to do with the stolen wine coolers, in retrospect.

We were looking for somewhere remote enough to enjoy our spoils, but close enough to a bathroom that we weren't actually camping. Volare decided that we should go to the construction site of her father and stepmom's new house. She said there would be a porta-john there for us to use, and maybe even a cooler of beer left by the construction guys.

Looking back, it was clear that Volare and I had a comfort with each other, an ease and camaraderie, to which Terre could only ever be adjacent. Sometimes, it felt sad that there was distance between us. In other moments, I felt resentful of her, and I often suspected this was mutual. Part of that was her burning desire to be cool. We had it, too, of course: we were all 14. Hers, however, felt so much more apparent, and palpable, and intrusive. It felt that much more difficult to ignore our discomfort with ourselves when Terre was around. She was skinny, and we were not, and maybe popularity just felt slightly more achievable for her than it ever would be for us because we were fat. She wasn't taunted daily in the halls of our high school with catcalls of "lardass," or known mostly by nicknames like "thunder thighs" the way we were.

Maybe she resented us for holding her back: we were her excess baggage, so to speak.

We got there, set up our sleeping bags, and cracked open our first round of the sickly sweet wine coolers. As we began to pass around my older brother's blown-glass bowl, Terre heaved a great, unsettled sigh.

"What?" I asked Terre with more hostility than was necessary.

"It's just...we could have gone to Mark Johnson's party tonight. Catie Peters asked me on Tuesday if I was going," Terre replied, resting her face on her hand so that it stretched into a mask of misery.

Volare and I looked at each other. Mark Johnson was one of our frontline tormentors. At school, it felt like he was everywhere—always just around the corner, prepared with vicious insults, machete words to cut us down to his preferred size.

"It sounds like *you* could have gone, Terre. *We* weren't invited," Volare said, carefully. Her words rendered Terre silent, though no less discontented.

After about an hour, Volare had to use the bathroom. Due to the fact that we were ride-or-die best friends, I immediately said I'd venture out with her in search of the promised porta-john. We had bonded instantly the previous year over our diagnoses of panic disorder and our shared realities of being fat and mentally ill in a small New England town. Even before that night, I'd have had her back anywhere. Terre, not wanting to be alone, insisted on joining us.

As we walked away from our sleeping bags, we immediately noticed a strange, surreal mist in the air. The haze was thin, at first, but got thicker as we walked, and before the dewy grass had soaked through my canvas high-tops, the mist was around us, so dense that we couldn't see anything else. There was a strange quality to it, too. It wasn't just gray, or white, like you'd expect mist to be on a late July night near the woods. Instead, like cotton candy, it contained layered pink, and blue, and sometimes yellow, with deep purples and bursts of red light. There was something warm and musical about it.

Terre called out to us, nervously. We answered, because we weren't monsters, and because we were unsettled, too. In the mist, we found each other. Terre clutched the sleeve of my sweatshirt while Volare and I grasped each other's hands, fingers intertwined, and held on tight.

We had no idea where the construction site was, or whether the elusive porta-john had ever even been, but we kept moving forward. I felt that Volare was leading, but she, to this day, insists that she followed me.

The mist gradually faded to a purplish gray-white, and became less dense. As my eyes adjusted, I realized that we had come to a clearing, where we were surrounded by the strangest flowers. We also appeared to be at the top of a hill, though I had, and still have, no memory of walking up an incline. Above us spread the night sky, absolutely packed with brilliant stars. And before us the dense, bizarre flowers whose light perfume filled the air.

To me, it smelled like flash summer rains on my screened-in porch, mixed with the particular blanket that my mother and I would huddle under on our porch-swing when we watched lightning flash. Volare said it smelled like the river down the street from her mom's house where we'd swim every spring in the freezing mountain runoff, then shriek with cold and cling to each other under quilts all the way home. Terre never told us what it smelled like to her, but she did agree, later that year, that it smelled good, and thrilling, and comforting at the same time.

The flowers themselves looked a bit like Lily of the Valley, but bigger—much bigger, by at least five times. They weren't white, like that flower, either. Instead, they displayed every vibrant shade of a blushing sunset: deepest magenta, burnt orange, and jewel-bright golden yellow.

Surrounded by that exciting and familiar scent, all around the colors of the sunset, we wanted to feel those blooms on our skin. Both of us first bent forward, then fell to our bellies among the teacup-shaped blossoms. The petals felt like the finest suede on our full cheeks.

My body was tempered by the strange flora. I had always felt encumbered by my softness; that I was supposed to hate it into firming or disappearing. In that moment, though, my fatness felt like those luscious flowers made flesh. We rolled around, never seeming to crush the blossoms, all soft and still holding hands, and came to rest on our backs.

The sky stretched, endless. It contained far more stars than any night sky we'd ever seen, as if we could see beyond our galaxy and into the bottomless wild multitudes of space and time. The stars didn't all glow the same color, either. We could see planets—purple, red, orange, blue—and their rings and moons, as clear as if they were painted across the black velvet night. It was all luminous, and infinite, and gave us a feeling of vertigo.

"What are you two *doing?*" Terre's unsettled voice rang out from somewhere, eons away.

She stood stiffly, thin arms crossed over her petite chest. There was judgement and fear etched into every line of her small, angular face. She looked at once like the most insolent child and the frailest and wariest adult.

"Come on, Terre! Join us!" Volare laughed. Volare was always more generous than I was; I wanted it to be just the two of us.

Terre sneered, "No, I won't! You're just, you're just like..."

"Glowing," Volare interjected, as much to Terre as to the universe itself.

Volare was, in fact, glowing. She was completely illuminated, seemingly from within, electric silver-blue, like bioluminescence. She stared at me in disbelief. I, too, was alight with a million phosphorescent particles, radiating from beneath my skin. I still don't quite know why, but we began to laugh together. I saw her—her lips, her teeth, her skin, all glowing. I could feel my smile hurting, but I couldn't stop it.

"*You fat, queer freaks!*" Terre's words ripped through our shared reverie. Our glow faded to a faint hum.

For one moment, I had been free of all the terror and shame of my chubby, closeted adolescence. Being reminded of it then was like being plunged into piercing ice water; I was shocked back to the cruelty of everything outside the flowers, the night sky, and Volare. Terre had landed on my deepest-held vulnerabilities in that moment. I wonder still if it was a coincidence, or something she'd been burning to say, lingering just under the surface of her resentment.

My legs felt strange as I tried to stand up. In fact, my whole body did. It felt like I'd been in the ocean and a wave had knocked me over, and I was struggling against the forces of the whole sea to regain my footing.

"Okay, Terre, we can go," I said solemnly.

I felt guilty, if I'm being honest. Looking back on it, I can't imagine for what, except that back then I felt guilty for everything. I felt guilty for existing in a world that didn't want me.

Terre's eyes were wide as she surveyed me. "Wh-what are you *doing*?" she asked again, her indignation replaced with terror.

"What do you mean?" I asked, but looked down at myself anyway.

I was never what you'd call graceful, or feminine, or any of that. I was never good at sports, or at being a girl, and I was too awkward a teenager to have yet developed any modicum of swagger to make up for it.

It was especially shocking to me, then, that I was floating.

And there, beside me in the air, was Volare. It was the first time I'd seen her fly. Her brown hair, now woven with a golden glow, whipped about her face as she hovered, weightless. She looked like a Renaissance painting, an angel alight from within.

We let ourselves rise up, away from the flowers, from Terre, and into the night. Slowly at first, and then with uneven bursts of speed. We were unused to all of it, but something in it felt deliciously organic, somehow. Maybe it was because Volare was there, too, but I wasn't scared at all. I flew up into that star-filled night and wanted to keep going, to leave everything behind.

"We can't just leave her," Volare shouted to me. Volare shined, a singular glowing beacon in the infinite sparkling black. She read my face and smiled, adding, "Plus, I still have to pee."

I acquiesced, following Volare as she descended. We landed just where we'd taken off, though the mist was beginning to clear. We found Terre on the ground, small and terrified as before.

I stood guard as Volare used the grass in lieu of the fabled porta-john, and Terre waited nearby, arms still crossed, mumbling and cursing under her breath. The mist seemed to have cleared completely now, the ground even, and the flowers were nowhere to be seen.

By the time we returned to the construction site and our sleeping bags, Terre's temper had cooled. Terre's words to us were never mentioned, and any reason on her part for not diving into the flowers was strategically omitted. She did lament not having joined us, but only half-heartedly that first night. Later, she would show far more determination for being part of our adventure than we ever could have anticipated.

Terre joined in as we speculated what They would do if our new ability ever got out. We'd seen enough alien movies to know that The Government would definitely lock us in a lab, and probably experiment on us.

We three agreed that night—swore a blood oath on our teenage hearts, in fact—that none of us would ever tell.

✿ ✿ ✿

Here Volare sits, though, convinced that Terre has broken that promise.

Volare always looks so obviously capable of flight to me that I can't imagine how anyone would believe that she's earth-bound. On nights when we meet to go flying, in a remote field outside town, that is when I get to see her, truly. She always glows brighter when she flies.

"What will we do if she told?" I ask, my familiar anxiety spiking.

Just as Volare opens her red-painted mouth to reply, a voice that has not changed at all carries across the cafe.

"Hey, ladies!" Terre shouts for all the restaurant to hear.

I cringe.

I'm sorry, Volare mouths to me. I hate being referred to as a lady.

Terre hugs us quickly. She looks as I thought she'd look: like she got married young, to a mediocre man, had two kids, and settled into a life of wearing peasant tops and yoga pants and shopping in bulk stores. She has become her teenage vision board. Adult Terre is the fit soccer mom who always remembers to bring the orange slices.

"Terre, you need to tell us if you told," Volare starts, ripping off the metaphorical band-aid.

Terre looks from myself to Volare, performatively incredulous.

"Volare, Cielo, you *must* know I'd never!" she gasps, clutching her chest and cocking her shoulders, the international gesture for being offended at the very thought. "I simply messaged you to get together with old friends."

Volare's eyes narrow. The silence settles uncomfortably, and Terre shifts irritably in her chair.

"Alright, alright, Volare. You always did know how to peer pressure," Terre laughs falsely. "I wanted to know...do you think...you'd be able to find *that place* again?"

"No, we wouldn't," I retort matter-of-factly. It's the truth. The amount of times Terre had us fly over every inch of Volare's dad's land that summer, looking for the spot with the enchanted flowers, had told us that it was a one-time deal.

Every year afterwards until the year we graduated, on that same day, at approximately the same time, Terre had carefully arranged for us all to find ourselves there. No matter how scrupulously she combed the area, and obsessed over us having the same amount of pot, or even the same brand of wine coolers, there was no recreating it. Terre had opted out, and four years of searching told us that there was no going back.

Terre's false smile fades as my answer sinks in. "It's not just for me, you know! It's for...my family!" Her face and voice are desperate, the last words spoken more as an appeal than anything.

"Terre, you are more than welcome to take your children and your husband and go hiking all over my dad's land tomorrow," Volare says, sympathetically. "I won't deny you that, but I'm certain it's gone. I'm sorry you missed your chance, but it's gone." Volare does look truly sorry.

We fill the remainder of our afternoon with strained small talk. Terre shows us vacation photos of her children—18 months and two years, she tells us. No one's heart is really in it, not even

Terre's. She brought us here for one reason: a long-shot that she maybe even knew, deep down, was useless.

We leave together, Volare and I. I find myself preoccupied with the wave and the smell of her hair, the scent-memory of those flowers lingering there. As we walk out onto the sidewalk, she turns to me with her mismatched eyes.

Volare often points out how Terre was right about us that night. We were fat queers, though we hadn't accepted either of those facts 14 years ago, when Terre tried to use those words to call us away from our joy. We wouldn't have gone to those flowers, though, if we hadn't believed that we were worth more than the world had allowed us to know. We were freaks, too, and always would be, to people like Terre. Thanks to that night, we're flying freaks. Fat, queer freaks—Volare always says—is a lot better than being straight and skinny on the ground.

"Fly tonight?" she asks, smiling, her dimples pronounced in the shadow of the sinking sun. In the orange afternoon light, her smile and skin are still more luminous than average, flightless humans.

I nod in response to her question, a quake of excitement in my abdomen at the thought of another night spent flying with Volare.

It was five years from the moment Terre said it that Volare and I told each other who we were for the first time. Now, it's laughable to me that I was scared to say I'm queer to the one person in the world who I could fly with. Nights with the other women I've loved have been exciting, but nothing has ever felt like the way we feel.

Above everything but the stars, full of our own queer magic.

"Sweet Revenge"

Leah Harris

I was raised by a large-breasted, loud-mouthed Jewish grandmother who kept my weight under surveillance with the relentless focus of the Terminator tracking Sarah Connor. From an early age, I learned that the only way to enjoy food was to eat it in secret, and to consume it fast, before I got caught.

Grandma Sylvia had an assortment of polyester clothes in her closet, ranging from sizes 8 to 22, a testament to her lifelong proclivity to yo-yo dieting. She'd say, *You don't want to be like me, stuck with this weight problem all your life. You've got such a pretty face. Nip it in the bud early, Leah!* I always hated that phrase, *nip it in the bud,* as if she was demanding that I never bloom.

Grandma Sylvia would force me to join her in Richard Simmons' "Sweatin' to the Oldies" workouts three times a week. I trailed five feet behind her at all times, shuffling like a teenaged zombie in a baggy t-shirt and gym shorts, carefully disregarding Simmons' impassioned demands to *LIFT! AND LIFT!* I also refused to *PONY!* under any circumstances.

Around 1992, Susan Powter's *Stop the Insanity* program was taking America by storm. I was less interested in Susan's fat-free diet tips than in Susan herself. I taped her late-night infomercial and watched it a bunch of times. Her quarter-inch blonde buzzcut, her white half-shirt, and her authoritative presence as she belted out *YOU GUYS READY TO STOP THE INSANITY?* consistently evoked a delightful little clench in my gut.

I processed my confusion and humiliation by bingeing on Double Stuf Oreo cookies I'd bought with my babysitting money and smuggled in. Defiant, I'd cram those Double Stufs into my mouth while watching late-night reruns of *Monty Python's Flying Circus* on MTV.

✿ ✿ ✿

When I was between the ages of zero and five, Mama trained me how to hunt Nazis. Snapshots of her in her altered states have situated themselves in my limbic system. Mama's kinky Jew-fro fanned out un-brushed around her face. She leaned down and got real close to me. Her eyes shone and darted around like hypervigilant hazel searchlights, seeking out signs of danger. *Leah, I've been informed that Dr. Mengele is poisoning the food supply as an experiment in mind control.*

We stopped eating, since we couldn't be sure which foods were poisoned by Mengele's evil army. We headed out into the streets, sometimes in the thick of Milwaukee winters, weak from our self-imposed starvation. We wandered for what seemed like hours while she mumbled to herself, *Fuck you, Nazi bastard operatives!* I looked in storefront windows, trying to distract myself from the hunger which was rapidly escalating from a tolerable gnaw into a sharp pain in my upper gut. I tugged on her sleeve. *Mamhja, do you think these potato chips are safe?* She didn't hear me. I felt instantly guilty for interfering with the plan to take down Mengele.

Mama stopped answering the telephone and wouldn't open the door to anyone. Then Grandpa Harold and the police arrived and took her away to the psycho bin. Grandpa Harold lured me out from my hiding place under the bed with the promise of a vanilla hot fudge sundae, my favorite. *With whipped cream and a cherry on top,* he said. I asked Grandpa Harold, *How do you know it isn't poisoned by the bad men?* He said that was just Mama's crazy talk and not to worry. After days of eating almost nothing, I remember the sundae being impossibly sweet. I scraped every ribbon of hot fudge from the bottom of the glass bowl until it was clean.

* * *

When I was five, the State revoked Mama's parental rights and gave custody to her mother, Grandma Sylvia, and her second husband, Al. First, we lived in Allentown, Pennsylvania, then in Coral Springs, Florida. By the early 1990s, we were living in San Diego. Always far from Mama.

It's better this way. Otherwise, she'd always be trying to see you, Grandma Sylvia explained.

Mama became phone calls. She became letters. She became short visits on winter break and two weeks in the summer. The madwoman who gave birth to me became equal measures of shame and fascination.

I loved going to visit Mama in Milwaukee on winter and summer breaks. No bedtime. No rules. Total freedom. I didn't get to stay with her for more than one or two days at a stretch, presumably due to her nonstop pot-smoking and other detrimental influences, like her madness.

When it came to food, Mama and Grandma Sylvia could not have been more polar opposites. Mama gave zero fucks about calories or grams of fat, and ate and drank whatever she wanted. When we strolled down the soda aisle during her weekly shopping trip with Grandpa Harold, he would say, *How about the Diet Coke this time, Gail? Gotta watch those sugars with your diabetes!* And she'd smile real big with her half-toothless grin and say cheerily *Whatever, Pops!* while reaching for the regular Coke and putting it in the cart.

On those rare overnights, Mama let me buy as much candy and junk food as we both could afford. We shared Funyuns, Twizzlers, and homemade milkshakes made of real Reese's Peanut Butter Cups and chocolate ice cream in front of the TV until late into the night. She smoked joint after joint, sweet smoke curling through the room.

After days and sometimes weeks of indulging beyond Grandma Sylvia's watchful eye, I'd inevitably come home several pounds heavier. She'd wordlessly scan me up and down. While my body was bigger, I grew ever smaller inside under her disgusted gaze.

As I grew older, Grandma Sylvia would sometimes show me pictures of Mama when she was the same age as me, long before they broke her with all the institutions and forced Haldol shots. She showed me 17-year-old Mama with her hair in two straightened black pigtails, stretched out with long lean legs on a lounge chair. Smiling. Eyes full of vitality and youth. By the fucked-up patriarchal Western standard, she was thin.

Grandma Sylvia shook her head. *I don't know why I was always nagging about her weight back then. Look how pretty she was! You could be that pretty.*

I'd retreat to my bedroom to binge on a frozen Entenmann's coffee cake I'd stolen out of the freezer, knowing I'd pay the price for it later. I hacked off pieces of the defrosting coffee cake with a sharp knife and consumed them while watching *The Terminator*, which I'd taped on the VCR and watched so many times that I had memorized all the dialogue, including the staccato noise of the machine gun sounds, until the tape broke. I watched it so much, because my first girl crush was Linda Hamilton as Sarah Connor.

She had me at that first scene, where she rolled up on her scooter, wearing those aviator sunglasses. I loved when she parked it and said flirtatiously to the Big Buns statue outside the restaurant, *Guard it for me, Big Buns.*

And then, Sarah Connor was hiding out with Michael Biehn as Kyle Reese in a tunnel, and he gave her a message from her son: *Thank you, Sarah, for your courage through the dark years. I can't help you with what you are about to face, except to say that the future is not set. You must be stronger than you imagine you can be.*

Of course, I watched the 30-second sex scene a bunch of times. It begins where Kyle is shoving the bombs they made together into that green duffel bag, and Sarah disarms him with a kiss. My favorite part was when Sarah was on top, and I could kind of ignore Kyle for those five or ten seconds. What was hottest in my recollections was the expression of pure abandon on Sarah's face when she was on top and in charge. I thought it was cool that she appeared to be having a big O while surrounded by handmade explosives.

But I loved the way the closing scene in *The Terminator* made me feel most of all. (If you have not seen *The Terminator*, spoiler alert ahead, skip over this paragraph.) After Linda/Sarah has destroyed Arnold Schwarzenegger, her transformation into a badass witch unto herself is complete. She's rolling through Mexico under a threatening sky, driving a red Jeep and wearing her aviator glasses, a gun in her lap, inexplicably pointed at her unborn child, and a canine by her side. I think I both wanted to be transformed like that, and I wanted to be with someone like that. Someone so willing to go into the storm.

She said, *You must be stronger than you imagine you can be*, and I would have liked to try, for the promise of a someone like that.

❀ ❀ ❀

When I was 15, Grandma Sylvia joined Weight Watchers, and the nagging became unbearable. *Just try one meeting. The weight is falling off me. It's falling off!*

For a few months, I begged off with excuses like homework, television, and pizza. Finally, I was so worn down from the daily badgering, I agreed, on one condition: *I'm NOT going to the same meetings as you, Grandma.*

Grandma Sylvia dropped me off at a strip-mall Weight Watchers nestled between a Baskin Robbins and a taco shop. As I walked up to the door, I stepped into a *let the ground open and swallow me whole right now* full-body humiliated state, as only a 15-year-old fat girl in the early 1990s could feel, gingerly moving forward, all the while looking around to make sure that no one from school was in the vicinity. If they were, I'd make a quick fake to the left, or to the right, as necessary.

The Weight Watchers room was filled with women of varying sizes and, I'm guessing, levels of repressed rage. I was the only person there under the age of 45. As I surveyed the scene, I cursed Grandma Sylvia over and over in my mind. The Weight Watchers leader, a bird-like soccer mom, informed me with saccharine cheer: *I lost 72.6 pounds on the program in 11.7 months and have kept it off for 13.4 years!*

She gestured for me to step up onto the scale. *Um-hm*, she murmured in a sing-songy tone as she wrote the number down on this little yellow folding accordion card where my weight was supposed to be recorded each week. She then handed me the folded-up card with her scrawny bird-claw hand, on the cover of which was written my assigned goal weight. I stared hard at that number, a number that I had last weighed in the third grade.

Something in me snapped. I thought to myself, *I am going to show Grandma Sylvia that I can reach this fucking number. Maybe she'll finally shut up and leave me alone!* This other part of me, a part I barely wished to acknowledge to myself, wanted her approval, which could only be won if I was small enough to earn it.

I never stayed for the stupid meetings after the weigh-ins. Who wants to hear a bunch of middle-aged housewives complaining about their stupid husbands, and how they didn't trust themselves to be alone with their kids' Halloween candy stash? I began religiously following the food plan the bird-lady gave me: chopping veggies, sautéing palm-of-the-hand-sized portions of protein in a scant teaspoon of olive oil, forcing myself to eat gobs of plain non-fat yogurt for breakfast. The more I dieted, the more I began to enjoy the sensation of depriving myself. There was a certain masochistic, authoritarian pride in restricting calories. I rarely cheated, even when my friends were gorging themselves on my favorite Mexican fast foods: carne asada fries or rolled tacos liberally topped with lettuce, cheese, and guacamole. Week after week of ignoring the smell of fried tortillas wafting from the taco shop next to the Weight Watchers had steeled my reserve.

For exercise, I marched up and down the hills in my neighborhood for hours every week, blasting Eazy-E and NWA on cassette at top volume in my Walkman. (I was an angry, adolescent Jewish girl on a crash diet, and nothing else would do.) I pounded the safe, suburban San Diego terrain, miles from whatever was going on in Compton, but as I mouthed the lyrics, I projected myself into a parallel universe as a ruthless rapper with access to endless women and weapons. My favorite lyric from "Boyz in the Hood" was when Kilo G is in court, and he yells "fire! and in comes Suzi with a sub-machine Uzi." At the time, I didn't know why I was so turned on by the combination of women and weapons, or women who knew how to use weapons. Now I know that it's about power, and the ability to defend what is yours.

Just as Grandma Sylvia predicted, by closely following the Weight Watchers food plan and power-walking daily to the raging strains of Ice Cube and Dr. Dre, the pounds fell off. Within five months, I was hovering just a few pounds from the goal weight written on my Weight Watchers accordion card.

Grandma Sylvia wept audibly with joy when I stepped into a straight sized pair of acid-washed denim shorts with lace trim that she had bought for me from Marshall's. For a moment, I basked in the glory of my win, in the approval I didn't want to admit to myself that I wanted. But, like Sweet-N-Low, it all left a terrible aftertaste in my mouth. Mama always looked at me the same, no matter what size my body was. Grandma Sylvia's love was conditioned on the size of the acid-washed denim shorts that fitted over my ass.

After Grandma Sylvia stopped crying, she looked up and smiled with moist eyes as she regarded my body without a shred of disgust. *I'm kvelling you look so good! Now, never gain it back! After your Grandfather Harold left me for that bitch secretary of his, I lost 50 pounds from the stress of it all. And we were dealing with your mom's illness too. It was such a nightmare of a time. But wow, did I look good. Men came out of the woodwork to woo me. I had my choice of suitors, let me tell you, until your Grandpa Al swept me off my feet. Listen to me. I've been fat and I've been thin, and it's always better to be thin.*

She hugged me as she said softly once more, *Never gain it back.*

Mean girls in the hallways of my high school who used to threaten to "kick my fat ass" when they were bored went silent, as if I had become completely invisible to them in my thinness. Mark, this kid I had crushed on since seventh grade, and whom I had sat near in several classes over the years, asked me one day: *Are you new here?*

I occasionally got invited to the popular kids' parties, but never went.

❧ ❧ ❧

When it happened for the first time, I was 15, and the time was around 11 o'clock at night. I was still watching my reruns of *Monty Python's Flying Circus* on MTV, just without the Double Stuf Oreos at this point. Then it came out of nowhere, like someone had stuck a burning metal rod through what felt like my solar plexus and right out of my back. Just this searing, gnawing pain in my mid-section, like nothing I had ever felt before. I could not get any relief from it, no matter what I did. It hurt to lie down and it hurt to stand up and it hurt to sit, so I just kind of curled into a fetal position and whimpered as it went on and on, my breaths really shallow in my chest. The drilling, stabbing sensation caused cold sweat to erupt from practically every pore. All I could think was, *I'm going to die now. Just let it happen.*

When Grandma Sylvia happened to walk by and saw me doubled over in that state she said, *Oh my GOD! I'm taking you to the emergency room now.*

The ER doctor informed us that I was having a textbook gallbladder attack. *You've got gallstones. To be more precise, you've* got what is known as "sludge." Dozens and dozens of tiny little gallstones that are blocking your bile duct, causing the pressure and pain. It's going to have to come out.

I remember being more excited about the surgery than scared. I'd get to stay home from school! And I'd finally get a break from all the power-walking and veggie-chopping!

At the pre-op appointment, the surgeon looked at my chart and said, *You're one of the youngest patients I've ever had for this procedure. Are you by any chance on a low-calorie, low-fat, high-protein diet?*

I looked over at Grandma Sylvia.

I've been doing Weight Watchers.

He nodded. *Well that's it, then. Weight Watchers is pretty much the definition of a low-calorie, low-fat, high-protein diet. There's some new research out about this kind of diet causing gallbladder disease in teens.*

Grandma Sylvia was quiet, studying her fuchsia fingernails.

You're lucky, the surgeon went on. *This used to be a major surgery, with a large incision and significant recovery time. But there is a new surgical procedure now: laparoscopic chol-ecystectomy. We make just a few tiny incisions, and then we insert a camera and pull your gallbladder out just below your navel. You'll be walking around the same day and back to school within a week.* His eyes lit up as he talked and his hands moved around a lot. He seemed genuinely excited about this scientific advance. All I could do was curse science. I wanted the big incision and the long recovery. I wanted the break from everything. But I knew better than to ask for it. The surgery date was set.

The night before surgery, the reality of what was happening began to sink in. Waves of fear gave way to tsunamis of rage, which gave way to insomnia. All I could think about, as I willed my eyes to close, was what an idiot I had been to follow Grandma Sylvia's advice and how I was going to exact my revenge. *I can't wait to gain it all back. I'll show her.*

In the car ride to the hospital that morning, we had a big fight. I screamed at her, *You pushed me to do this dumb diet, and now I have to have an ORGAN removed! ARE YOU HAPPY NOW?* She stared straight ahead as she drove and screamed back, *DON'T YOU BLAME THIS ON ME. HOW WAS I SUPPOSED TO KNOW? I'VE BEEN DIETING ALL MY LIFE AND I STILL HAVE ALL MY ORGANS!*

In the recovery room, high from the post-op morphine drip, I was ravenously hungry. I wolfed down as many cups of strawberry ice cream, the kind they serve in the little paper cups with a wooden paddle spoon, as they would allow me to have. Exactly three cups. It was the first sugar that had passed my lips in months.

A tidal wave of pink vomit rose up out of me and a projectile shot across the room, landing on Grandma Sylvia, who was standing at the foot of the bed. And she just froze there in her polyester suit, shocked and covered in my rosy, creamy puke, calling *NURSE!* It was everything I could do to stop laughing once I had started, because even with that morphine drip, it hurt too fucking much.

✿ ✿ ✿

Back home, Grandma Sylvia stared hard at the recent pictures of Mama that the family had sent us from Milwaukee, from a recent birthday. Mama was the biggest she had ever been, and was smiling her gap-toothed smile over a cake, a lit cigarette trailing smoke from her hand.

Grandma Sylvia audibly gasped. *Look at her. She is absolutely gigantic. Whoo, boy! What is she here, three hundred pounds? Aren't they doing anything about her diabetes over there? Did you even try to talk to her about her sugars?*

Grandma, you know she doesn't listen to anyone, I said.

She shook her head and looked for a minute as if she were about to cry. *You can't imagine how beautiful she was once. So beautiful. Look at her now. Don't be like her. You look gorgeous now. Never gain it back.*

❀ ❀ ❀

Not long after my surgery, I tried to take my own life by ingesting a fuck ton of pills. It wasn't the first time I had tried such a thing, but it was the most lethal attempt by far. I do not have some dramatic trauma porn story to share with you about why I tried to kill myself. To be honest, I don't even really remember specifically what precipitated that suicide attempt. It was 1992 and I was still dieting. Life without food as a comfort felt all raw and jaggedy; the fat loss felt like a loss of skin, of safety, of protection from the world outside my body.

My family decided to put me into a long-term residential treatment facility for troubled teens called Oak Grove, in Temecula, California—basically, the middle of nowhere.

Someone who worked at Oak Grove took a Polaroid photo of me on arrival. *We're giving this to all the local police stations, so if you try to run away, we'll have an APB out on you so fast, you won't stand a chance of getting far.* They asked me to smile. I refused, my mouth frozen in a petulant, uncooperative, line.

It wasn't a conversion therapy program, but it could have been, because that place was fairly crawling with gay. I'm not sure if it was a coincidence, or if it is because queers tend to have mental health issues, and also tend to be disproportionately represented in the helping professions.

The education I got at Oak Grove was definitely not the one that was intended for me. For the first time in my life, I met a whole bunch of other queer and nonbinary kids. Even a lot of the staff were gay. Almost every kid in there was either queer, black, brown, or on the autism spectrum.

The freaks in this place were not an assortment of marginalized and invisible subcultures, like I was used to at my high school. We were the majority in this place for marginalized, traumatized, and abused kids. Our "treatment" consisted of family, group, and individual therapy. We were forced to participate in "women's group" sessions together, where each of us were asked to confess our darkest secrets to the group. All of us had battle-scarred wastelands of childhoods, and, sooner or later, we all knew each other's histories intimately.

Sue Ann, a quiet, freckled girl with stringy brown hair and the deeply slumped shoulders of a 40-year old, was said to have had had Satanists for parents. It was the 1990s and the height of the "Satanic Panic" in America, so I am not sure if that was indeed the case, or if it was a "false memory" implanted by the weird therapies that prevailed at the time. Lizzie, a fat ginger with frizzy hair and impossibly white skin, had an alcoholic mother who used to abuse her. She coped by developing what the staff said was an "unhealthy" obsession with Michael Jackson—listening to his music during every free moment, plastering the walls of her room with images of him, and writing him a fan letter every day. *Michael Jackson is gonna invite me to Wonderland, I know he is, soon,* she would say. It was cringeworthy even back then, but what with the more recent revelations about Michael Jackson, it's doubly painful to recall.

Two of the girls were goths from Los Angeles. Next to them, I felt so uncool with my weirdly cobbled-together hippie-grunge look. Claudia was a stocky Latinx femme with black and cherry-red hair, who wouldn't be seen without her black or dark burgundy lipstick. Angie had beautiful long braids, and wore different colored fishnet stockings, black dresses, and chunky silver spider rings. She always smelled like patchouli.

We were a bunch of hormonal teens thrown together in one place, but we were explicitly not allowed to have romantic relationships of any kind. If the staff or doctors got wind of you loving someone, it could very well mean time added on to your "sentence." This no-love rule was universal to all adolescent psych wards, but was especially surreal in a place like Oak Grove, where you might be placed with the same young people for months, or even years.

Lots of little romances sprang up anyway, of course. Lisa, one of the staff, discovered Sue Ann and Lizzie in their room sixty-nining. They were separated, put on ten-foot restriction, and not allowed to talk to each other. The two were subjected to incessant taunts of "lesbo," "dyke," and "muff-diver" from many of the other kids, all of which were ignored by the staff, except for Lisa. *Shut it, or that's a write-up* she'd say whenever anyone used homophobic slurs within her earshot, her face and neck turning red with fury underneath her buttoned-up men's polo shirts.

By the winter, a long-time Oak Grove resident kid named Jamie and I were sort of dating. They had spent nearly their entire adolescence in Oak Grove. Jamie's dad was a semi-functional heroin addict, but Jamie was the one who was locked up. When Jamie was 13, they tried to take their own life by hanging, which is what landed them in there, and which I thought was dreadfully cool.

Jamie was tiny, skinny, and delicate, with a mane of thick blond hair. Next to them I felt big and fat and uncomfortably masculine, but since Jamie never seemed to care, I learned to brush those feelings off. Jamie was born as a boy, but liked to wear women's clothing. Oddly enough, the staff tolerated it—as long as Jamie didn't wear any makeup, because somehow, that was crossing some unspoken institutional line demarcating acceptable forms of gender nonconformity. Jamie would borrow my dresses. I thought they looked beautiful in my clothes, especially in my polyester orange-and-purple vintage paisley dress. We even wore the same size shoes, so they would frequently borrow my Docs and my creepers.

Jamie and I shared a love of the exploding grunge scene. They let me borrow their Nirvana *Nevermind* cassette to listen to on my busted-up Walkman. "Smells Like Teen Spirit" had been a recent hit, but I hadn't heard the rest of the songs.

"Lithium" spoke the most to Jamie and me, and we'd sing the refrain together, imitating Kurt Cobain's sustained rasp:

I'm not gonna craaaaaaaaaaaaack.

Now, while I had started skipping school, and getting into trouble, I had been a nerd all my life and I really did want to go to college. But I had begun to give up on that. Some of the kids at Oak Grove were bussed over to the local high school every day. But because I was considered a flight risk, I couldn't go. I had to go to the "school" at the institution, which wasn't actually school. There weren't even any books.

Randy, a 30-something-year-old guy with a bald head and glasses, was our teacher. *So, yeah, I wanted to become a filmmaker when I was your age, but I never got into film school, so I ended up here teaching you fuck-ups.* But his life's failure was our gain: he created a syllabus for us that would have been a winner at any film school. He called it "Cult Classics 101." We'd watch the films, read some articles about them, and give presentations on our reflections. One of the first films we watched was *Harold and Maude*. This is another spoiler alert, but looking back, I find it really interesting that Randy would show a bunch of suicidal teenagers a film that featured multiple scenes of Bud Cort attempting to kill himself by hanging, wrist slashing, and even an elaborate hari kari ceremony. We all loved it.

It was in Randy's class that I was introduced to the world of John Waters—a man so strange, so twisted, so unabashedly bizarre, that he said in a commencement address that he was proud to be called "the people's pervert." He would become my "filth angel" in that place, where I was locked up for nearly a year. I was obsessed.

The highlight of my high school education, to this day, was when I got to watch a bunch of Waters' films and write papers on them for high school credit. I still have the paper I wrote about *Hairspray*, where I analyzed its social justice themes:

Tracy Turnblad is a sort of anti-hero, failing to adhere to societal norms—being overweight, having big hair, and supporting desegregation. Another theme throughout the film is how difference is punished and discipline is executed. Tracy is given degrading labels like "hair hopper" and "whore." She is sent to the principal for having big hair, goes to jail for her role in demanding desegregation at Tilted Acres. Tracy's best friend Penny, who is having an interracial relationship, is dragged into a paddy wagon and subjected to a psychiatric de-programming session conducted by John Waters himself as punishment. In both films [*Hairspray* and *Cry-Baby*], there is a clash of power between the underdogs, the Drapes, and the establishment, as represented by the Squares. In summary, I think Mr. Waters would be really happy that his films were being showed in a facility designed for troubled teens who are rebelling against societal standards of normalcy. He said, and I quote: "Parents should worry if their children haven't been arrested by the time they turn sixteen. Being a juvenile delinquent is a birthright and as much a part of healthy adolescence as smoking cigarettes or getting pimples."

Randy gave me an "A" in Cult Classics 101.

John Waters' films were some of the best therapy I could have had. Waters was the first adult I encountered who make it okay to be queer and weird. I said to myself, *When I get out of this place, I am going to do outrageous, epic shit that John Waters would approve of.*

Jamie and I were an item for the entire time I was in Oak Grove, just a little short of a year. Eventually, they let me out. I was 17. I got out before Jamie. Eventually they let them out too, but they were in Northern California and I was in Southern California, so we had trouble making a long-distance relationship work at that age. But we are still friends and still in touch, almost 30 years later.

After Oak Grove, I stopped dieting altogether, and let myself eat whatever I fucking wanted. I slowly escaped the psychiatric system, exchanging it for an only slightly less oppressive system: academia. I ended up going to UC Santa Cruz, and being as absolutely fat and queer as I could manage at the time. I'd do things like get high and watch *Xena: Warrior Princess* in the dorm's common room with my best friend Joelle, who had a crush on me, but who wasn't my type. I shyly courted some of the older women who had placed their profiles in the binder at Herland, the local lesbian coffee shop, although I was never brave enough to place a profile of my own in there.

❀ ❀ ❀

In 1996, I applied to study abroad for a year in Cairo, Egypt. It was a place I'd always dreamed of going, and something about losing myself in a completely different culture felt like an attractive option. I remember thinking at the time that John Waters would be proud of such an unconventional choice for an American student. Mama was also ecstatic that I was getting to see the world. "CAIRO – WOW!" she wrote in all caps in a letter, after I broke the news to her that I would be leaving the country.

A few months later, Mama dropped her body.

The official cause of death was cardiovascular failure, which I have decided is medical code for a broken heart.

She was 46.

The gathering after the funeral at Grandpa Harold's house in the Milwaukee suburbs was pure torture, the motions of mourning the family's most shameful member. I didn't want to talk to Grandma Sylvia or to any of the other relatives who had always regarded Mama's size and her psychiatric diagnosis of schizophrenia with disdain. She was invisible to them, except when she activated their own fear of fatness or madness. I avoided my Uncle Bob, who had told me when I was 13 *I hate you because you remind me of my schizophrenic sister* with so much venom it still makes me shiver.

I overheard Grandma Sylvia say to people:

She didn't watch her sugars.

All that cigarette smoking.

If only she took better care of herself.

She was a talented artist...

She never lived up to her potential, poor thing.

There was no way I could spend another minute in that house, with those people. People who never cared to know Mama, who only pretended at loving her. I grabbed two plates and loaded onto each one an enormous piece of vanilla sheet cake with pastel flowered frosting, jamming a fork into each one. Grandma Sylvia regarded me warily from across the room. I knew I was too fat for her liking at this funeral, stuffed into a black, frumpy polyester dress I found on sale in the plus-sized section at Marshalls.

I looked around for Mama's best friend Mary, the last person to see her alive on the night she died. Mary was smoking a cigarette, small and alone on the couch, her eyes swollen from crying.

Let's get out of here, I said, and Mary nodded blankly. We shrugged on our coats and headed outside into the April air, unusually cold even for Wisconsin, sitting on the front stoop chain smoking, shivering, and eating our giant hunks of cake.

Your mother used to cook for me every night. Her spaghetti with meat sauce was so good! Mary parked her cigarette between her lips, balancing the plate and the cake on her lap, and gestured with both hands to simulate a huge mound of pasta. It occurred to me that Mary had enjoyed more of my mother's cooking than I ever had.

Mary had lived with Mama in falling-apart Section 8 housing in one of the city's most under-served zip codes, b. But they always managed to cook and eat like kings. Mary, who dated a series of unfortunate, abusive alcoholic men that Mama was always rescuing her from. Mary, who after Mama died, devoid of her friendship and her cooking, would eventually succumb to crack cocaine, stop eating, and disappear altogether.

She used to heap the food on my plate so high. So high!

And I'd say, Gail, you're gonna make me fat! *And your mom would say,* Mary, there's nothing wrong with being fat. Big is beautiful.

Yep, Mary said. Big is beautiful, *she'd say*.

Her features suddenly clouded. *I feel guilty about not calling 911 that night. Her color was bad. She couldn't even hold her cigarettes. She kept dropping them. She was, like grayish in color. I know about that stuff, I learned CPR and rescue stuff. How to splint legs, you know? You put them between two boards.*

It's not your fault. You couldn't have known, I said weakly, my mind spinning as it envisioned the scene. Mary trying to figure out what to do with my stubborn, ashen-faced Mama. She was always the dominant personality in their friendship. Even on the eve of her death, her will had prevailed over Mary's.

I'm the jerk. I'm the jerk. I'm the jerk, Mary kept repeating, staring down into her half-eaten slice of cake.

No, Mary. No. It's okay. I tried desperately to comfort her, as my mind filled up with if onlys. If only she did not have to leave so soon. If only everything had turned out differently.

Mary's eyes found mine, and took on an almost fevered sheen.

Jesus is going to raise her from the dead, you know, she said with her mouth half full of sheet cake. *You know that, right?*

I let Mary hold on to whatever she had left of Mama, to whatever beliefs brought her release from the pain, and said nothing, chewing my cake slowly, savoring its sweetness, the way the frosting melted on the back of my tongue. After I ate every bite, I used my fingers, not my fork, to retrieve the smeared remnants of frosting from the paper plate. I let my body have what it wanted.

Mama wouldn't have had it any other way.

"seven nights of noodles"

Jay Audrey

Sunday, I realize I have new stretch marks
across the top of my stomach
reddish purple like an overripe raspberry.
I have thrown out my scales by now but
honor this gain by making a rich beef broth
for stroganoff (my mother would
pre-portion it on my 10-year-old plate)
I eat it in heaps.

Monday, I have her—*her*—over and sit
with a glass of crisp rosé
as she tosses shrimp, mussels, crab
with lemony linguine. The steam collects on
her forehead like sweat as she concentrates
the same look as when she grips the headboard.

Tuesday, I discover a new recipe
tucked inside a secondhand book;
it has tamarind paste, scallions, biting red chiles
that coat my tongue and we are alone in my kitchen,
me and my appetite. It tastes of a peace I never knew
until *she* held my round woman hips and thanked me
for my abundance (she studies art history and points out
that my stomach rolls like Aphrodite's).

Wednesday, I marinate chicken thighs
as the afternoon sun dies out the window.
I'm picking away at work that needs to be done
while they soak up garlicky buttery goodness.
The recipe called for breasts but
thighs have the fat and so the flavor
(her thighs are all the glory of the world).
The pasta will drink up the schmaltz
and it will be worth the heartburn to taste.

Thursday, she tells me I only need five ingredients
for the best pasta I'll ever eat—
finally she trusts me enough to share the secrets
passed down by her mother's mother's mother,
listing them off one by one, the way
she counts the freckles on my neck with her lips,
black peppercorns, guanciale, fava beans, pecorino
and, of course, her favorite, bucatini. *bu-ca-tin-i.*
If my want for her had a taste, it would be this
and she is right—it's the best I've ever had.

Friday, I am joined by one of the friends made
in the latest group therapy session
we are making carbonara, which I say slowly,
over and over, let the savory yolk word burst
on my tastebuds. I invited him over because his mother
is like mine, all harsh corners and skipped desserts,
so it's no wonder we've ended up here, together, afraid of
adding too much fat. To eat, to savor, is to regain
all that has been taken from us.

Saturday, I visit with my mother
promising to make my famous recipe for
dill yogurt orecchiette with spiced lamb
(which I ripped from a magazine—*shhh*).
I tell this woman who bore me about the girl
I've been seeing, that it's getting serious,
and she responds that I do not need seconds
so I tell her for the first time
after twenty-two years of sitting alongside it
that my body is not her battlefield
and I leave with my leftovers
go home where I
am waited for.

"Lessons Learned and Unlearned"

Edward Kelsey Moore

As a musician, I hold fast to the notion that a sub-par performance can be redeemed by the ways it teaches me to improve my preparation for the next concert. When I sit at my desk to write, it is with the certainty that each shaky chapter or lackluster short story of the past will enable me to find a clearer approach in the future. I believe that I'm a better husband because I've paid attention to the ways in which I was a less than stellar partner in my youth. After years of good and bad concerts, successful and unsuccessful literary efforts, miserable and joyful love relationships, I have come to trust that there is value in even the worst of my experiences as long as I glean some sort of lesson from it. Learning can be a complicated and messy process, though. It took me decades to acquire the ability to differentiate between the lessons that I needed to take to heart for my future happiness and those that should be buried before they leap up and bite my ass.

When I was 12 years old, I was given my first instruction in how and why to be thin. I had run out of clothes to wear that summer after a lengthy eating binge added 20 pounds to my already stout frame in a matter of months. My mother woke me on a Saturday morning, instructed me to squeeze into the one pair of pants that almost fit, and drove me to a Weight Watchers meeting.

By 12, I already knew that I was fat. My schoolmates and my older siblings made sure I harbored no delusions of thinness. However, I had believed until that morning that my mother and I were on the same side. When I had overheard her saying to my aunts that "Edward Junior eats just like a grown man. I can hardly keep up with him," I had heard only pride in her voice. I was an emotional, artistic, and defiantly nelly boy. I happily spent most of my weekends adding photos to my Diana Ross collage, reading *Rona Barrett's Hollywood* magazine (I had a sub-scription), and snacking. Eating was the only thing I did "like a grown man," as far as I'd ever heard. I had convinced myself that my mother and I had settled into a mutually beneficial arrange-ment in which she supplied delicious food and I flattered her culinary skills by eating massive, manly amounts of it. That Saturday morning, I discovered that I had been mistaken. My weight was a problem, apparently, and it had to be dealt with immediately. As my mother put it during the drive to my first Weight Watchers meeting, "We have to do something about this now or you'll start thinking no woman will want you. Then you'll really be in trouble."

I am embarrassed to admit that many years would pass before I gave serious thought to my mother's belief that a woman wanting me and, presumably, me wanting a woman were crucial goals whose achievement merited the reconfiguring of my body. I would have to experience many more failures and successes before obtaining the fortitude to fully digest the lesson at the bottom of that particular well.

My first Weight Watchers leader, Audrey, was a charming woman with towering, lacquered hair that looked like a mass of glistening black cotton candy. At the end of that first meeting, Audrey took me aside and told me the story of a fat friend of hers who had refused Audrey's many entreaties to join Weight Watchers. After suffering the health crisis that Audrey had long seen coming, that friend's fate had been to end up enormous, ill, and immobile, reduced to begging her overburdened caretakers to bring Oreo cookies to her sick bed. "Edward," Audrey said to me while sadly shaking her head, "she just refused to learn her lesson." Audrey would later permanently cement her place in my affections when she brought five pounds of pork fat to a meeting, tossed the fat onto the floor, pounded her foot on it several times, and then gleefully invited everyone to come up and have a turn at stomping on "the enemy." With her big hair and her flair for drama, she was a nascent novelist's dream.

The day that I met Audrey, I didn't know that there would be countless weight-loss attempts in my future. Most would be marked by promising beginnings and disheartening endings. Some would be dangerously unhealthy. None achieved, or could ever have achieved, the unreasonable results I'd envisioned. I never managed to starve myself into heterosexuality. Unlike Audrey's friend, though, I learned from my missteps. I learned to view each uncompleted stab at shedding fat as a personal failure. I learned to see myself as physically unattractive and lacking in resolve. Strangers, schoolmates, and even people who claimed to love me reinforced those feelings, and I absorbed them more deeply every time I stepped onto a scale.

It took decades for me to tire of beating myself up, but I eventually started dodging my punches. With middle age approaching, I took a closer look at some of the uglier lessons I had learned and at the people who had taught them to me. While I can't claim to have completely shed the self-sabotaging beliefs I drilled into my soul for decades, new lessons have presented themselves to me and, over time, crowded out many of the old ones.

After half a century of trial and error, I have learned to be thankful for every version of the body that has carried me from adventure to adventure. I can work toward better health, whether that comes with a more compact frame or not, and still love my body for what it has done and continues to do for me. I have learned that when anyone other than my physician offers an unsolicited opinion about my body, what they are really saying is that they want me to become smaller in some other way. They are saying that I should be less successful, less gay, less black, less smart. The motivations and messengers change, but the goal is always to lessen me, and it is rarely for my benefit. I have learned that whatever amount of space I take up, I have the right to occupy.

I wish Audrey had told me when I was 12 that the most important lessons I would learn about my body had nothing to do with inches and pounds. But Audrey was younger when I met her than I am now, and maybe she still believed that nothing lay between thinness and begging for Oreos. I hope she learned a new lesson, though, for her own sake and for the sake of the next kid who showed up at one of her meetings. I hope that she was able to tell the next fat 12-year-old that looking into a mirror and loving who they saw was the first step of their journey, not the last. I hope that kid listened carefully and learned their lesson faster than I did.

"Faithful Food"

Ruth Gibbs

The strangest part of fatness is the presumption of
the sacred.
My thin friends expect to find me worshipping
in the ice cream aisle head tilted back to bask
in the holiness of Our Lord and Savior Lard.
They see me as a thing profane always less than thinness.

Their eyes read me into paragraphs upon paragraphs
of excuses.
I am the creature in their wobbling, softening nightmares
of gluten and caloric intake, a pariah.
The unsainted bitch of all that is wrong in the world.
They are not wrong, they are not right.

"Faithful Food"

There is no evangelism to the art of fatness.
There is only the pagan celebration of the things that are.
I worship in the restaurants where food is made as beautiful
as I.
My prayers go up with the smokehouse fires,
cooking meats with methods that span millennia.

The foremothers tending flames in caves smile
upon my softness and weep with joy.
I find my warmth, my house, my home,
in the bread made with hands as soft as the dough they work.

I am the patron saint of hedonism.
I am not the good fat, bad fat, chaotic neutral fat
who will never speak of food or eat nothing
but butter sticks for days.
I am neither parody nor ideal.

I am saint and sinner. I exist as a contradiction.
I will challenge every petty word and lie you tell
to make me smaller in your mind.

Women like me walk with the goddesses.

Venus swans behind me
collecting the flowers I drop,
broad hips swaying in the sun.

Ishtar laughs with me
over leftovers, pasta made by hand,
full of love and dedication.

Lilith screams with me,
women villainized for daring
to be beasts and monsters.

Eve arranges apple slices
and pomegranate seeds to stain
excited fingers with no regrets.

We all feast, women too big for history
and shaped to slip happily between
the thighs of myth.

The first sin was a woman eating.

"cherry popsicle"

Jay Audrey

cherry juice on her skin
drips down
through her valleys
her slopes and hills
(our ripened, plump bodies)
(seem to have been made)
(for the kiss of light)
(the lick of cherry)
(I crave her)
she is an August landscape
firefly freckles
butterfly lashes
I cannot catch her unless
she lets me
her smile
(the taste of a daisy)
(sun on water)
liberates my hands

from their tentativeness
she is all red and sticky and sweet
and spreading herself
on me, too,
my canyons and shorelines
I have never been held like this—
the sacred way a popsicle
is lusted over on
a summer day

"cantaloupe season"

LJ Sitler

My lover—
They say they love to watch me eat
as together we share grease and potential on my couch.
I, prone to redness, blush but
keep eating anyway.

I am not fat solely
because of my joy in eating—
nor am I naive enough to believe this is not
part of the equation.
I make these sounds, joyful,
an alternation between savoring and devouring.

Please lover, do not turn on me
and eat my heart.
Do not say you love this body and then rescind.
Give me time to savor still.

My lover—
their body is beloved. (As lovers are.)
Their body is much like mine, I feel sometimes
they want to slip into an old skin and instead slip
into me.

I will hold them—my body encircling—
us two pale and sturdy creatures.
Do they know I couldn't dare dream of this—
an imperfect skin blurring the lines of fat and woman
and fat and human and fat and something othered.
Something that did not conceive of a lover.

Crawl into me, use this body as your second home—
I will care for you and cook for you and all I ask in exchange
Is that you look at me with fondness as juice runs down my
chin.

My lover
feeds me musty cantaloupe in bed
after fucking.
Even in Paris in summertime it is distant universe dark.
I cannot see and there is no ounce of the voyeur here.
We are, we are, we are
two bodies beyond identity in the anonymity of this room.
Sex drunk, hazy at the promise of sleep
and hungry.

I take what you give—I give
my body and a firm and steady heartbeat.
I've stumbled for years—with size, with label, with body
Into the beds of both men and fear
and here my lover—
I am warm, I am sated, I am full.
I am, we are, I am—
we are together.

"The Gender Nonconformity of My Fatness"

Caleb Luna

Last month, I was in a public space, meaning, I was in a space that left my body vulnerable to the interpretations of those around me and their responses.

Two strangers met nearby, and one asked the other a question that necessitated acknowledging me. Stranger #2 responded to Stranger #1's question, referring to me as "she" ("She's waiting in line"). I noted this internally, bemused. He then immediately stammered and corrected himself—or so he thought—to gender me as "he." I wanted to tell him, *It's okay, you didn't do anything wrong; both and neither are right.*

Instead, I waited for my pizza to be ready, picked it up, and left.

This was not the first time a stranger in a public space directly or indirectly expressed confusion about my gender.

It won't be the last.

Last week I was walking to my bus stop when I passed a stranger who was talking to several people on the street as they walked by. He said hi, so I responded in turn. This led him to walk up to me, put his arm around me, and ask if I was gonna let him fuck me. I shrunk away, said "no," and he took his arm away and went back to talking to other people on the street.

This is not the first time a man on the street has sexually harassed me in ways that mimic the street harassment so many women face daily. It won't be the last. One difference, I'm sure, was not only my comfort in telling him no, but also him hearing my no and responding accordingly, though this has not always been the case when I tell men no.

Still, the interaction was interesting to me in the way this person clearly interpreted my body in a way that was, if not woman, woman or feminine-adjacent. He clearly read me as woman, or femme, or gay, or queer, or bottom—some experiences I identify with and some I don't. I wondered, would he have approached someone in the same way who was taller? Hairier? Less fat? Fat in a different way? Darker? Would he have asked to be fucked rather than to fuck? Would he have needed to interpret someone as not straight to do so? And what identifiers is he looking for to do so?

As a person who was assigned male at birth, my fatness produces my gender in a very specific way. I have a big, soft belly and what might be called breasts on a different body. This is a feminized fatness that is different from the hard, muscular guts found on athletes and those in masculinized spaces like the bear community. I have very little body hair that follows the patterns of my father and other Indigenous men I see who look like him. This is another marker of masculinity that my body fails, which, along with my fatness, locates me in a kind of gender purgatory—both, neither, all, and none.

The way I experience my gender getting produced the most—the way it feels most present and prominent—is through sexual currency. In these moments and spaces, it becomes obvious that most men who are attracted to men have ideas of manhood that are not just cis, but non-disabled and thin or muscular as well.

For me, this begs the question, *What makes a man?*, particularly when thinking about the ways that normative queer spaces construct gender, manhood, and masculinity.

Those men who are attracted to me seem to be already especially attracted to a specific type of fat body that aligns with mine. These bodies are called "man" or "male," but the physicality of our interactions, the language they use to refer to my body, the assumptions they make about my sexual positions and habits, and, especially, how they position themselves and their own gender in relation to my body and my gender suggest that a multiplicity of genders are actually present in these interactions, though we might both use the shorthand of "man" to refer to ourselves.

Sometimes these interactions vary depending on how I'm dressed—whether I am wearing big hoops or more subtle studs, makeup or nail polish, or even a skirt or a dress—but many times not. Sometimes when I am not wearing obviously feminine-coded attire, they ask for it. The way this becomes an access point to desire for me is not lost on me.

In addition to thinking back to my experiences of street harassment by men who presumably consider themselves straight—or, approach me in a way that feels as if they experience me as adjacent to womanhood—I think of the class of straight-identified men who specifically like to sleep with fat men. This implicitly differentiates fat embodiment as its own gendered population, contra to the way cis gay men who identify as attracted to men often imply a specific population of men who are cis, thin/muscular, not-disabled, often white, and so on, as the gendered objects of their desire. What, then, are those who fail or fall outside these standards?

There are many activists today doing amazing work around breaking down gender and challenging the binary. This is necessary work. But what gets left out of the conversation are all the subtle intricacies of a body beyond genitals and the secondary sex characteristics that gender relies on, like race, ability, body size, and even shape.

Similar to the way my fatness interacts with my gender to position me outside manhood, many fat women activists have pointed out how the fat positive movement and especially fatshion movements are dominated by pear-shaped smaller fat women. This highlights how womanhood, as well, relies on specific body shapes and proportions to remain legible. What about the women who are apple-shaped, or merely round without the normal, appropriate, or acceptable "curves"?

Disabled, queer activists have already talked about the way that normative gender performances rely on a non-disabled body, that the gestures and posturing necessary to render a gender legible on a body rely on movements not available to everyone. I think this analysis needs to extended to fatness, as well. What of people whose fatness produces a body where otherwise presumably obvious secondary sex characteristics become more ambiguous? Whose bodies challenge a presumably clear and defined binary of dichotomous and easily definable bodies?

Further, black, queer, gender non-conforming activists and scholars, most notably Hortense Spillers, have theorized that gender is always already racialized. Under colonialism, racialized and colonized people and black folks especially are set against a white gender standard that we will always fail. We are always set against white masculinity and white femininity, which are always already cis, muscular or thin, and not disabled.

The more I have experienced this the more that, in some ways, I feel like my fatness arrests my gender. Regardless of how I *feel* and how I view my gender, there are material limits to what gender my body is allowed or—more appropriately—disallowed to access. While I don't have a desire to participate in it, I feel as if my fatness has excommunicated me from masculinity and perhaps gender as a whole. This complicates the journey for me, as someone whose gender feels at different times coerced, contextual, erased, invisible, absent, aspirational, and failing.

The limits fatness places on my gender possibilities can be overwhelming. And I must acknowledge the other fat trans and gender non-conforming people who have very different relationships to their fatness and their gender, whose fatness may help, hinder, or place no bearing on their gender. I do not want my experience to minimize, undermine, or diminish theirs.

But as for me, I have come to a place of gender apathy, where gender becomes an experience much larger than me that I have little to no control over, and have forsaken any attempts. I feel no pressure to "figure" out my gender, and have rejected any responsibility to reach a destination, to decipher what gender means for me and what role it occupies in my life and experiences, to present a road map or answers to a system that refuses to acknowledge the complexity of what informs all of our genders. The closest I can come to articulating my gender is fat, and even this feels like offering more than what is deserved, like retrofitting a body to a system that never wanted it.

The feeling is mutual.

"Incorrect Attribution: A Collision of Fatness and Gender"

Alyssah Roth

In "The Gender Nonconformity of My Fatness" by Caleb Luna, a fat, brown, queer, femme writer, Luna discusses their experiences of how their fatness entangles with their gender. Reading this was perhaps the first time I began to consider how my own gender and fatness impact each other.

I am a dyke. To be more precise, I am a (small-to-mid) fat, brown, nonbinary, masc, AFAB (assigned female at birth) dyke. My gender and my fatness are inextricably linked and sometimes even undo each other. I have often searched for reflections of myself in writings about gender and fatness, but seldom have I found them until Luna's piece. While I resonated with their piece in many ways, there are aspects of our experiences that are also different. For instance, Luna discusses their experiences of fatness and gender by writing about the sexual currency of their body. I, however, have not had those experiences. What I have come to understand about myself in writing this piece is that I experience the collision of my fatness and gender most often through clothing.

Luna writes:

> The limits fatness places on my gender possibilities can be overwhelming. And I must acknowledge the other fat trans and gender non-conforming people who have very different relationships to their fatness and their gender, whose fatness may help, hinder, or place no bearing on their gender.

My hopes in writing this are to see myself, and others like me, at the intersection of all of our pieces, as well as do Luna justice in this informal response.

The earliest and clearest memories I have of the terror that clothing has imparted on my body are from middle school—both right before and right after I came out. I attended private, Catholic school from kindergarten to 12th grade, where we were required to wear uniforms. Up through about fifth grade—at which point I was already fat—most of the girls wore jumpers, simple plaid dresses that buttoned at the shoulders. It was like wearing a potato sack in that it just felt like a piece of fabric draped over my body. Around fifth or sixth grade, however, the girls enthusiastically traded the jumpers for skirts, to my chagrin. It's not a surprise that most of the girls who were enthusiastic about this change were the athletes and/or pretty girls, many of whom were already dating boys. I, a preteen, felt a lot of social pressure. I went to school every day hoping to see another girl in my class show up in a jumper, but eventually I understood that the transition to wearing skirts also signified a transition in age and growth; I inevitably had to retire the jumper. So I begrudgingly came out of it, but I was so uncomfortable in the skirt. I didn't know what to wear underneath. At that point, I only owned baggy shorts that would hang below the skirt.

The only shorts that wouldn't peek out were the boxers that I slept in. I hated the way my tucked-in polo revealed my two bellies, how the skirt rested right in between them at my belly button. Even into the 90-plus-degree desert spring and summer, I did everything I could to keep my sweater on to avoid showing anyone how I looked.

Every once in a while, I had some reprieve from the uniforms. Though Spirit and Free Dress days came with their own sets of problems (no one, especially I, knew how to dress a fat, awkward, tomboy-soon-to-be-baby-gay with no fashion sense or desire for one), they did take some pressure off me. And one day, I thought I'd found a way to completely evade the whole skirt situation. See, the boys had to wear green pants or shorts and a polo. Wearing the pants never crossed my mind, but one day, I realized I could wear the shorts. Shorts are gender neutral, right? Girls wear shorts, right? So one day in October, I showed up to school in these shorts and my tucked-in polo, and I felt really good. The shorts did something different to my bellies, and I didn't feel exposed when I sat down or went to pick something up. But as soon as I stepped into homeroom, everyone was looking at me. I saw eyes moving up and down my body, and I immediately felt embarrassed. No one said anything mean to me, but they did stare. I found my seat, and then Lucas, a short, wiry, loud, arrogant red-head, turned around to talk to me.

"Why are you wearing shorts?" I didn't know what he was asking or which way to answer.

"Because they're comfortable, I guess?"

"Oh, cool," he responded. I was confused by his simple statement. "You know, you're not allowed to wear shorts after September."

My heart sank, and I immediately remembered the rule book. He was right: October through January, we were not allowed to wear shorts. I was still confused, though. Why did everyone stare at me? Was it because they all remembered the rules as well? Or was it because I was a "girl" who'd shown up in shorts? All day, it was as if the shorts were a target on me, and this choice I had made to feel much more comfortable in my body instead made me feel terrible and embarrassed.

Unfortunately, I experienced the same kind of terror at the hands of parental figures as well. The next summer, my dad and stepmom drove me out to Palm Springs to attend a basketball camp my uncle was running. I was there for a little less than two months, and what started as a hard experience for me turned into a really lovely one. I also lost a significant amount of weight that summer, mostly because I was running a lot more, both for basketball and also because it was Palm Springs, and it literally felt less hot to be running. Towards the beginning of the summer, my uncle gifted me a t-shirt with the logo of the team which was attending the camp. It was a simple heather gray shirt with a blue logo. It fit snugly initially, but by the end of the summer, I was so proud of how it fitted me.

The day my dad and stepmom drove me back to El Paso, I was wearing some shorts and the team shirt as a memento. I got into the back of the car, my dad and stepmom in the front. Out of nowhere, my stepmom said to me, "You're never going to get a boyfriend if you dress like that." I was both amused and confused. Sad and also not. I had just come out a few months prior, though not to my stepmom. But even then, at 12, I knew that it probably wasn't appropriate to be commenting on something I was wearing and threatening a lack of boys' interest. I felt hurt by her comment, and confused that an adult would make me feel this way. Even now, I still do wonder what would have been more acceptable road trip attire for her. (In another instance, a couple years later when I was in high school, my mom said something similar to me: "Girls are never going to like you if you dress like that," which, though maybe not kinder, was at least more accurate.)

In both of these childhood experiences, I chose to wear something that I felt really good in: shorts instead of a skirt, and a t-shirt that commemorated a very sweet summer. And both times, my choices resulted in shame. In the first instance, Lucas did not outright shame me (and dare I say was nicer than my stepmom?), but I certainly felt a lot of embarrassment, and the stares and questioning made me feel very insecure about my choice. In the second instance, there was outright shame. A shirt I felt deeply good in (and an experience I was proud of) was disregarded because it was not "girly" enough, and because it probably was not good enough to attract the attention of a boy.

In both instances, my fatness was the driving force behind these choices in clothing that I felt most comfortable in. Both articles lived at the borders of what was acceptable for a girl to wear, at least on my fat, queer body. Maybe it would have been different if I was skinny, or straight. I think about all the other girls—athletes—who I went to camp with and wonder how boys were still interested in them, or how they still seemed so girly. I think about all the clothes I owned at that point in my life, and how seldom they felt great, and how most often they were a little too big on me. Because, again, what was a fat, awkward, tomboy-soon-to-be-baby-gay with no fashion sense or desire for one supposed to wear? Where was one supposed to even shop?

That time in my life feels gender-less. But in some ways, I think saying that reduces gender to clothing. Surely clothing *is* a large part of gender, and for me, at that point in time, everything about clothing felt hopeless—and so did gender. Nothing fitted. I was fat and short, and not girly. I was too big for boys' sizes and too small for men's, and I did not want to touch the girls' section. So, in essence, I dressed the way I dressed primarily because of my fatness. Though uniforms were hard at times, there is a part of me that thinks they maybe saved me from having to create my own gender-affirming fashion identity and having dysphoria every day of my young adult life.

Thankfully, as I grew up, I slowly learned how to find clothes that fitted my body and my desires. There was a lot of give and take, though. The jeans I found, for example, fitted me really well, but the ass pockets were bejeweled. And even though I was starting to feel better about how I was dressing, there was still a huge chasm between where I was and where I wanted to be. I remember going to the mall, to Hot Topic and Zumiez, and feeling inspired, but nowhere trendy carried my size. So I stuck to bejeweled jeans and three packs of solid-color t-shirts from the men's underwear section at Target. Eventually, for me, this translated into a masc gender, a deep dykehood. Then, once I went to high school and was around other gays, girls were attracted to me, to my gender, and that was very validating.

Now, as an old sea dyke, I have sunk into a lot of comfort with my gender—for the most part. I have an aesthetic, and I know the places to shop that carry things I like. I know how things fit. I am largely surrounded by queers my own age who can recognize who or what I am trying to be. I understand the choices and nuance behind my gender.

However, there are still aspects of gender that I long for that are halted by my fatness. At 27, I have been binding for about seven years, but because of the size of my chest, even in a binder, I look as if I just have a slightly smaller mound of uniboob. At almost the fattest I've ever been, I am pushing the top (in-store, regular-priced) sizes of my trusted brands. And at this size, there is not much room for me to explore the styles I really want, most of which lean towards men's fashion. So I've settled for women's jeans and button ups that I can pass as fairly neutral, or masc up with my shoes or even just my gait. I spend hours looking at masc clothing made for "women's" bodies, and mark the page as a favorite for when I have the money to make the purchase. And I've learned how to suppress a lot of sadness, and maybe even some anger, when my tall, straight-sized partner walks into the men's section and finds a beautiful pair of corduroy pants that fit her perfectly.

So maybe you could say I've *learned* how to be comfortable, and maybe how to compartmentalize some things I cannot change. I have figured out how to live with my fatness, again—for the most part. But I would be lying if I said I sometimes did not resent the fattest parts of myself for how they interact with my gender, for how I cannot consent to how they interact with my gender. In "The Gender Nonconformity of My Fatness," Luna writes:

> Regardless of how I *feel* and how I view my gender, there are material limits to what gender my body is allowed or—more appropriately—disallowed to access.

> While I don't have a desire to participate in it, I feel as if my fatness has excommunicated me from masculinity and per- haps gender as a whole.

The gender I am most often incorrectly attributed—most often incorrectly allowed to access—is butch woman. I am forever loyal to womanhood, and there are some ways that feel lovely to be claimed by it: the people I love the most, the people who have taught me everything good, the people who help me grow are women and queer femmes. But still, I am not a woman, and I am certainly not a butch one. I know why the attribution happens, though. It's my short haircuts, my voice, my clothes, my big body—the things that queer me—and also the parts of my body that outsiders can identify as *woman*. However, I think butch womanhood is often forced on to me by people who are not queer, or people who cannot understand how else to comprehend a fat person who *could-be-maybe-probably-is* a woman.

See, growing up, my understanding of butchness was shaped by the brown butch lesbians I saw as a baby gay stumbling through El Paso's tiny Pride Square, most of them emulating brown border manhood, many of them in ill-fitting men's clothing, romanticizing chivalry, and existing in direct opposition to femmeness. The butches through whom I learned about butchness wanted to be adjacent to manhood. And I think because I grew up understanding this particular way of butchness—a way that never inspired me and a way that I deeply do not resonate with—I am always fearful of being gendered as a butch woman (this, and the fact that I am just not a woman).

However, my body lives at this particular intersection of attributed gender, and I cannot divorce my fatness from the reasons why. Essentially, my fatness sometimes betrays me, allows others to misgender me. I was never able to articulate this interconnectedness until I read Luna's piece. The way they contextualized how their fatness shapes their gender has helped me have a greater understanding of those two instances in middle school, as well as many other moments since then, of grief and rage towards my own body. As an adult, though, the shame I've felt has been a bit more complicated.

When I first bought a binder, I accidentally bought one that compacted not only my chest, but also my hips and bellies. I remember putting it on—a struggle—pulling it down over all of my rolls, and then slipping on jeans and a t-shirt. The lust I felt when I looked in the mirror was unreal, and I've never felt anything like that again. My clothes fitted well. You couldn't make out my hips or my bellies. My chest was so flat. So I took it off immediately. I couldn't do it. What I was seeing was not my true body, just a body that I wanted so badly. I tried to imagine the thought of having sex with someone, having to tell them that I was actually binding my entire body, and I looked a whole lot different without it. I couldn't do it. It is a complicated moment to think back on because with that frame of mind, does that also mean I think binding does not show a true body? I don't think that. I bind, and it feels so true to me. I think the difference is that it feels easier to change this one part of my body that is sometimes hard—my chest—rather than change my entire image. And there might come a day when I no longer have anything to bind on my chest, but I don't think I necessarily see a future where my body will look significantly different from how it did then or how it does now.

I felt a lot of sadness in that moment, then, in sending back the binder, and now, thinking back on it. I felt sadness about not being able to have the body that would have allowed me to wear the kinds of clothes I've always wanted, and I felt sadness that I was enamored with how thin it made me feel. Flatter than I'd ever been. I resented my fatness for not allowing me a body that could access the gender and clothes I most desired.

It's not a secret that in the queer/dyke community, thin mascs have the most social capital. Probably because their thinness grants them the most access to the in-between spaces of gender and often, by default, masculinity. My fatness, as Luna wrote, arrests my gender, it disallows me from accessing that in-between gender. However, contrary to Luna, I have a much stronger desire to be accepted into mascness, and for the most part, I think I have achieved that. There are some ways I know that my frame actually lends itself more easily to mascness.

But whose mascness? What kind of masc do people see when they look at me? Will I ever be able to wear the type of clothes I most desire and step fully into my gender? Or will I have to reconcile with the fact that I will probably never find gender euphoria through clothing? Will womanhood ever not be attributed to me, or will my fatness always misgender me?

One of the hardest lessons I've had to grapple with is that with fatness, at least for me, there's not a lot of changing things, not a lot of transformation. I've tried more diets than I can remember and have been excited by countless exercise regimens. I have experienced many weight fluctuations, but my body often gravitates toward this weight. And I won't say it's the weight my body is *happy* at; my back hurts, and my ankles are wobbly. But this is kinda where I've landed. And sometimes it's HARD. Not only because of how other people see me, but because of how I also see me. Sometimes, I can't even get dressed because I am so dysphoric about my chest, or binding, or about how most of my button-ups fit. Often, I have to blunt my own emotions while shopping so I don't have a breakdown. Usually, those feelings lift. I lie down for a bit, I cry, I do whatever, and they lift momentarily, but they always come back. I could do things differently; for instance, I *could* change how I dress, I could spend money on bigger sized clothing, then spend more money on getting them hemmed and tapered. I could put everything into changing my body. But after a childhood of shame around fatness and eating, I just don't think that's where

I'm at. I don't know if I see another point in my life where I will actively try to lose weight—and I feel great about that decision, even if it means I may have a life of hard body feelings.

But that means I'm also left in an in-between space. I can buy women's jeans, but only very plain ones. I can probably even buy women's button-ups, but only if they don't dip too high on the hip. I can search for more affordable gender-affirming clothing, and I can maybe even try to be more explicit about my own gender. But no matter what, I will still be a fat, brown, nonbinary, masc, AFAB dyke, and I will probably still be attributed an alien gender at those crossroads.

"A Sexy Fat Shower Time Playlist Confessional"

Eddy Francisco Alvarez Jr.

I

Getting ready to shower
My playlist is on
Jenni Rivera, *Inolvidable*
Gloria Trevi, *Todos me miran*
Whitney Houston, *I want to dance with somebody*
India Arie, *Video*
And *I* too am in that video
Not the average boy in a video, I am fat, and queer and sexy
bears, chubs, they call us, queer in size and sizzle.
Hot
como tortillas calientitas, like lock the bathroom door, spur
    of the moment calenturas
Standing in front of the full-length mirror,

Naked, I sing along, I dance, watch myself dance,
This is a sacred moment
me and my body, in worship,
Yes.
A moment of worship.
A ship, yes a ship, a vessel, yes, yes, yes!!
This is my fat and sexy vessel, come ride in it, swim to my
    edges, rock this boat, paddle me, I
paddle you, drink from these waters, as they spill like my
    stomach onto yours,
This vessel carries me forward, in breath, in movement, in
    ecstasy, in orgasm, in forgiveness,
of myself, for blasphemy against myself,
for internalizing the blasphemy of others, hurtful words,
    eyes and gestures erasing my existence in the club, on the
    Boulevard, on the app, no fats no femmes? Fuck that.
For internalizing their false claims, their sugar coated
    ofensas in the name of health, of my well-being, well I
    don't buy it.
I forgive and love this cintura, this textured cuerpo de
    exceso, de estrillas, scars, and invisible
wounds,
Don't you want to know what I can do with this body?

I dance, and swing my hips, "moviendo la cadera, moviendo
    la cadera"
Me gusta ver mi propia sabrosura. Yeah, that's right, my
    deliciousness

"When I look in the mirror and the only one there is me,"
    Arie sings,
and reminds me that my body is no mistake
a work in progress always, but not your idea of progress and
    not a mistake, not unfinished, not
on the way to be skinny.
"My feet, my thighs, my lips, my eyes," yeah baby!
And, yes, I too am LOVING the image in front of me, of
    beautiful imperfection, dripping oozing sexiness, my
    belly, my thighs, this is where it's at.

This is a fuck you to the haters and the naysayers and the
Fatphobic Karens and Beckys the tías metiches saying, "It's
    about your health."
"Es por tu bien."

II

This is a wet dance confession
Of a fat queer jotx
Confessing in the nude
This is a letter to myself
An affirmation
A negotiation
A convocation
To honor and love my body, always

"A Fat Lot of Good That Did: How an Art Studio Transformed My Eyes"

Jerome Stueart

I had a little art studio for one year. A place for all my paints, my canvases, my artistic dreams. A place to be alone, to create masterpieces, to rock out to music, to be myself, to grow and learn.

Then the art studio was completely erased, as if it had never been there. All the walls taken down, the room swallowed by a much larger gallery. You couldn't find it if you didn't know where it had been. If you didn't know my window, you couldn't see any fingerprint of where I was.

While the studio was there, that brief year, it changed my life. It gave me a better understanding of my body—something I had never really seen before. It gave me back my sexuality—something taken from me by churches. It let me see myself as a work of art—something I never would have believed.

While I struggled to create art, the studio worked on creating *me*.

❀   ❀   ❀

For decades, Front Street Studios in Dayton, Ohio, had used an old Singer Sewing Machine factory as living space for artists. It was a set of imposing red brick buildings, some two story, some three, with giant 15-foot windows, built next to a very active set of railroad tracks, with a river not far away. Over the last few decades, the old factory had gone to seed, become unliveable, a place for drug deals and fire hazards. A few years before I got there, it was taken over by new management. The new owners cleaned it up, bought out whoever was still there, and turned it into studio spaces for artists, with open studios twice a month where people from Dayton could come through, wine in hand, and visit your studio and buy your art. The new owners brought in live bands outside, and sold burgers and hot dogs on those open studio days. You would never have known the place was abandoned and trashed just a few years before.

In the summer of 2018, needing more studios to rent, the owners divided a larger studio space into smaller 300-square-foot slots with giant warehouse windows. They aimed these studios towards artists who didn't need a *lot* of space, and didn't have a lot of money.

Perfect for someone like me.

That summer, I had decided to turn my hobby of portrait painting into a small business, and I needed a small space. I was an adjunct English teacher at a local university, but that didn't really pay the bills. I struggled a lot. I knew that each semester I would have to beg the chair of the department for any classes he could give me.

So, I needed another source of income.

I had a passion for art. Why not turn it into something more? Why not give it a chance? The owners interviewed me, liked me, and gave me the space for a mere $250 a month. I was in! I had my own space.

It was the perfect size for me. High ceiling, tall, unfinished, white drywall, those giant windows that let in the sun—full blazing in the summer! And privacy. I could do anything I wanted in that room. I could wear what I wanted. I didn't have to share this "office space" or justify what I was doing to anyone. It wasn't part of a job. I had complete control of me in this space. I loved it. I loved that freedom. I still love it, in my memory, even though it is gone.

I had never owned a studio before, a place outside the apartment I lived in, but, to me, having a studio meant that I was taking my art seriously. I was taking *myself* seriously. So I was there every day that summer, working on painting, even as the studio worked on me.

❀　❀　❀

Queer people have to learn early to own themselves and their bodies because we are told that the spaces are not for us in this world, and sometimes, our own bodies are not for us. Society likes to tell people what they can and cannot do with their bodies, their behavior, their minds. They rent space in our heads, sometimes the whole factory in our head. And in those studios are how we should dress, how we should act, who we should be.

I was raised a Southern Baptist Christian boy—Baptists didn't dance, didn't cuss, didn't drink, and they were frightened of their bodies. In this fog of unreason, it took me till I was 34 to realize I was gay. I had no space in my head for what it meant to be gay. I was a kid during the AIDS crisis, and that was the first time I had heard about queer people. When you grew up in the Midwest or West Texas, in the rural areas, the queer trains didn't get that far, and the books, movies, and people who are strongest in their identities—who might show you who you could be—couldn't reach you. At least they couldn't in the eighties. So I didn't know myself.

I knew to be afraid of my body. I knew my body was supposed to be attracted to women, and attractive *to* women, and as a good Christian boy, I should be looking at marriage in my early twenties, if not before. I also knew that men around me did *not* talk about their bodies. The boys talked about their desires for women, but that's not the same thing. Once they were married, it was as if they had joined a secret cult where they were no longer allowed to discuss their bodies, their sexuality, or their desires anymore. "You'll learn about that when you get a girlfriend."

I knew to be careful not to show I had a sexual feeling because all sexual feelings were bad. Even the straight ones! And don't touch yourself, young man. I knew a young man who got married because he needed sex and he wasn't allowed to touch himself or God would be angry with him. So he married a woman as a sanctioned way to release.

Queer people were watched. Before we discovered I was queer, I was watched by my parents, by my friends, as they looked for signs that I was on the Path of Straight Salvation. I did not give them the right signals, and we all thought I was broken. The stuff just doesn't work on me. At my Baptist university, I got a reputation as a man who had mastered his body! I had overcome temptation! (I thought I was secretly immune!) Truth was, my sexuality was buried so deep, it was made invisible. It was erased.

I had to draw it out again.

I had to give it some time to grow and breathe.

But I had to discover it first. That would be when I was 34. When I discovered I was gay, it was such beautiful relief to know I wasn't broken. But I also didn't know the directions to my own body or mind, nor did I have people around me to mentor me at the time. I had a lot to learn about myself, and a lot to unlearn about my body, about my perception of myself, about what was attractive. It took me a long time to figure out who I was and what I wanted—and even by 2018, there was still work left to do inside my head. I didn't know that.

Queer people need a space to figure out who they are when they are surrounded by a world of people so unlike them. They need the time to figure out what they like, what they feel like doing, what aspects of gender conformity to keep, what to toss. Even queer people in the age of queer visibility still need to find their path in a highway system of How to Be Gay and How to Be Lesbian and That's All There Is messages given to us today. We are lucky that so many new voices are speaking out about their very different paths to find self-fulfillment, painting their own stories so vividly.

❀ ❀ ❀

At first, in my new studio, I didn't know what I wanted to paint, and I didn't want to waste time. I tried writing in there. I set up a little office. I attempted to tap out some stories. Instead, I just tapped out. It was *so* hot. It was about 85 degrees inside the studio. I had afternoon light, and a glorious sunset over Dayton in the evening, but no curtains. That afternoon sunlight turned the studio into an oven.

I bought a fan. I bought two fans. I bought three fans.

Eventually, I tried to regulate hours so that I didn't land there between 1pm and 6pm, but that was a good chunk of the part of the day that I liked. I preferred coming late morning and staying till 10 or 11pm. So, instead of escaping the afternoon heat, I opened windows, used the fans, and dressed accordingly.

I started wearing a sleeveless shirt with snaps that I could open when I was alone. I had a belly, and I was always raised to believe that men did not walk around a workplace showing their body. After all, there were other artists working in the building. No one else was around in my studio though, and so I wore the shirt like a vest, or went shirtless. I thought it was indulgent and kind of sexy. But I was also nervous of anyone seeing my body. I just thought it was wrong, especially if you looked like me.

Remember, I had never liked my body. I grew up skinny, way too thin, and then I started gaining weight when I was 30, and I kept going, and now I no longer had an accurate idea of what I looked like.

I had not seen what I looked like, lately—never as a full-bodied man, outside a Kohl's mirror in the dressing room—and had a very unrealistic view of myself. We all have the bathroom mirror impression (light in your face, mirror stops mid-chest) and the "I can look down at myself" view, which narrows the view as you look further down. And the arm-stretched-as-far-as-I-can-go selfie. I knew I wasn't that good looking. I knew I was not "well built," but soft around the edges. I had some major body dysmorphia going on. But I was getting curious to know what I looked like. I started taking pictures of myself in the studio to see what other people saw when they saw me.

I didn't know how big I was. I was always underweight for my height and I kept that image in my head for a long time until I noticed myself in other people's photos and thought—who is *that*? It would always surprise me how large I was compared to other people, especially other men. I always thought I was the smaller, "weaker" one when I compared myself to other men.

So I set up my iPad to take pictures of myself from a distance. I wanted to see my whole body from the side, from angles you can't catch in a mirror. I wanted to know what people saw when they saw me.

In my own private space, with my own iPad, I could take pictures of myself shirtless. I could take pictures of myself in my underwear! Hello, *Jesus*, I could take pictures of myself naked.

Guys had wanted naked pictures before when I had chatted online, and I never felt good about sending a picture of my body online. There are many good reasons not to send nudes through the internet. There are *no* good reasons not to take one though. You can learn a lot about yourself, about the way your body looks, and not just standing up, but relaxing against a window, or lying down, or with special sunlight on your body. I needed to see what I looked like naked. I know, it is hard to believe that I hadn't really seen myself naked, but I hadn't from a distance or in a full-length mirror.

So I started taking pictures of myself.

* * *

We all have our bodies we are attracted to. I was into "bears." Big, hairy men with soft curves and big arms and kind faces: Jack Black, Theodus Crane, Chad Coleman, Sebastian Cabot, David Harbour, Kevin James, Bob Hoskins, Questlove, Brendan Gleeson, James Gandolfini, Nick Offerman, Mark Addy, Nick Frost, Daniel Franzese. Santa Claus.

I was attracted to large men, fat men, big men, huggable men.

When I saw my pictures, the first thought I had was: I am one of those men.

I was not the size I thought I was. I was larger. I was much wider from back to front than I had ever seen. I was thick. My pecs were soft, wide pillows that stretched under my arms. My belly overlapped my belt. I had some really nice curves, and an undefined ass.

But my initial surprise gave way to love. I loved this body. I was not who I expected I was, but I was okay with that. I began to sympathize and empathize with the man in the pictures.

I started acting more comfortable in my body for different pictures, different poses.

You'd think I'd be painting!

Instead, I was creating with my body and my iPad these pictures of a heroic fat queer man, dancing, being sexy, being goofy. Just to see what that looked like. I changed filters and created some of the best pictures of my beautiful fat body. What about this Noir setting? Or this Dramatic Cool? Or Vivid Warm filters? I used the different adjustments to work the saturation levels, the definition, the exposure, and had fun using my body as the subject of my own artistic exploration.

I even chanced answering requests for pictures from long-time text friends, gaining consent, and sending these nudes to men I was talking to. I was suddenly not afraid if the nudes got out into the world. These were artistically done, and completely sent with consent. I had nothing to fear from my body. My body was teaching me who I was.

I wasn't perfect, but I wasn't as unattractive as I thought I was. And even if I was, I could work that body. And I noticed in the pictures how much more attractive I became when I became fearless in my mind. When I let loose. When I stood tall.

I was everything visually I admired in that long list of men.

Then I started wondering something even deeper, and more taboo. What did I look like having sex? I'll be honest. I had not had a lot of sex. Old beliefs. Fears of pain. Embarrassment over having so little experience. So, I never wanted to see myself or think of what I looked like during those moments. But while I had this studio, this private place, and this way to dissociate from my body by watching it through a screen and seeing it as both other and self, I needed to explore places of vulnerability and ecstasy.

Why was that important?

* * *

Sexuality, and queer sexuality especially, is taboo in religious circles where I grew up. I did not have the safety of a space—a studio—to talk to others about sexuality, about their bodies. I never talked about myself sexually with other people. I wanted them to pretend I never had sex. That was okay. I didn't want them to know. I really didn't want my straight friends and allies to know I had ever had a sexual thought. I didn't take my shirt off when we played basketball in high school. It took me a long time to feel comfortable undressing in a gym. My naked chest somehow was all about sex! My naked body in the gym was somehow talking about sex! Some of my straight friends seemed okay if I never brought it up, so why talk about it? With my queer friends, I felt embarrassed that I had not had as much as I (should?) have had. I felt sex was another world.

I wish we all felt more comfortable talking about sex, about ourselves and sex. I'm 51 now, and it's taken me this long to feel comfortable in my body, and talking about myself and sex. As a queer man, I saw that straight men had their sex talked about everywhere. If they weren't repressed by religion, they could see a very narrow idea of their sexuality presented on TV, in movies, books, magazines. But even they were suffering from not talking about real sexuality. What a body really felt like, really looked like, how it acted. Not what we're told to look like—the idealized form that is impossible to become, or the idealized way of having sex.

I was lucky to have had some great moments with other men where I was allowed to be goofy and to laugh and to be a human being having fun and having sex. But it was also important to have an "out of body" experience—to see myself as a sexual person—so I could understand my body having sex.

For the first time, I really felt this joy for the person in the video. I felt empathy and love. And I wanted him to have a great time, and to find love and to find positive sexual experiences in his life. It allowed me to love myself in a whole different way.

I also got to be a director and filmmaker and work those filters!

I wasn't going to do 75 of them, but I needed to see it once.

Evangelical religious dogma made me feel disgusted with my body for not being like other men. It made me feel ashamed to give in to passions. To have sexual feelings. To act on them.

I slowly tried to erase my body.

Over time, it worked. I had forgotten what I looked like.

But in that Studio of a Year, I got to know my body again as a work of art. I got to meet the Jerome who felt sexy and unashamed of that. I got to send those unashamed, sex-positive images to friends and lovers to share that part of myself. I got the same back from them. In this way, sharing our bodies through pictures, we created encouraging support for our bodies with each other. By sharing those pictures, I affirmed their bodies, and they affirmed my body. It wasn't just something that happened in the bed, or in the dark. It was a way of telling each other that we were good men. That we had great sexual feelings. And for me, seeing myself was about getting love from the Divine too. Because I knew that while the studio was private to me, I think God was pretty happy I had discovered and loved my body too. Because they gave me that body, and they loved that body too.

* * *

After the studio was destroyed and remade into a gallery, I went to an art school. I felt inspired by my studio experience to paint positive pictures of fat queer heroes having adventures. I picked out Yukon Cornelius as my character to develop. He was in about ten minutes of a Christmas special, *Rudolph the Red Nosed Reindeer*. But I wanted to give him a full queer life.

I had planned to take photos of men that looked more like what I wanted Yukon to look like—strong, hairy, large, heroic—and I had friends lined up to be models. But schedules never worked out and time forced me to use what I had at hand to get my paintings done. So I just substituted my own body in heroic poses. I looked at those pictures—and realized I could be the queer hero too. I didn't just love myself, but I saw that I could be the kind of hero I was looking for. So I posed for all my paintings. I was used to taking pics of myself now!

The studio only existed for one year, and I did paint in that art studio, but my time in this studio also taught me to see myself differently. To be proud of my body, to be unafraid of my body. To be sexual and not be ashamed. I was able to take back so much that had been taken from me. And in my year of art school, I worked more of that out.

It's a process.

"About My Breasts, Since You Asked"

Sherre Vernon

In the Russian sauna, two
old women scrub me without
consent. Through the birch-branch
steam I avert my eyes, but there are bodies
everywhere. Just this once, breasts like mine:
thank god. thank god. thank god.

❀　❀

My breasts believe in Archimedes, float
above my sinking body. With the water, they are
full & well-positioned. My lover, the mathematician,
wonders why they can't be like this
always. At least there is something lovely
in the contrast of my nipples against my skin.

❀　❀

I thought bosom was a chest in blossom,
the vowel a sigh into adulthood, the *ah*
both breath & connection. How disappointing,
the words that actually find me—*badonka-donks*,
tig-ol-bitties—and keep me wishing
for other skin.

❀ ❀

My classmates have decided the women
in the National Geographic must have
breasts like that for lack of underwire
or by nursing too many babies. Telling
them otherwise would expose me.

❀ ❀

My mother sleeps prophetic & topless
her breasts an advertisement. How
could I know—what did I know of
shirts strangling themselves around us
in our sleep?

❀ ❀

In order to breathe, girls like me, we
sleep in our bras. It's the closest we come
to sleek. In my twenties, for headstand,
an old man shows me how to strap myself in,
how to keep my boobs at bay.

❀ ❀

I'm thirteen & the man at the counter calls me
thick, makes a sweet exhale through
the side of his mouth. Another hollers
an invitation from the street. A third pushes by,
his breath hot in my ear & on my face, his
body scraping into the cotton on my skin.

❀ ❀

Running is two sports bras, layered
over circulation, each step a gravity punch.
I become a swimmer. We dress & undress
in paper-thin skins. I learn
a thousand ways to be unseen.

❀ ❀

The first doctor writes pendular in my file, tells
me with his face that I am vain & petty. I barely
dress before he shows me the door. A hundred
pounds later, a specialist traces the divots burrowing
into my shoulders, the red branding
circumscribing my ribs, tells me I
should have done this years ago.

❀ ❀

In two days, I'm making
love, surgical tape still
in place. I have never
felt so beautiful, never
so easy to move. I sleep

shirtless. I always sleep
shirtless.

❀ ❀

I want to talk about breasts. I am reduced! I am
lifted! Hallelujah & Amen. I know a woman
who has left her breasts behind. I want
to tell her—*I read that article you wrote—it meant
so much to me*—Why
does she look away?

❀ ❀

Women never say to me, you really shouldn't
have. They ask about nursing or pain,
even some about identity, if they ask
anything at all. The men though, it's always:
I wish you hadn't. What about me?

❀ ❀

What about her, my little love? I can feed her,
barely. My arms shake from holding her
up, my nipples are eroding & the milk is only
two ounces, ever. She is so hungry, so tired. I am
the one who did this.

❀ ❀

Here's something few people know: I
would have chosen a mastectomy, were I
braver. Might have transitioned this body, had I

known that was a choice. Might not
have done it at all, if I had believed
I'd allow myself a daughter.

❉   ❉

My baby inventories bodies: *Eyes. Toes.*
Ears. Nose. Hair. Bellybutton. Lifts her
shirt &—*Boobs!* She reaches across
to help me find mine, just in case
I missed them.

❉   ❉

& she tucks her palms between my breasts,
snuggles down to sleep, folds herself into
me. Nursing, we'd allow this. But for her,
my weaned one, who allows her
this skin?

❉   ❉

I have grown into these two
decades' gravity. I love these
faded key-hole scars, soft shelf
bras, and my body's simple refusal
to keep shape.

❉   ❉

At the day spa, a woman with large,
heavy & pendular breasts sits
near me. Her body is

what mine was almost. Still
is. We don't speak. I am
grateful, find her
beautiful.

"Heretic Body"

Ninamarie Ochoa

fistfuls of flesh
unruly as a creation myth

this heretic body
begs to be made legible

what do you read first?

stretchmarks
like the rippled veins of
light
at the bottom of a swimming pool

the darkened skin
between my legs,
scarred
from the friction
of walking miles

in humid heat
that left me
raw

this greedy mouth:
full
treacherous lips
that devour

her

what can she do
but worship
these apostatic hips?

hips
and a belly
that would strain the
ropes binding me
to the stake,
condemned
for my abundance

condemned
for the audacity of
my pain and pleasure

this heretic body
of multitudes
dares you
to set it
on fire

an alchemy of light and electricity

feral blooming
in hospital gowns
under the netted silhouette of chicken wire glass

a mind as dissident
as my body

kaleidoscopic rapture

on a bed with her
in summer
with the AC off
beads of sweat between my breasts
my shoulder blades
down my spine

bliss and suffering
inextricable
in this heretic
and celestial body

elemental and yearning

like the shattered floor of the desert
aching
under arcs of lighting

this body

whose joy is an insurrection

whose hymns
brand themselves
into her palms

this ecstatic body

made
to be held

too big
to be held

at once

"Soft Butch"

Nora E. Derrington

I. Soft

There's an onomatopoeia to the word. It begins with a sibilant, sinuous, sensual ess, then moves on to a gentle ah that caresses the palate. Then the quick succession of consonants hitting the lips and teeth like a playful kitten batting a toy mouse. The word is a delicacy, smooth and subtle.

As a descriptor, it can be tactile: pliable, cushioned, comfortable. Cotton sheets worn silky smooth. Downy puppy fur. Velvet rose petals drawn across bare skin. But of course, the negative associations slip in quickly: pliable becomes yielding, yielding becomes weak. A soft touch. Soft-hearted. A big softie. An antonym not just for hard but for strong.

For as long as I can remember, I wanted to be strong, to be tough. I didn't want to be soft. How could I be anything but soft, though, when PE was my worst subject and I was so sensitive that the slightest injustice—Nikki's mom yelling at me for wearing shoes on Nikki's waterbed, even though the tell-tale footprint clearly came from Nikki's shoe—or most mundane tragedy—restless teens dismembering a cheap claw-machine teddy bear in my presence—never failed to make me cry?

II. Butch

More onomatopoeia here, too: a voiced plosive, a deep vowel, three consonants in a row. Similar in feel to "macho"—but subtly different in meaning. Stereotypically masculine. Nothing about me has ever been masculine, so how could I ever be butch?

Dickies pants became the rage when I was in high school. As an alternative-rock aficionado who obsessed over the sound and aesthetics of the movie *Singles*—it came out when I was 12 and changed my life—I knew I needed them. When I was 16 and had both a job and transportation, I made my way to the local Tillys to snag a pair. The black cotton twill was stiff under my fingers as I stepped into the pants and pulled them up.

The Dickies pulled against my hips, uncomfortably snug, and gaped so wide at my waist I could fit a fist between my skin and the cloth. I left the store disappointed. Why did I even bother? "Good, child-bearing hips," people would tell me, even as an adolescent. I resigned myself to a presentation that never quite matched the ideal in my head.

III. Thin

When I was an adolescent, the parts of my appearance I was most satisfied with, even proud of—and, not incidentally, these were also the things I got the most compliments and praise for—were my hair, long and fine and honey-brown, and my thinness.

At 14 I was paired with another girl for a dance routine, and she openly admired my prominent collarbones: "You have those," she exclaimed, gesturing at the neckline of my t-shirt. "I want those!" So rarely did I have anything someone else wanted!

I was plenty thin, then, despite my wide-set hips, and it felt right. But my frame was clearly all wrong. I should have looked like Linda Hamilton in *Terminator 2*, strong and hard and fierce. Instead I was still somehow soft—one time I substituted for one of the bass drum regulars in the winter drumline, and the drum harness left big enough bruises on my hip bones that I had to tape folded dish towels across my abdomen for the performance.

So I was thin, and I was soft, and somehow that made it easier to believe I was straight.

IV. Fat

These days, I'm Schrodinger's fat girl, simultaneously existing in a state of thinness and fatness depending on who's observing me and how they're doing so. In the doctor's office, I am fat. Nurses look at my BMI (body mass index), waist circumference, and body fat percentage—which I dutifully submit myself to measurements of every year in exchange for benefits through my workplace's employee wellness program—and tut. I need to get more exercise and eat better. They say—not in so many words, but they say it nonetheless—that I take up too much space. There should be less of me—and what there is of me ought to be more socially acceptable. None of this perpetually messy hair or sprawling limbs or visible tattoos or constant fidgeting.

In the rest of my life, though, I'm not really fat, which is to say that I don't face most of the marginalizations fat people have to deal with. Sure, I might have a relative see photos of me online (from a relay race, no less!) and email me to say I really ought to lose weight, but I can mostly buy clothes off the rack. I fit into airplane and movie seats without discomfort. I don't get more street harassment than the average woman or femme.

But somehow, at the same time, in groups of thin people—particularly women, particularly straight women—I'm definitely fat. Once I stood by quietly while two women friends bonded over having (allegedly) put on a few pounds, and how unattractive it made them. "I'm bigger than both of you," I eventually murmured, "so you must think I'm a monster." Oh, no, they assured me, "you've just got those child-bearing hips!"

Good, child-bearing hips. The structure of my frame says I'm meant to procreate. Is that why it took me until I was almost 30 to realize I didn't want to?

V. Straight

I had this boyfriend in ninth grade that I adored. Sure, he had an anger problem and a way of making all his issues feel as if they were my responsibility, if not my fault, but I really did love everything about him. Everything about him was soft and gentle. I talked about how the moment I fell in love with him was when I realized he was crying with me over a fight within our friend group (precipitated, it occurs to me now, by a friend calling me a "two-timing slut," "as a joke").

He came out as gay three years later, long after we broke up. The fact that he'd never wanted to do more than gently smooch me suddenly made sense.

Meanwhile, I attributed the fact that I'd never wanted to do more than gently smooch him back to my being a girl. There seemed to be a sort of basic logic to it: soft boys and soft girls must like boys. Hard boys and hard girls must like girls. The idea that any of those dichotomies—soft/hard, boy/girl, straight/gay—might point to people who existed in a place of "both/and" or "neither/nor" didn't occur to me until much later.

Perhaps it's more accurate to say that I didn't question how those labels applied to me, personally, until much later.

After I graduated from college, I gained weight slowly but steadily—and the world didn't end, as my adolescent self would have expected it to. I got rounder and softer, but also stronger, inside and out—surprising friends with how much I could carry when I helped them move, beginning to learn when and how to prioritize my own needs. If I could break the rule that thin was the only right way to be and come out the other side even stronger, even more comfortable in my skin, what other rules could I break?

VI. Queer

The use of "queer" to mean "strange" dates back to the 16th century. I lost track of the number of times I was called "weird" as a kid and adolescent. Part of the weirdness was that I frequently had my nose stuck in a book, which means I first encountered the word "queer" in that older, "odd duck" sense, while reading. I think I encountered it in its derogatory sense the same way. The reclamation of the word as an umbrella term happened in the late 20th century, around the same time I was growing up. I heard it at the first Pride festival I attended as a tween in the early 90s, helping my mom staff a booth for the psychology clinic she worked at.

When I was a sophomore in high school, my French class was assigned a group project highlighting a region in France. I don't remember the exact region my group was assigned; I just remember it was a region that produced leather. We were at one group member's house, putting the final touches on the project. I have no memory of how this came up, but the group member dug out a pair of shorts his mom had kept around for decades: burgundy suede hot pants. I was usually fairly draped in fabric: baggy jeans; big t-shirts I tucked in, then tugged out a bit so they'd blouse around my waist; loose hoodies—but somehow the group decided the shorts would fit me. And indeed they did. Picture this, then: a mid-1990s camcorder slowly pans up an awkward teenager's body as she models a vintage pair of hot pants. A voice-over—me? another group member? all four of us?—intoned the French word for leather: cuir. "Cuir, cuir, cuir," we chanted in our best advertising voices—pronunciation shaped by suburban southern California, the edges of the consonants sanded off, the vowels pushed forward in our mouths, so we might as well have been saying "queer."

I modeled vintage hot pants while a handful of people—myself included—chanted "queer," like a ritual of invocation.

I'd be hard-pressed to come up with a more apt origin story. I had my first crush on a girl sometime in the next year, though several more years would pass before I realized that's what it was. Once awareness arrived, I tried various labels on, but none quite fitted. Queer always fitted me like those hot pants: unexpectedly but perfectly.

VII. Soft butch

Despite my fitting comfortably under the queer umbrella, I'd never really given all that much thought to the specifics of my gender identity and expression. I met a trans man when I was 24 who used the same nickname I do, which made it easier to see our similarities, but I knew immediately that his path wasn't mine. Later that year I met someone who epitomizes high femme, and, again, I could immediately see both how perfectly she embodied that expression, and how poorly it would suit me.

The person I thought of at the time as my boyfriend, then my husband, used to joke that I was the man in the relationship—despite my tender heart, my frequent tears, my undeniable softness—but I was more or less content in just knowing what I wasn't. It seems possible I could have stayed in that liminal place forever, but then when we were in our mid-thirties, my wife came out as trans.

This is not a story of my adapting to my wife being trans. I'd always known we were both queer, and discovering I was married to a woman came more as a pleasant surprise than anything else.

What did happen, though, was that her coming out gave me permission to do more soul-searching, to try to pinpoint my gender identity and ideal gender expression. I first encountered the term "soft butch" in one of those joke "futch scale" charts—the ones that sort musical instruments or tropical fruits on a scale from high femme to stone butch—but it stuck with me. It didn't seem to be something I was allowed to call myself, though: image searches on Google or Pinterest just led to rows of photos of beautiful slender white people with artful short haircuts and distressed jeans. Lots of Kristen Stewart and Elliot Page and occasionally Justin Bieber. I am definitely too old and too fat to try to emulate those folks! Eventually I lamented on Twitter that I was drawn to the soft butch aesthetic but didn't know if I could pull it off, given that I'm not thin. I quickly received a slightly baffled but firm response from a genderqueer acquaintance that of course I could. In some ways I'm still a kid, seeking others' permission to accept myself.

I realize as I write this that I'm wearing what might be my quintessential soft butch outfit—it fits me almost without my trying. Distressed jeans—a pair that I stole from my wife long before she transitioned. They fit my hips and thighs beautifully, which means I have to cinch a belt tight to make them stay up around my waist, but I know how to manage that now. A close-fitting t-shirt celebrating a punk band I've seen in concert a good dozen times. Hair pulled back into a messy bun. Fuzzy gray slippers with arch support, because I'm a middle-aged fat person, so of course I have plantar fasciitis. A gentle breath before a firm statement: the perfect mixture of soft and butch.

"F-Words"

Jonathan Hillman

When I was young, I was afraid of F-words.
Fat.
Fem.
Faggot.
Red marks, like stretch marks,
on my social report card,
reminding me that I was
Failing.

Failing to fit.
Failing to become the man
my Family and Father wanted.
A test with two boxes:
☐ **M** or ☐ **F**
I was too Fat, too Fem,
to fit inside the M.

Capital M. Masculinity.
My doctor showed me
a graph of all the boys
my age, my height—

MY WEIGHT

floating blimp-like above
them.
Chad told me
in the middle school hallway—
he pointed, he shot me blank
with, **"You're a Faggot"**
They told me
    my body,
        my belly,
            my S's,
                my wrists,
threatened a paradigm built
on barbells and beer cans
and belts pulled tight.

We, the Fat Faggots,
We, the doubly queer,
We were afraid of you,
but we make you feel Fear.
Fatphobia.
Homophobia.
Effemiphobia.

F-words.
Fatal Flaws in my Facade.
Freshman year,
I lost forty-five pounds.
A fresh man, a real boy.
Puppet strings pulled straight,
lanky-limbed
lines memorized.
But no matter how I sucked
it in, pierced the hole, and let it hiss,
Fatness followed me.

He followed me back to my locker,
the first boy I wanted to kiss.
He leaned back, belly big.
I wanted to touch him, to feel his fat flesh.
I wanted to become him.
I wanted
I wanted
Liberation,
a combination I couldn't unlock.
Could I be like him?
Could I be with him without
Failing?

Can a man be a man without
Fading

"You're Too Fat to be Androgynous"

Nicole Oquendo

You're right, based on the definition you hold
so tight your nails dig into your palm.

Let's not romanticize it—my body
is heavy, and the space I take up
is more than the multiple rounds of my belly
and the inconvenient width of my arms.

Let's talk about buying a suit. How, eyes wet with want,
there's a symbol of androgyny orbiting just outside,
and I can feel it in my hands, the material that won't
rest just right.

Yes, we can discuss symbols more.
I own so many ties, none of which I wear.
My hands shake too much to work the knots.

"You're Too Fat to be Androgynous"

I stopped shaving the sides of my head because
sitting in the barber's chair, so often and so public,
was a coming out as regular as the period I can't carve out.

You're right, in the way that this is not
a conversation, that my width makes me more.
My body is haunted by the ghost of a young girl,
the boy who almost was,

yes, and the frame we see with our own eyes.

"Enough"

Tiff Joshua TJ Ferentini

`00.00`

My mother is crying in our local Applebee's.

It's not the first time nor the most ridiculous place my mother has cried in public: there was the diner by our house (after we got the call that my aunt passed away), the A&P my uncle worked at (after we went to see the plaque of his employee of the month photo after *he* passed away), but this is the first time I've seen her cry in public without it being over someone dying.

Well, I guess someone *did* die. To her, at least.

My mother blows her nose in a napkin as our waitress comes over, asking us if we're ready to have our order taken. She smiles, through tears: it's the same smile I make when someone tells me bad news, an awkward smile to defuse an even more awkward situation, the kind of smile you make when you couldn't be further from being happy or laughing.

"I'm sorry, we just haven't seen each other in so long," she apologizes.

We see each other every week.

128

"We're going to need a few more moments to see what we want."

She's planning on ordering the same thing she always has: an oriental chicken salad, grilled, dressing on the side. Because if you get the dressing on the side, the 1,000 calories claimed on the menu no longer apply.

The waitress sympathetically smiles, setting down our previously ordered two waters with lemon and glasses of diet ginger ale—our drinks of choice when we dine out—before exiting.

My mother blows her nose, honking in her napkin tissue again.

"It's just..." she continues from where she left off before she started crying, dapping at her eyes with her napkin, goopy black mascara joining the yellow stains of snot. "You've just gained so much *weight*... You shouldn't be changing the body you were born with... It's *unnatural*... So can you tell me... are you still on *those hormones*...?"

I respond by taking a sip of my ice water, the swirl of lemon immediately going sour in my stomach.

Testosterone—"those hormones"—and I have been on a break for a year and a half, after I decided I needed space to see if continuing to be on them was something I still wanted. For the year I was on them, my body began to change, slowly but surely: my voice began to crack as if in a second puberty; body hair started to come in, thicker in places it already was and coarse in places where it was making its debut; my arms and legs grew more toned. The body hair I could live without, but noticing my voice crack in freedom and grow deeper, my limbs growing slimmer and stronger, filled me with a power and happiness I never could have imagined existed.

When I first came out—both as queer and as nonbinary—my mother asked me "if the doctors thought it had something to do with the fact I was born premature," as if the human body, *my* human body, were a turkey or a cake, taken out of the oven too soon before it could fully cook; as if there had to have been a *reason* for me to not only be queer, but also trans on top of it.

I don't know what hurts more—that first dismissal where instead of acceptance, my mother kept searching for a reason for my queerness, or that the only element of my transition that she chooses to notice isn't even my physical transition itself, but my weight gain. Hearing her vocalize her disgust at not only my body, but my nonbinary, trans identity as well, makes my stomach grow more nauseous than any lemon ever could, a nausea that not even a ginger ale cure-all could sate.

01:00

Food was my family's love language.

Name any holiday, any occasion, and it was celebrated with the entire family. With both sets of grandparents as my next door neighbors and both sets of aunts and uncles not more than ten minutes away, there was no such thing as a "mom's side" or a "dad's side"; we were all part of the Ferentini family: a small, Italian army of 17.

Palm Sunday (the Lamb holiday); Easter (the Lasagna holiday); Thanksgiving (Manicotti before turkey was a requirement); Christmas Eve, Christmas Day (the double feature of seven fishes, antipasto, and homemade pizza, two kinds: plain and with anchovies); New Year's Eve, New Year's Day (the post-credits scene that came after Christmas, featuring appetizers and aunt's special cheesecake). With every occasion, everyone brought their own dish—always made from scratch, always made with love.

Sometimes, there wasn't an occasion at all: it was just afternoon snacks of pieces of parmigiano and soppressata, dried and hung from my nonno's garage; Wednesday nights with chicken cacciatore or spinach raviolis with Aunt Marie and Uncle Carmine; Thursday nights of Nonno Gino's homemade wine and Nonna Lina's polenta or rigatoni or salad grown fresh from the garden; or afternoon Sunday dinners of my mother's meatballs and sauce.

No matter whose house we were in, the scent of sauces and spices clung to the air like music, my family's dinner table conversations serving as the accompanying lyrics.

Who made this?

Pass the bread.

Pass the cheese.

This is amazing!

But eating food wasn't always joyful, and the times it wasn't was whenever I'd eat in secret, alone, or when I was the subject of my family's criticism, observed under the microscope of 17 pairs of eyes, the lyric changing into:

You finished all that already?

02.00

I'd always been really good at hiding.

It started off with food wrappers: Gusher packets, chips!

Ahoy packages, string cheese plastic, Go-Gurt tubes. Snacks were a rarity in our house—chips were the distant relative you only saw at family barbeques and holidays, cakes and cookies making their special appearances only when family friends came over—so I treasured it when my mother allowed my siblings and me to add the occasional fruits snack or cookie package to our shopping cart. When they were in our house, I'd treat them like house guests, saving our time together but instantly missing them the moment they'd leave.

When I was younger and came home after school, I'd snack on whatever I could find, whatever I was craving, whatever sweet or saltiness gave me the most momentary pleasure that lasted longer than the guilt that followed it. My snacking had meticulous rules: never be the one to open a package to avoid being the first one accused of opening it, always eat cookies in threes, destroy the evidence.

I'd bury my Gusher wrappers, cookie packages, Go-Gurt tubes, and whatever other snack packaging was my victim of the day as deeply as I could in the garbage in our kitchen; wash my hands, making a show of washing up past my wrists, to my elbows, and getting my arms more wet and soapy than they needed to be; then use more paper towels than was necessary to dry myself, enough to hide the evidence in the garbage, the murder victim a trifle of snack wrappers.

As I grew older, I never broke the habit of hiding food wrappers. I squirreled them away as if the wrappers themselves were food I needed to last me through the winter—Party Mix and sour cream and onion chip bags buried beneath colored pencils in the pockets of my school backpacks, sweet Entenmann's and Hostess cellophane wrappers squished into clear white balls in my jacket pockets.

Clothes with pockets were a must, and oversized clothes even better—shirts and hoodies that fell past my butt, sleeves that dangled well past my fingertips, any fabric that was soft and warm in which I could bury myself, bury the shape of my body, the curves of my prepubescent body falling into straight lines at my sides, cotton and polyester replacing paper towels. My body was as shameful to me as the snack wrappers I buried in a shallow garbage grave.

The larger the clothes I wore, the smaller I thought they made me look, and I wanted to look smaller so badly, despite destroying the possibility of that ever happening with each extra snack I ate.

Despite that, the larger the sizes I bought, the sooner I'd grow into them.

And as I grew older, I had more to hide than snack wrappers, more to hide that was past what was beneath my clothing, beneath my body, more than skin and fat deep.

03.00

I was the youngest person in the group—a child of ten—when I attended my first Weight Watchers meeting. My mother had taken me with her and we had received a note from my doctor to allow me to attend, not just as a bystander or the child of a woman who was going for herself, but as a member.

At the age of ten.

I hated the meetings. I felt as if I was in Alcoholics Anonymous for fat people, that it was bad enough I needed to feel that I should apologize, be ashamed for not only being in a fat body, but for also being a child who loved sweets and food that maybe wasn't the healthiest for you—as if I wasn't like every other kid.

The chairs were set up in a semicircle, and in the center stood the meeting leader, always a woman in her forties or fifties who was the poster image of a Weight Watchers "after" picture, who knew the struggle we were all going through because she had gone through it herself. Each meeting started by celebrating the latest member milestone—someone who had hit a goal of 5 or 10 or 20 lbs, or, if they were lucky, their long sought-after goal weight. One week, we celebrated the milestone of a woman who had lost 5 lbs—*in a week*! When asked what was "her secret," the woman smiled sheepishly, awkwardly leaning into the microphone the meeting leader offered her.

"Get sick."

04.00

From the ages of eight to 14, I took sewing classes after school every Tuesday in a family friend's sewing shop. By that age, I was already bigger than the largest children's size McCall's had to offer. That's what pins and chalk were for: whenever I started a project, I laid down and pinned the largest size pattern pieces to whatever fabric I was using at the time. I used measuring tape to measure out what the pattern *should* have been if it fitted my measurements, drew out and mirrored the pattern shape with fabric chalk, and then finally cut the fabric; an extension of my bones and body as I measured myself, comparing how much larger I was than the outermost line of the outfit pattern: my body, a second body, made of pins and dust.

Of all the projects I made, I can't remember one where I didn't have to draw my own body, extend a preexisting pattern because I didn't perfectly conform to the sizes Macy's or McCall's or Singer expected of a child of my age to have been.

When I was 12 or 13, there was an older girl in my class, 15 or 16, which, to a preteen like me, seemed like an older, mature woman. Her name escapes me, but I can still recall the smoothness of her voice and her flaxen, golden locks, which she kept tied up in a high ponytail during our lessons so that she wouldn't accidentally snip off some of her hair when cutting her fabric or get it caught in the machine as she pushed her fabric along with her fingertips as she sewed, disjoined pattern pieces slowly becoming a finished ensemble.

I was still trying to decide which high schools I should look at, when I asked her where she went to school.

"Ursula," she said with a smile, her voice, strong, almost proud, as she looked up from her work. A strand of blonde hair escaped from her ponytail, and I recall admiring its color, the way it traced her sharp jawline. Her blue eyes and the mere sight of her face and sound of her voice made my heart pound for reasons I now know why but didn't have a name for until nearly ten years later. "A lot of lesbians go there."

She didn't tell me what a lesbian was, but I didn't need her to. I don't know how, but I already knew the word.

Ursula, she explained, was an all-girls school. I didn't even know that you could go to all-girls school, that it was something that existed, but after I had heard of it, I kept it in the back pocket of my mind for when I began looking into high schools. (Later, my family would tell me, "It's better to go to an all-girls school anyway; that way you won't be distracted by boys." I wasn't distracted by boys as it was, so I didn't understand the validity of their argument.)

She continued, telling me stories of girls linking their arms around each other's waists in gym class as they waited for their turn to run around the school's track, stories of girls hiding under bleachers or in bathroom stalls, making out while avoiding the watchful eyes of teachers, but public enough to risk getting caught by their peers.

I played out those scenes in my mind's eye over and over again, wondering what it would feel like for my waist to be on the requited end of a girl's arm, my body warmed by her touch and the overhead sun; what it would feel like to hold a girl in my arms behind the closed door of a bathroom stall, sighs and kisses and giggles echoing off the wall.

I didn't know why, but the fantasy made my heart pound in my throat, and I silently decided that I wanted to go to Ursula, because that's where all the lesbians were, and for some reason, I wanted to be near them.

05.00

I didn't end up going to Ursula, but I did go to an all-girls school.

Having graduated from an elementary school with a graduating class of eight, one of whom was a boy, I didn't feel as if I was "missing anything" or, as my family members had commented, "had anything to distract me" by being in a school of all girls. I walked down perfumed halls of light blue and gray skirts, just trying to get from classroom to classroom without getting anyone to notice me.

Instead of tall, slender lockers, we had stocky ones on top of one another to accommodate space, and so that everyone had their very own locker buddy. The lockers were assigned in alphabetical order by homeroom class, and, as luck would have it, I was assigned a bottom locker.

Taylor, a girl with pin-straight, chest-length brown hair and marble blue eyes, was assigned the locker above me. I didn't know why, but each time Taylor and I crossed paths after home-room to get our books, I found my heart racing. I kept my head down as I burrowed through my bottom locker like a squirrel, pretending to look for a book I needed that was already in my backpack. The brief time we rendezvoused at our respective lockers was the only time we'd be relatively close to each other since we didn't share any classes aside from homeroom. I kept my head down in my locker, pretending not to catch the whiff of whatever body spray she used, pretending not to notice the way her hair fell in front of her face whenever she bent over, as I wondered what it was about her that made me think she was *so* pretty.

I didn't have the fortune to think it over for that long. Taylor joined the school choir not long after school started, and since they practiced in the mornings, all the choir girls were soon transferred into their own homeroom. Taylor's locker got cleared out as she moved to one closer to her new homeroom, and I found other reasons to keep my eyes down, not wanting my classmates to meet my eyes, not wanting to risk them being able to read my confused, turbulent thoughts.

06.00

There were no top and bottom lockers in the gym locker rooms, thankfully, but instead of having to avert my eyes from one girl fully dressed, I now had a full locker room full of peers that I couldn't bring myself to look at.

It wasn't that I *wanted* to look, but more that I felt I didn't deserve to look. I didn't need to see my classmates in a state of semi-undress, without their Catholic schoolgirl uniforms on, to know that they were thinner than me—and by association, *prettier* than me. As one of the heavier ones in my friend circle, I felt ashamed to look at them, ashamed that my body wasn't as slender or as tall as theirs, ashamed that my heart shot up into my throat in embarrassment the same way it did when Taylor hovered at her locker above me.

I kept my head down and my clothes held tight to my body as I tried to navigate my own semi-state of awkward undress from pleated uniform skirt and a white polo to gym shorts and a t-shirt, the shuffling all the faster and more hurried from having worn my shorts underneath my skirt in an attempt to save my thighs from chafing.

07.00

"Hey, do you mind reading this?"

A hushed voice asked me from behind and I straightened my posture, feeling the diamond of the corner of a small stack of printer paper poke me in the back.

The voice, and the stack of papers, belonged to Giana, one of the girls in the friend circle I was in. Similar to Taylor, I found myself drawn to Giana as well; she had a husky voice, played drums in our school's guitar club, and to me captured what I thought was the epitome of cool.

I took the stack of papers from her and clicked the red pen in my hands, having nothing better to do in our study hall session. It was a fanfiction she had written: focused on the relationship between Spencer Carlin and Ashley Davies from the teen drama *South of Nowhere*. I had no frame of reference—having no access to The N channel and never having watched the show before—but I liked Giana, and loved writing, which is why Giana had asked me to read the fanfic over.

I didn't need to know about the show, having soon found myself completely immersed in the fanfiction Giana had crafted. Spencer's dimly lit bedroom after school, a steady rainstorm pitter pattering against and crying down her bedroom window; Ashley in her arms; their hands tangled and twirling in each other's hair; the two girls crying as they kissed, either in the middle of a break-up or getting back together, I can't remember. I just remember being charmed by the intimacy, allured by the little taste of Spencer and Ashley's relationship that I was reading, by the tug on my heart as I finished the piece, my own red pen marks on the page the closest I would get to such a scene, quietly longing for it past ink and paper.

"It's really good," I whispered with a smile, meaning it, as I passed Giana back her papers, wondering how I could find a way to watch *South of Nowhere*.

08.00

I weighed 125 lbs in high school, and I told myself I was fat because my mother acted as if I was.

She'd never called me fat, not directly, but instead would always encourage and prod me to lose weight, that I needed to.

The doctor says you should be 110 or 115 lbs.

I'm not saying it's not hard; I've been on a diet my whole life, I know.

You don't want to wind up having all these health problems like those we have in the family.

My mother always had her nose in a new diet book or magazine, humming and hawing whenever she found whatever sounded like the next best fad to make you lose the most weight the fastest, without ever even trying said diet first.

By high school, both of our relationships with Weight Watchers had been on and off, and by the time I had started college, we had moved on to Jenny Craig. Jenny Craig had managed to help me keep the freshman 15 off, but it soon turned into another failed diet, and by the time I had reached my college heaviest, I was over 160 lbs.

One weekend, when I had returned home from campus, my

mother was going through some old albums when she came across an album of pictures of me from high school.

"Look at you," she sighed wistfully. "You used to be so thin..."

It took all I had to swallow back tears that had threatened to burst, words that had threatened to fire off my tongue.

Then why did you want me to lose weight?

09.00

"Are you gay?"

We were in my freshman dorm when a friend of mine asked me this, after seeing the collage of Aya Matsuura print-outs on the wall over my bed.

It wasn't the first time I had been asked this. My earliest memory dated back to my early preteen years of using Gaia Online, when the question was posed to me by a fellow forum user and online friend who I had been casually private messaging.

Are you gay?

There was more to his message: he said if I was, that was okay, that I shouldn't be ashamed or embarrassed about it, that it sounded as if I was because of the kinds of anime series I loved and because I had been working on a sapphic romance story that I had been telling him about. But any text after those three words escaped me; I was too consumed by the waterfall that roared like white noise through my ears, how sweat began to pool under my armpits, and how my heart started to pound so fast, it ached so hard I was unable to breathe.

The same way that I lied in my message response to my

online friend, I lied to my friend in my dorm room, trying to ignore how my face burned and flushed as it had those few years ago.

10.00

I wouldn't say I sought it out, but I kept finding myself coming back to and being drawn to lesbian content: Giana's *South of Nowhere* fanfic, the DVD copy of *But I'm a Cheerleader* tucked in between the other gay films on my cousin's bookshelf that my cousin thought no one noticed. The word lesbian and I walked alongside each other, as if we were friends taking a stroll down a beach boardwalk. I couldn't see myself in it, but there was something about it that I kept finding myself increasingly drawn to: the excitement of two girls kissing, of a love that was soft, passionate, tender, and sapphic.

I discovered *Revolutionary Girl Utena* in the brief 48 hours when my parents switched from cable to Verizon Fios (which we ultimately cancelled, after my father couldn't stand the excessive number of channels, unable to easily find his favorite go-tos). It was nearly midnight when I was flipping channels and stumbled on the Funimation channel playing the second to last episode of *Utena*. As fragmented as it was, having missed the 37 episodes that came before it, I immediately became captivated with Utena as I learned more about her, piece by little piece: A tomboyish girl who, instead of wanting to be saved, vowed to be a prince herself, and who wielded a sword in her hands in the name of defending and keeping the hand of Anthy, her Rose Bride.

Within the span of the next week, I hunted down all three, nearly out-of-production DVD box sets of *Revolutionary Girl Utena*. I remember sitting on the floor of my parents' bedroom, swapping out disk after disk as I binged the series, wearing the pair of purple silk pajamas that I was upset were so snug on me but refused to take off. I was unsure if I wanted to be *with* or be *like* Utena, a girl who seemed to defy gender roles, who cast aside her femininity in favor of wearing her school's boys' uniform, vowing to do the saving instead of waiting for someone else to save her.

Who unapologetically loved herself for who she was, and didn't apologize to anyone for it.

11.00

My interest in anime eventually led to an interest in cosplaying—dressing up as characters from my favorite series—and soon led to me binding my chest.

I started out binding only while I was in cosplay, but the more I cosplayed, the more I loved the look of my chest in a binder: how my size 38 chest seemed to flatten, almost disappear, beneath the short pleather jacket of my Survey Corps uniform when I dressed as Armin Arlert or Levi Ackerman, or wore my Nekoma volleyball track jacket when I became Kozume Kenma.

After months of cosplaying at conventions as male characters, I decided to try binding dressed as myself.

I pulled my binder over my head as I always had, tugging the tight fabric down over my chest. The binder pressed my breasts to my chest and I smoothed them out, pressing my fat down and to the sides—a tip in the binding community to get one's chest to appear as flat as possible, especially if you have more chest to work with.

My chest now smoothed out, I pulled a t-shirt over my head, observing my new, flattened chest in the mirror. My breath caught in my throat as I ran my hands down the flattened surface, the tight fabric squeezing my ribs, but I had never felt more free, the air in my lungs never tasting so crisp.

12.00

Tumblr became popular towards the tail end of my college career, and reached its peak when I was in grad school. Gone were the days of Gaia Online and Xanga and LiveJournal, and without having a virtual hub on the internet to meet fellow users engaged in fandom, I found that Tumblr soon became that new hub.

Amid reblogged posts of fanfiction, fanart, and anime screencaps, Tumblr hosted a treasure-trove of queer content: EveryoneIsGay, informative blog posts delving into the various letters found under the LGBTQ+ umbrella, and users blogging their own gender and sexuality struggles and experiences. There were stories of losing one's self, of discovering who they were, of trying to survive in a world where people didn't want them to exist, or if they did, didn't want to see them be their true, authentic selves.

I didn't blog about it, but I had spent every day of that year waking up and asking myself if I was, in fact, gay. While I was trying to figure that out, I'd spend hours and hours scrolling on Tumblr, learning more and more about the various queer identities that existed outside gay, lesbian, bi, and pansexual; the genders that existed outside male and female.

It was during one of those nights of mindless scrolling where I came across a post going into the details of demisexuality and other identities, gender and sexual, falling under the gray-ace spectrum, including the gender nonbinary. In addition to the term *demisexual*, my eyes immediately widened at the word *agender*. I copied and pasted the post into a Word document, reading and rereading it again, bolding and highlighting the bullet points that seemed to put words to the fractions of myself that I had been struggling to find a name for over the years.

Needs to experience an emotional connection with someone in order to feel sexual attraction.

Likely to be monogamous or attracted to only one person at a time.

May find self attracted to someone's personality, rather than their gender.

Does not identify as either male or female.

Suddenly, years of questioning, of blood and heat rushing to my cheeks in embarrassment, in shame; years of ducking my head down as I walked through the halls of my high school, of feeling as if I had something to hide whenever I was questioned about my sexuality—all suddenly made sense.

I never identified as a lesbian because I was never a woman, even though the people I mostly found myself emotionally attracted to were women.

I could never tell if what I was experiencing was attraction because I never got far enough to feel such a deep, emotional connection.

I felt so euphoric when I bound my chest because there were aspects of my body, I learned, that gave me a sense of dysphoria that binding helped sate.

I had always responded the way I had to the word gay—with confusion, shame, and embarrassment—because I knew deep down that, somehow, I was; I just didn't have a word for it.

Now, I finally found the words for myself.

13.00

Once I realized I was nonbinary, binding had evolved for me: going beyond something I would do only in the casual, seldom context of cosplaying to something I would incorporate into my natural, everyday routine. The same way I had woken up every day asking myself if I was gay, I began to wake up and start asking myself if I wanted to go on hormones, my flat chest looking at me in the mirror, filling me with such relief, and leading me to question if I wanted something more. I took the plunge the same way as I had when I reclaimed the word gay as a word that applied to me—in honor, not in shame. If I had been waking up asking myself if it was something I wanted to do for so long, the chances were it was something I really *did* want to do.

After all, someone who was straight, who was cis, wouldn't wake up and have to ask themselves if they were straight or cis.

It had taken nearly half a year—between finding a clinic, going through the appropriate physical and mental health treatment, and getting the proper letters and evaluations from doctors—but eventually, I began medically transitioning.

I arranged to have my first shot of testosterone on November 22—three-and-a-half months after my birthday, the day I was supposed to be born.

14.00

There are two ways to inject testosterone into one's body: subcutaneous, or intramuscular.

Subcutaneous, I learned, meant injecting testosterone directly into your fat.

It's how we typically start people off, my GP explained, *but we can change it down the road after you get used to it.* She went on to explain that most people started off injecting into their stomach, changing the injection points every week to prevent scarring.

That sounded fine, I said. After all, I had a lot of stomach fat to work with.

After five weeks of going down to my clinic every Monday before work to have a nurse help me, to steady my hands and walk me through it as I injected myself, I started to do my injections at home.

It was like an art, a craft, not unsimilar to those years of sewing lessons when I laid myself out on fabric with pins. If I wasn't wearing a binder, I needed to carefully part my breasts to see past them, to make sure I was pinching the proper area of my stomach, that I was squeezing just the right amount of fat between my left pointer finger and thumb, that the needle I had in my right hand was pointed exactly at 45 degrees, my finger as steady as it could possibly be on the plunger.

What started off as a lesson in patience and fear—of making my breathing even and calming myself down, of steadying my hand as I drove the needle into my fat, injecting myself with testosterone once a week—soon became routine.

15.00

Until it didn't.

16.00

I've bought a scale, because it's been a month since my mother's Public Applebee's Cry, a year since I've moved into my apartment, and even longer since I've last weighed myself. The last time I did, I was in the 180s, and if the number on the scale today is even close to that, it will be a miracle.

The clear blue screen of the scale lights up as I pull out the plastic tab from its battery casing and set it down on the tile of my living room, the 0.0 clear as day even for me with my poor eyesight, but when I eventually stand up tall to straighten myself on the scale, I'll need to shift if I want to read it past the barrier of my chest.

It's been months since I've last bound my chest—and even longer since I have been on hormones. While I loved some of the changes testosterone brought me—a slightly deeper, huskier voice; more muscular and more slender arms and legs—as the weeks turned into months, and the months turned into a year, and I walked deeper and deeper down the road of my transition, the same dysphoria that brought me to seek out hormones in the first place started to make me feel uncomfortable in the new skin I was creating for myself. As the fat that was once on my arms and legs shifted to my stomach, it brought me back to the years under the judgemental gaze of Weight Watchers meeting leaders, my family, and my own self-hatred.

I began to hate the reflection that looked back at me in the mirror, the reflection that once gave me comfort—not because I didn't love who I was becoming, but because I didn't know how to love myself as someone who was nonbinary without hating myself for being fat.

The feeling of my own fat pressed against my stomach and my sides triggered my issues with my body and my weight, and soon became just as bad as, if not worse than, my dysphoria.

In the same way that I started hormones because I couldn't stand my gender dysphoria any longer, I stopped because my body dysmorphia became just as debilitating. I was unable to stop myself from thinking that I was less of a trans person because the shifting of my weight to my stomach made my chest tighten more than any binder, any dysphoric panic attack ever could.

Because my waist curved instead of falling into a straight line.

Because I could only look so flat when I bound my chest.

Because I was still deadnamed and misgendered by family and strangers, even when on hormones.

Because I stopped taking hormones.

I bring myself back to my body, back to my breath, and begin my weighing ritual, back from the days when I used to weigh myself: I strip down to my underwear; remove all my jewelry, one, two, three, four rings and a watch, not wanting to risk a single ounce on the scale not being my own. I let out a breath, immediately sucking it back in to draw in my stomach, the zeros on the screen flashing as they configure, tell me my weight. I rock back on my heels, trying to see the blue backlit screen past my chest.

Finally, the number displays on the screen.

It's higher than 180, but is around what I had expected it to be. I perform the second part of my ritual—stepping off the scale, waiting for the number to clear on the screen, and then stepping back on, seeing if the second reading is the same as the first, or, if I'm lucky, a few pounds lighter.

The number on the scale remains the same.

I keep my eyes downward, towards the screen, letting the blue lit digits sink in as I realize they are my new reality. No more lying to myself, no more excuses, no more thinking that I'm not plus sized.

This is my truth. This is me.

I laugh. Ugly, joyful. Still standing on the scale, I sink down, my body now shaking in laughter as I hug my knees to my chest, laughing so hard tears stream down my cheeks, my laughter muffled by the flesh of my kneecaps.

When my laughter finally dies down, I stand up, the number ever present on the scale. And for the first time in my life, for the first time since I've weighed myself in the name of weight loss, I smile. A reassuring, warm glow begins to spread up my sternum, across my chest, up my throat, to my cheeks, and I smile.

I'm heavier than I have ever been but I smile, feeling lighter than any number on the scale could make me feel, believing for the first time ever that I'm more than just a number.

"How I Found Fat Acceptance and My Nonbinary Truth"

Benny Hope

From the get go, I took up space, demanding to be seen and, I can only imagine, heard. When I was born, I weighed nearly ten pounds. My mom tells me I was a happy baby, that I loved to play with my older siblings. I have pictures of the three of us in some long-ago backyard, little toddler me with a huge smile on my face. How surreal it is now to look back on those photos, to not be able to warn or protect myself from the lifetime of trials ahead.

My dad left when I was three, and that's when my issues with food started. I was so angry, and I wouldn't stop being angry for a very long time. It wasn't until I was an adult that I figured out the connection. I never wanted to admit that I had a problem with food, because I felt as if that was giving in to fat-shamers, but the truth was that I was very unhappy for most of my life and eating was a way for me to self-soothe. I refused to feel shame for wanting to eat, and I still do, but I didn't have a loving and healthy relationship with food. I just wanted to feel joy, and food was one of the few things that brought me that joy.

I grew swiftly, becoming one of the tallest in my class, and always the tallest girl, from a young age. I didn't really want to stand out (does any child?) but I didn't have much of a choice. I was picked on in elementary school for wearing clothes from Goodwill, and white sneakers I decorated myself with puffy fabric paint. I loved those sneakers, until someone laughed at them. I quickly grew to dread school every day, not knowing at the time that I was experiencing the start of a lifelong battle with anxiety.

Despite being smart enough to excel in school, I stopped even trying to do homework. I would hide it in the drawer of a table in the living room where I thought no one would find it. I constantly said I was sick to try to get out of school, and would cry when I had to go. This continued through middle school. In the meantime, I was still bigger than most kids in every grade, every year. I thought I was a giant. Little girls were supposed to be dainty, petite, light, and delicate. I was none of those things. I couldn't be even if I tried. I remember finding a photograph of my middle school self as an adult, and seeing myself at a birthday party sitting next to my girlfriends. I was barely any bigger than them, but I remembered thinking I was massive compared to them at the time. My heart broke for little me, feeling so ashamed of her body at such an early age.

I remember when I stopped being able to fit into kids' clothes. I shopped in the "women's" section of Target, and once in middle school my mom took me to a plus size clothing store. I was embarrassed to be seen walking out of that store, which is something I can't even fathom feeling now. I now walk around like "Yes, you're damn right I'm fat, what of it?" but I was not even close to that mindset when I was just a sad preteen.

In "physical education," the least aptly named class ever, we started having to wear uniforms when I was in middle school. Of course, they didn't come in my size. They never came in my size. I took the biggest size available, and it barely fitted me. Everyone else was in roomy, comfy gym wear, and I was uncomfortable and self-conscious in skin-tight red shorts and a gray t-shirt. I faked sickness and injuries to get out of class as often as I could.

I had friends in middle school, but I didn't really let anyone in. I don't think I could let people really know me, because I didn't really know myself. I was also extremely socially awkward, and had no idea how to act naturally when I wanted to get to know people. At the time, I assumed people didn't like me because I was fat, and that might have been true for some people, but I don't think I made myself an easy person to befriend. I was still struggling with feeling lost, angry, and out of place.

As difficult as middle school was, high school was when I reached my breaking point. All of my middle school friends went to a different high school, and I would only see them at the occasional birthday party. I met a few new people to walk to school with in the morning and eat lunch with, but we almost never saw each other outside school. My miserable experiences with gym class and too-tight uniforms continued. I kept making up stories as often as possible to get out of running the mile or playing basketball.

After years of faking sickness, ignoring homework, and crying at the thought of going to school on Monday mornings, I dropped out my junior year of high school. I remember making my case to my mom, telling her how miserable I was. I knew there was no other option. I never tried to do my schoolwork and I was so unhappy. I was made fun of for my weight, I felt that I had no friends, and I didn't fit in anywhere. I wish I could go back in time and tell my younger self to walk up to the weird, cool punk kids and ask if I could hang out with them. I know they would have said yes.

One day when I was in my late teens, I was browsing a bookstore when something caught my eye. I saw the word "Zines" on the spine of a book, and pulled the book out of the shelf. It was *The Book of Zines: Readings from the Fringe*, edited by Chip Rowe. It was a collection of pages from a wide variety of zines. At the time, I had a burgeoning love of zine culture, and had even made one myself.

I bought the book, and, as I flipped through it, was delighted by the variety and creativity of the works inside. It was fun and playful, silly and exciting, but on page 101, I found the best treasure of all. Butts. To be more specific, it was a page taken from the zine *Fat!So?* by Marilyn Wann, and was a selection of photos of beautiful human butts. The top of the page had the heading "Revolution," and it would certainly be the start of a revolution in the way I thought about my body.

Here were big butts, small butts, lumpy butts. Butts with back fat on top of them. Butts that looked like mine! Actual human variety was present on this page. It was glorious. I had never seen anything like it. I had never seen body parts like mine presented without shame or embarrassment. I was used to seeing my body as a "before" picture. Here, for the first time, was someone saying it was fine just how it was.

After finding *The Book of Zines*, I desperately wanted a copy of *Fat!So?* for myself. One day a few months later, I was perusing the stacks in the nonfiction section of my local library, when a title popped out at me. It was *Fat!So?* I couldn't believe it. I checked it out immediately and poured through it at home. I found out that *Fat!So?* started as a digital zine, but was eventually published as the book I held in my hands.

It's not an exaggeration to say that this book changed the course of my entire life. This is the book that opened the door into fat acceptance for me. I started looking for more people in this new-to-me movement. I felt as if I stepped into an absolute wonderland of incredible people and ideas. I found more books and blogs and became fascinated and awestruck by this world. Here were so many people telling me it was okay to be me. Other large, beautiful women telling me I didn't have to change, that I wasn't disgusting or shameful or broken. Through *Fat!So?*, I found Kate Harding, Marianne Kirby, Linda Bacon, and Lesley Kinzel. They wrote about accepting your body as it was, they wrote about fat fashion, they wrote about being yourself in a big, bold way. It shook my world.

These people started to teach me how to heal my relationship with food. I didn't need to change the way I ate in order to lose weight or please anybody else, but I could eat in a way that would nourish my body. I didn't have to diet or step on a scale if

I didn't want to (and lordy, I never wanted to). I could eat intuitively. I could listen to, and trust, my body. The idea of trusting and loving my fat body was completely groundbreaking. I had only ever been taught embarrassment and shame about my body. The women around me only ever wanted to be smaller. These were the first people teaching me that maybe it was okay to be who I was. That I could take care of myself out of love, not as a punishment for being fat.

I was assigned female at birth, and I was never uncomfortable with that. It fitted to me. As I grew up, I embraced my own personal idea of womanhood. Being a chubby girl and then a fat woman, I never felt accepted. Once I found fat acceptance and feminism, I was okay with not being acceptable. I was okay with my loud laugh and my big belly. Fat acceptance changed my views on what it meant to be a woman. I felt as if I was okay as myself for the first time in my entire life. I felt that I had the approval of all these strong, fabulous women whose books and blogs I was devouring.

I still had a long way to go in understanding who I was, but I didn't know it at the time. When I was in my late twenties, I went to college, and it was there I started to meet more nonbinary and genderqueer people, and all kinds of wonderful people under the trans umbrella. I still identified as a cis woman, but I was learning more about the wide and beautiful variety of gender expressions in the world. Ultimately, it was all these amazing people around me who allowed me to finally find my truth.

I started questioning my gender when I was about 31. There was just an inkling, a little something in my mind that made me think "hmmm, maybe I am different." I started to not nec-essarily feel that the label of cis woman still fitted me. I started using the term genderqueer to identify myself. It's hard for me to explain exactly what shifted or how, but I've always been the kind of person who decides things fast. I get an idea and I want to act on it as soon as possible. Turns out, the same is true for my gender. I still used the name I was given at birth, and I still used she/her pronouns, but I was learning so much about the possibilities of gender and gender expression from the people around me, and my world view was constantly expanding. Looking back, what came next feels as if it was inevitable in the best way.

I was 32. It was Trans Day of Remembrance. I was spending too much of the day on Twitter as I so often did, but that day it was different because that day it was filled with beautiful expressions of love, acceptance, and countless people honoring the trans people that we have lost far too soon. It was also a day to call people to action. Do not simply mourn those who have passed, but celebrate the living while they are still here. I was reading stories about trans people coming out, and something clicked in my brain. I didn't feel as if I was a woman anymore. I didn't feel genderqueer. I was nonbinary. It was that sudden. I just knew and it felt right. I wanted to change my name and my pronouns and leave womanhood behind me.

Fat acceptance helped me define the kind of woman I want-ed to be, and that carried over when I knew I wasn't a woman anymore. Finding fat acceptance let me know that I didn't need a certain kind of body to be nonbinary. I didn't need to be thin, or flat-chested. I didn't have to change anything if I didn't want to. Being nonbinary helped me to further embrace my fat body because as a woman, it was never considered acceptable to look the way I did. Well I wasn't a woman anymore, so now what? Now there were no rules. I felt as if I was getting away with something. Haha, you can't shame me for not looking like a "proper" woman, because I'm not a woman!

Being nonbinary makes me feel powerful. I feel that I'm part of an incredibly cool secret club, but anyone can join if they feel it in their hearts. If fat acceptance opened the door into a new world for me, being nonbinary took that door and ran it through a wood chipper. The rule book wasn't just thrown out, it was set on fire and the ashes were scattered. There were no limits to what I could do or who I could be. No matter my size, no matter how big, lumpy, bumpy, saggy, or flabby, I was allowed to accept myself. There was no one way to be a woman, and there was no one way to be nonbinary.

I don't wake up every day loving myself. Discovering fat acceptance and my nonbinary identity did not magically heal my pain and trauma, but it changed how I see myself and the world. Now I walk through the world with a sense of admiration for myself. I have made it through so much. I have survived. This body has survived. My fat, queer, trans, loud, outspoken self has survived. I now know I am capable of transformation. Like a caterpillar, I went through my gooey transformation phase, and came out changed and new. I learned to trust myself. I learned to feel the fear, and do the thing anyway. With the help of so many incredible people, I have discovered a new world, and myself along with it.

"To All the Fat Queers on the First Day of School"

Hannah Propp

Happy first day of school to you, and just to you.
Happy first day to you who hold so much,
whose uniforms and backpacks burst
at the seams with truths
you long to name.

Happy first day to you who have been planning,
trying on,
crying on,
cursing,
that One Outfit That Will Determine Everything.

Happy first day to the ones who will still get called
"Dyke" and
"Fag" and
"Queer" and
"Fat Whale" and
"Hippo."

Happy first day to the ones who
keep looking down as if
those words
are painted on their chests,
against that perfect outfit.

One outfit can't mask your truth.
An outfit can't disguise that which lives
in your flesh
in your bones
in your veins
in your beautiful, secret hearts.

You *are* a hippo
wild, ferocious, able to crush the skull of a lion
like ripe, dripping, fruit
between your wicked jaws.
With skin thick and powerful as iron,
you wait in quiet, deep waters.

One day, you will rage and roar and bellow.
One day, you will emerge in an eruption
of river spray and mud and glory.
One day, your truths will ring in their ears;
Undeniable.

You are a Whale,
making beautiful, sad, longing music.
All gentle ripples
of undulating blue—full, deliberate grace.
You have more magic in one quavering, mournful note
than they will know in their lifetimes.
You are fat, you are queer, you are a Whale.

You are a Dyke.
You are a Fag.
You are Queer with a capital "Q."
You come from generations of power.

They think they insult you?
They invoke warriors of the past
who made you in their image;
crowns of flowers,
stilettos as weapons,
holding each other close,
protecting each other.

They think they isolate you with these names?
We exist in multitudes throughout the country and the
world, and the universe.
You are not alone.

They name you as One of Us
We Claim You.
We see you.
Stay here with us and
we shall survive them, together.

So, happy first day of school to you,
musical beings of infinite magic
and might and light.

Happy first day of school you
Textured, Rippling,
vast forces of nature.

Happy first day of school in this lifetime,
where you stand, in the steps of those
who fought this battle before you
and will continue to fight.
Should your feet shake the ground,
know it is because each step contains
the love and
loss and
stories of us all.

You are Fat.
You are Queer.
You are Everything Everywhere.

Happy First Day of School.

"Fat Top/Switch"

Emilia Phillips

When fucking you, my belly hangs over
the harness, its scars and stretchmarks
milk-blue, and wobbles—look away,
I used to but missed the strap emerge
slick and your lips draw in when I pushed
but then you reached for my hips, thumbs
shadow-deep, pulling me toward you. *Closer*,
you whispered. *Juntas*—together.
That's when I began to look, to see
myself, to *be* my body, *in* my body,
to claim it, my belly *me*, to feel
strong, my thigh muscles hard
as vulnerability. I confess: before our first
time, I worried you'd somehow realize
how fat I am once I took off my clothes,
as if I was hiding behind my skinny
tie printed with bluebonnets I wore to
the hotel bar and that you used to pull me

onto the bench in front of the window.
I love how different your body is
from mine, you told me, *I love your body,*
unbuttoning every button then
that ever held me back or in.

"I'm Not Masc of Center Because I'm Fat"

Emilia Phillips

My fatness doesn't mean it's harder for me
to cross my legs at the knee. Sometimes I sit that way
but other times I spread, especially next to a man
who's taking up space on a plane or train.
But if it did, that wouldn't mean I was any less
femme or any more masc. Some days I put on lipstick
to walk around my apartment in only boxers,
which do, I admit, prevent my thighs from rubbing
together and chaffing. But that's not why I wear them.
I buy online some button-ups marketed to butches
but even those make a little peephole between the buttons
over my breasts, all of their models flat-chested
in the way so many call "androgenous." But I have tits
and hips and ass. A belly as voluminous as my laughter
whenever I'm called *sir* or *ma'am* or *miss*, all as ill-fitting
as believing anything about my body a disaster.

"She Doesn't Need Any More Dresses"

M.P. Armstrong

pattern

I inherited fatness like a quilt. My chest from my grandmother, who I watched dress for church on Sunday mornings only to see permanent dips in her shoulders from 50 years of bra straps. My protruding stomach from my father, whose silhouette I mirror in every Christmas family photo, along with the slightly stretched-out pattern of a festive sweater. My knowledge from my mother, who taught me to cut down on sweets when my double chin started to appear, to celebrate the opening of each branch of Catherine's and Torrid like the birth of another child, to expect the weight to stay unless I fought it off.

I sometimes hear fatness discussed as a process, a gradual gain, but I was fat from the moment I was born, looking like the Gerber baby in my first hospital photos. As a toddler, tired of napping, I managed to get my chubby legs stuck between the bars of my crib. And throughout elementary school, when plenty of kids still had little round bellies and dimples in their cheeks, I never felt out of place. I went to dance classes, soccer and baseball practice, even swim lessons without thinking about the way I needed larger leotards, uniforms, and suits than the other kids.

But I collected my scraps of fabric diligently. And among the fragments were spools of memory: sitting down at the glass-topped kitchen table with my parents, who explained to me that my aunt and uncle were going to my uncle's daughter's wedding in Washington D.C., and they might not talk about it much because she's marrying another woman and that makes some people angry. Watching *Dancing with the Stars* with my grandparents, my grandpa pointing out one of the contestants and telling me "he used to be a woman," and when my grandma tucked me into bed that night, she muttered, "I don't know why he told you about that nonsense."

Over the years, the collected snippets drifted into place, the full patchwork laid out on a table, forming the design of a girl who was definitely too big and definitely too butch and just hadn't realized it yet.

draping

I was no longer the standard mannequin in middle school. Kids shed their extra pounds left and right, joining sports teams, trying out diets, and obsessing over their looks in pursuit of a glossy perfection only available between the pages of a magazine. Although I definitely didn't like the image in the mirror, I never cared enough to change; my strategy was more about disguise. Hiding the hair starting to grow under my arms and on my legs for as long as possible, until my mom noticed one day in the grocery store when I reached up to grab a carton of eggs, and she made me learn to shave. Trying to hide my growing chest, too, but the next thing I knew, I was strapping myself into a beige bra.

That year, my dance costume was a bright pink tank top and black spandex shorts under a jean jacket, and my parents wouldn't let me wear it outside the studio. The next week, I swore off pink forever and bought my first clothes from the boys' section, where each piece camouflaged the boobs, the curves, *and* the fat: the triple threat of everything I wanted to disappear. By high school, I had mastered the uniform that cloaked me in confidence: Converse, jeans, an oversized concert t-shirt, and a blazer.

I had also started to meet queer kids for the first time and, though I certainly wasn't admitting it yet, felt like we belonged in the fabric of each other's lives. So I joined our school's brand-new Gay-Straight Alliance. At one of our first meetings, we had an activity called Alphabet Soup: we went through the letters of the acronym LGBTQ+, defining those and other terms related to the community. There I heard the word butch for the first time.

I assumed I'd found my identity. I was a butch lesbian. I was, as the boys started yelling at me in the hall, a dyke, and that didn't have to be a bad thing. I could be Rachel Maddow, Hannah Gadsby, any of the characters in the panels of *Dykes to Watch Out For* or the badass women with Dykes on Bikes. And these women weren't thin, either. I could throw on all black, buy a motorcycle, and fit in, short haircut, men's clothing, extra weight, and all. I came out. I got bigger. I felt better.

alterations

I was a sophomore when the Fates' scissors started hovering over my thread and I suddenly stopped feeling better. First, a chronic cough and lingering headache. Then, mouth sores and red eyes; thrush from my increased inhaler use, and pinkeye from the infection, we assumed. But soon, the sores erupted on my ears, my arms, and across my entire body, and I was admitted to the hospital with the mysterious diagnosis of Stevens-Johnson Syndrome.

I stopped eating. I drank my meals from protein-packed bottles, Muscle Milk and Ensure, and there was the threat of a PIC line if I couldn't force them down. I forced them down. I counted calories and ounces, created drinking games to go along with Disney movies, did shots and chugged like a college student at a frat party. I spent two weeks confined to a hospital bed, my 16th birthday crying yellow dye out of my eyes in the ophthalmologist's office, and two more weeks resting on the couch before going back to school. The scissors never made that final snip; I survived what most don't.

I also lost weight. I wore a dress to prom. And I didn't know who I was anymore. Not without fatness and androgyny. But I didn't know how to gain back one without the other. While I didn't like being heavier than all the other girls, I did like being visibly different; but now that I looked good in their clothes, I didn't have an excuse to go back to the men's button-downs in the back of my closet. And while I wasn't getting called a dyke in the halls anymore, I was getting catcalled and, somehow, that felt worse.

I compartmentalized. I would be queer quietly, not quite

back in the closet but not quite out of it anymore, either. And I waited. I would see which alterations lasted.

backtack

The pins of my old garment immediately pricked at my heels. I returned to the overweight person who refused to wear makeup and had a crush on the girl who sat behind me in math. It was hard, but became increasingly easier. The concept of being nonbinary danced across my consciousness for the first time as I met Sam, a New Yorker I encountered because we both loved Broadway. They were nonbinary and fat and wore skirts sometimes, simply because they wanted to. While the burgeoning media portrayal of gender-nonconforming people was telling me that I had to be skinny and androgynous to have a place in that community, the community itself was telling me that wasn't true. So I experimented, reading everything I could, adjusting my presentation, and trying on different labels.

And it became easier when I graduated high school and left my small, conservative hometown for Florence, Italy. There, removed from anyone who had known me, relieved of American pressures, I bought clothes in the men's sections of Italian stores and never received even a questioning glance from an employee. After a few glasses of wine, I came out for the first time at the weathered wooden dining room table, and my roommate—who at first seemed lukewarm—offered to accompany me to a queer bar in Dublin. Threads were pulled taut, seams were straightened, and identity ironed itself out.

I realized I didn't simply resent femininity because everyone expected me to perform it. I resented the entire one-or-the-other construct of femininity versus masculinity. And the pressures to have a certain type of body were just more divisions I didn't want. Male versus female, thin versus fat, healthy versus unhealthy, good versus bad, normal versus abnormal—I didn't want to choose between arbitrary categories. And suddenly, the complex patchwork of queerness and fatness fell into place.

embroidery

I return to America and arrive for my sophomore year of college wearing queerness and fatness with pride. My campus job prints me a name tag that includes my new pronouns and stops questioning what size staff shirt I want. Old friends adapt; new friends adopt without questioning; I decide I don't care who sees me while I'm changing.

I dress the way I want—women's jeans paired with men's sweaters, boys' dress shoes and a girl's watch—and eat what I want, whether that's a salad from Panera Delivery or a dining hall hamburger. When stress makes me lose weight, I feel worse, not better; when I make sure I start eating again, everyone comments that I look much healthier. And when I stop home for Christmas, a former teacher tells me she had always thought I was nonbinary, and comments how much happier I look now, too.

Every morning, I wake up and Chase Twichell's poem "The Phantoms for Which Clothes are Designed" greets me from the wall above my bed, reminding me that the 1930s WPA (Works Progress Administration) average woman doesn't need any more dresses.

And neither do I.

"So Not a Big Deal"

Haley Sherif

My outfits stopped being a form of armor the night I was raped. Or maybe there is no way for me to know really what purpose clothing served for me. Maybe what I choose (or don't choose) to wear or eat has more to do with protection—a kind of disguise like a Halloween costume that never comes off—than it does with my style or the world in general. Maybe this is the way it is for all of us who have experienced trauma (so that is to say, everyone). We look at a clock, pass an awning, unpack a box, eat a food, or feel a change in weather and automatically are transported back to before what we now refer to as "trauma" occurred. Fall in Boston around midnight at a dirty bar downtown, my pants almost falling off my hips, was the moment "before" and everything else, well, everything else is after.

I was raped in the fall of my sophomore year of college. Newly 21, going out for a drink with a woman had nearly been a fantasy. The night I met my rapist was warm, too warm for the black skinny jeans that my hips curved around and the blue and white striped button-down, sleeves rolled up as I walked up Boylston Street.

Then it was: beer, sticky floors, eyes met, kisses in the stairwell, my keys in my hand, stop. "You can sleep here," I said with no intention of sleeping with her or anyone. I was a virgin. I had been dressing my body—hiding my body—for years. I was not ready for whatever happened below the belt—whatever strange fate awaited me when someone's body touched mine that wasn't family or a friend. And so, I hid, first by trying to make my body smaller and then by making it bigger, filling out my curves, my breasts, morphing into a woman—a change I had yearned for for years.

Resume. "Your body wants it," this red-head would be my albatross—a burden I would shoulder for the years, partners, one night stands, my marriage, and the unraveling of it to come. Before I knew what was happening she was inside me, her sweaty skin rubbing against mine, my eyes devoted to the red flashing numbers of my clock: how long until morning?

Being raped made me believe something was wrong with me. Why else would someone take something so precious from me? But what made things especially difficult was the complete lack of resources and conversations happening around homosexual rape and assault. I was in uncharted territory and so I kept quiet. My rape did not: I tried on partners, pants, and positions. I shed one black leather jacket for a multicolored kimono. I straightened my hair then cut it all off: dyed it blonde, purple, and red. My body grew too. I stopped being able to look in the mirror. I settled for lovers the way one buys off-brand toilet paper when their preferred brand is out of stock. I felt worse.

Depressed. Suicidal. Anxious. I devoted myself to sobriety, to alcohol, to girls, to women, to waking up naked with a stranger, to obsessing, sleeping late, and eating more.

Always more.

I was bullied starting in fourth or fifth grade. I didn't tell anyone. The girls (wasn't it Anne Carson who said, "Girls are meanest to themselves"?) clambered over themselves, provoking a tightly stuck bobby pin out of the ballerina bun my nanny had preciously crafted the night before. Ha. They snicker. Again, a mean girl's laugh is comparable to nothing. Or maybe... like the sound of a bottle tie caught in the garbage disposal. Or maybe...the phantom sound fear makes: omnipotent, afar, yet so close.

Fear became my second language the night I was raped, yet it was a familiar sounding in the way you might walk into a deli caught off guard suddenly by the allure of that scent: you are back in middle school, awkward and gangly, so young. I got dressed with fear that one day I would again be stripped of my clothes—my armor—my freedom, my choices, and my youth. It took me a long time to recognize that my gain was bigger than my loss—owning my body, commanding my heart, devoting myself to lean in to listen deeper and better to my gut was a self-taught art. I was a virgin and then I wasn't—akin to shuffling a deck of tarot cards or reading tea leaves, I kept looking for a confirmation that this was all meant to be, but all I could come up with was momentum to move forward, to go on despite what had happened to me, to adorn my body not because it needed to be hid, but because it deserved to be shown. This momentum was encouraged by reading other writers who wrote about pain: Cheryl Strayed, Maggie Nelson, Melissa Febos, and Carmen Maria Machado.

My stomach will never be small, but one day it will swell with a child. My arms remind me of the stories they tell in each tattoo, a forever reminder of where I have been, what I have seen. The words are purposes. The words are maps. I don't know how to do this, but something inside me does. And yet. Go. My legs are sturdy, holding me up when my world comes crashing down: a rape, a divorce, a mirror, a scar. My heart has always been my biggest asset—bold and assertive, not far from my sleeve. I am willing to love hard and then harder, now knowing I am worthy of the same in return.

I exist in a body that once existed inside my mama. She is a woman so beautiful she cannot be reckoned with. She is a reminder of what it means to feel stable, to come back to, and to embrace. Every year that goes by between my birth, I stop feeling further from her and instead draw closer. "Mama," I say, "thank you."

I think about my bones, the ones that make up my body. To write. To eat. To make love. To laugh. To cry, workshop, yell, and deny. The moment I choose to change the narrative: I am no longer a girl who had a story, but a woman who has a life. I am living it every time I fuel my body with foods that make my insides smile, read or talk or laugh in ways that make my heart sparkle, or cleanse myself, my body, my thighs, the hair between my legs and on top of my head.

I am not shy to say that the greatest love affair I have is with myself. What happens when I begin to trust the ground I stand on, the words I hear and speak, the faith I have in someone somewhere whispering "keep going, baby," is this: I continue to expand, I hesitate less at the light switch too eager to see what my smile looks like, my tummy, my arms, the veins on my chest and the stretch marks on my thighs. That is beauty. In the magazines we read or the shows we watch, the ads we listen to, and the fads we chase we are taught a more superficial, performative acceptance—we will be safe/happy/okay when we have X.

I remember being about 15 when I decided to make myself smaller. It was easy: I couldn't control anything else, so I learned to control what I ate, subsisting on Luna Bars and too much coffee. I shrunk. Today, I think about my sweet teenage self and tell her, "Sweet love, hold on. This is the ride of your life. We will be banged up, but we will refuse to ever break."

For a long time sex is difficult, getting dressed is difficult, and life feels insurmountable. Therapy. Faith. Friendship. Boundaries. Hobbies. Self-care. Homemade food. Home. Me.

It is roughly six years after my rape. I walk home late at night. My gray boots, slightly heeled, cling to the ground announcing their presence with each step, unperturbed by ice, slush, sleet.

My hands nestled are inside my white knit gloves. I glance upwards catching the setting sun behind the buildings in Jamaica Plain, a town full of families big and small, white and black, gay and straight. I carry my scars in my pocket, thumbing them like worry stones, thinking, this, this is the whole point.

❀ ❀ ❀

Recently, looking in the mirror of my childhood bedroom closet, all I could see was my longer curly hair (my dad's hair), my brown eyes, corners crinkled from smiling, a white and yellow striped dress not clinging, but encircling. I am beautiful. Big. Fat. Queer. I have another chance at life, and this time, I refuse to make myself smaller or sadder for anyone.

"They Does Not Fit Like a Thundershirt Should"

after Wren Hanks

Nicole Oquendo

I have written at length about the pronouns *wolf/wulf*—
trust that I am better suited to gnaw
at the raw flesh of another animal
than to wear the *femme* (yes, this is a whole other language).

He, no, and not for lack of trying. I have slipped
in and out of pronouns as if this body was a fitting room.

The lighting isn't right here, and each curve of my body
is a segment that, deep down, I'd like to carve out, but *she*
is all I'm left with—not because the sound is right, but
    because that's
all my ears have heard for over thirty years:

She is this,
She is that.

My hair is too long. The body I inhabit is neither here nor

—not the right body; I am missing so much—

there. This binary is a rotten egg
we are too afraid to crack open
for fear of what is inside churning.

"Growing Up Fat Made Coming Out Harder (But Now I'm Queer, Fat, and Thriving)"

Samantha Puc

I don't remember when I first realized I was queer, but I do remember the first time I got a crush on a woman. I was three years old and fell head over heels for a grocery store clerk; my mom left me standing there, staring, and I hadn't noticed she'd left until the pretty girl pointed it out. I ran out of the store, cheeks burning.

I've embarrassed myself in front of more beautiful women since.

Still, the idea that I might *like*-like women didn't take root for many years. Here's what I remember: I was coloring in the living room while my mom watched a movie and worked on a cross-stitch project. It was the summer before fourth grade, and I looked up at the screen just in time to see Sarah Michelle Gellar kiss Selma Blair in *Cruel Intentions*—with tongue.

I was nine years old and I loved romantic comedies; I'd been watching people—men and women—kiss for years. Never had it made me feel quite so *alive*. Although I couldn't put my finger on why, seeing two women kiss felt different from seeing men and women kiss. Some small, soft, secret part of me wondered how it would feel, to kiss another girl; I thought it might feel really nice, because girls had soft mouths and pretty smiles.

Lit up from the inside and enraptured by that scene in *Cruel Intentions*, I barely noticed when my mom told me that perhaps I should go color in my room while she watched this movie. She had to ask twice before I did, and for the next hour I sought every possible opportunity to pass through the living room in the hopes of seeing those two women kiss once more.

The concept of lesbianism wasn't entirely lost on me then, but it was framed in my mind in a very specific way: fat butch loves thin femme. This was how lesbianism was presented in most media, where I saw it presented at all—although my clearest queer media memory, prior to *Cruel Intentions*, was seeing two men kiss in an Adam Sandler movie. The scene was clearly played for laughs; in the theater with my grandfather and uncle, I remember wondering how often men kissed each other, and why my grandfather was so disgusted by it.

In fact, he even threatened to leave, with me in tow, if the two men kissed again.

Any time I saw queerness after that—on screen or in real life—I felt hyper-aware of how my family reacted to the scene. More often than not, they'd make snide comments that made my stomach flip and squirm. They were always quick to comment on butch women being fat and "manly," and femme women being thin and "so pretty." I didn't yet realize I was one of the people they so clearly hated, but my gut knew. Of course it did.

Hence why my stomach filled with so many butterflies when I saw that brief scene from *Cruel Intentions*. When I saw Sarah Michelle Gellar kiss Selma Blair, it subverted my understanding of queerness insofar as I had one, at age nine. Neither of these women were fat. Neither of them presented as butch. Yet, they kissed with open mouths and probing tongues and, perhaps because I didn't know the context of the scene—I didn't see *Cruel Intentions* in its entirety until high school—this brief moment gave me some unexpected, but intense spark of hope. Could I be with a woman if I was fat, but not butch? Could I have what these women had, even if I didn't fully realize that was what I wanted at the time?

But they don't end up together, which I only found out later. It was a fluke, then; not a measurement of what real lesbians look like, of what kinds of women are attracted to each other. The disappointment in this, once I had finally begun to realize I was very much *not* attracted to men, was almost as impactful as the initial thrill of seeing them kiss.

If I liked women, and I was fat—I've always, always been fat—I thought it meant that I had to be butch, too. I didn't want that. I thought it would be easier to hide my queerness than to hide my fatness, so that became my goal, especially when I started to grow breasts in fourth grade. My family made comments about my weight—ironic, since I come from a lineage of people with fat bodies—but those comments were less hurtful than the ones they made about queer people. About lesbians. About me.

I was fat, I had boobs, and I had to shave my armpits; I fluctuated between super-femme and femme-lite, placing Beanie Babies and avoiding Pokémon cards because "they were for boys." I didn't play video games. I listened exclusively to pop music. And whenever someone made mention of media that was "for boys," I'd mock it or avoid it, so no one would suspect my growing desire to kiss girls. Despite how I dressed, I still feared how people saw me when I played handball at recess or dressed as Sporty Spice for Halloween. I wore sports bras to make my chest less obvious, but because I wasn't an athlete, my peers thought that was weird. I took dance classes every week, but I didn't play soccer or basketball or any of the team sports that my peers played, all while remaining thin and "girly" even without ever putting on a skirt. Because I was fat, I felt I had to work extra hard to maintain that same status.

For a while, it felt as if maybe no one would notice that I probably—definitely—didn't like boys. Unfortunately, the cruelty of children lies in their ability to notice small details; it lies in their observation and their honesty, which is as brutal as it is welcome, depending on the circumstances. Being fat already made me an easy target for bullies; being fat and liking girls—no matter how well I thought I hid the latter—felt like kicking myself in the face and wondering why my nose was bleeding.

I was ten the first time someone called me a dyke. I wore a "real" bra—a white training one with a little pink bow between the cups—and a pink, velvet button-up with a *Looney Tunes* t-shirt and a skirt. I was in a femme phase; after that day, I'd remain in that phase for years, even once I started wearing baggy, goth clothing in middle and high school that was intended to hide as much of my fat body as it could. The slur surprised me; it also sent me into a tailspin that made me eschew sports bras and chunky sneakers for more than ten years.

"I don't want to be friends with a dyke," a peer told me that day, giving me a sneer so intense it made my insides curl. Weeks later, while I was "cheering" at recess with a friend (we were both obsessed with *Bring It On*), another girl gleefully called, "Don't quit your day job, fatty!" The latter was familiar, but so soon after the former, it made me want to crawl out of my skin.

That year, I started self-identifying as "boy crazy," and talked about my crushes until I was blue in the face. No one expected me to ever date any of the boys I said I liked; I was fat, after all, and everyone knew cute boys didn't date fat girls. I knew that intimately. The few times I tried—once in seventh grade, once in ninth, and once in college—I was rejected outright.

I never had the guts to ask boys out myself, so I did what anyone would do: sent in friends to do recon. After a while, I could predict what boys would say without having to reveal my feelings at all.

"Oh, Sam's cool, but...does she like boys?"

"Wait, the fat chick? Isn't she a lesbo?"

"If she lost a few pounds, I'd consider it."

Depictions of romance in media hadn't just fucked me up; they had fucked us all up. They taught us that abusive, co-dependent relationships were healthy and desirable; that fatness was inherently evil; that no one in a fat body could ever be beautiful or beloved or good. I came from the generation of fat kids and adolescents who saw *Shallow Hal* at a formative age and threw in the towel on forming genuine, romantic ties. I reluctantly related to Disney villains, not just because they were queer-coded, but because they were fat. I watched men kiss women and men kiss men and women kiss women and, all the while, wondered if I'd ever be kissed at all, because I was ugly and undesirable and disgusting.

These ideas were ubiquitous. Movies, television, children's books, and even music equivocated fatness and butchness and queerness until these things felt synonymous, even though they weren't. Girls who don't actively date boys in high school are often assumed to be gay; if we're fat, that's even more true, because hey, lesbians love big, masculine chicks, right? Not always. But at 10, 13, and 15, I didn't have the vocabulary to argue with those assumptions. And even when I finally, finally began to realize that being fat didn't mean I had to be a lesbian, or vice versa, and that my presentation didn't have to coincide with media stereotypes, I still struggled to reconcile my fatness, my queerness, that ever-elusive goal of real, legitimate happiness.

It wasn't until I finally embraced my queerness that I successfully asked someone out.

My first partner told me they liked my body, wanted me no matter how fat I was, and came up with a "pet name" that was supposed to make me feel safe. That "pet name" was "bebe whale," and I wanted so badly for that to be cute and normal that I not only adopted the name when referencing myself, but told my friends they could call me that, too.

In retrospect, that should have been the first red flag.

We lived on opposite sides of the globe, with a 12-hour time difference and not enough money or technology between us to do more than talk online—or later, the phone—for hours at a time. I lost my virginity through cyber and phone sex and believed, for a time, that this was what being in love was supposed to be like—that being worshipped from afar and compared to renaissance paintings was the kind of romance I'd been striving for my whole life. Those are the kinds of things that make women swoon, right? I certainly did. So when my partner's comments suddenly turned cruel, I told myself it was okay, because they still loved me. They would love me forever. They promised.

But after we met—and had sex—in person, their sweet, doting comments about my body changed drastically. They told me if I lost weight, we could have better sex; they told me not to get any more tattoos, because they liked to see my skin; they told me losing weight would make me more flexible, would allow us to share clothes, would make me "stick out less" when we were in public. And still, I stayed with them—for another year—because I was convinced that no one would ever love or want me like that again. They told me as much, whenever we would "take breaks." I believed them.

I was wrong. So were they.

It took me years to untangle the mess they made. Embracing my queerness made me feel free, lighter than I'd ever been, and intangibly, incredibly happy. Falling in love with someone who claimed to like my body, claimed to love that I was a fat, queer, femme woman, made me feel even better. But from the first moment they called me "bebe whale," my feelings changed.

I ignored the sinking of my stomach because I wanted the nickname to be cute. I wanted to believe my partner loved me, wanted me, embraced me completely.

For two years after I broke it off, I continued to allow my friends to call me "bebe whale." When I asked them to stop, at the urging of my partner at the time, I cried. I felt guilty for asking them to be *nice* to me, to not call me something that both invoked memories of my emotionally abusive ex and made me hate my body. Any progress I had made in accepting and loving my fat body was erased by my partner's behavior throughout the latter half of our relationship; asking my friends to drop this horrible nickname felt like the first real step toward loving myself again, even though it was utterly terrifying to do.

My therapist recently asked me what I would say to my younger self, if I could. I replied, "I'd say, break up before they throw this in your face. You're fat and fabulous and queer and smart, and someone better will love you for all of those things, not in spite of them. Don't let someone hurl your insecurities like daggers. They're not worth it. You deserve more."

Being fat and queer means entering into queer spaces, expecting to be embraced, but still being alienated for being fat. Being fat and queer means falling in love with people who may not have the language to talk to you about your body, but at least they don't expect you to be butch because you're big. Being fat and queer means slowly learning to embrace both, then unlearning and re-learning every time someone reminds you that just because you can be both, doesn't mean you *should* be.

Being fat and queer means remembering that girl who called me a dyke and wanting to laugh, because now I call myself that with pride. Being fat and queer means remembering all those boys who didn't want me because I was too big and wanting to laugh, because I didn't really want them either.

I was so afraid of my body then, afraid of what it wanted, how it yearned. Being thin, being straight—these were impossible goals for which I strived, but only because I didn't know any better. I bought into the lie that in order to fall in love and be happy—to have any kind of life at all—I had to lose weight. And even when I first realized, with startling acuity, just how nice it might be to kiss another girl, I lived in fear of what that meant, and how I could possibly be both fat *and* queer, if I didn't present myself a certain way.

It's been 20 years since I saw Sarah Michelle Gellar and Selma Blair kiss on my living room TV and wondered why I felt like my skin was on fire.

Now, I know better.

Now, my fat, queer self is so achingly alive.

"And Then..."

K.M. Steigleder

I'll start by stating a fact: I used to be skinny. Some would even say too skinny. I would suck in my stomach constantly, wearing high-waisted jeans so when I sat down my stomach wouldn't bulge over the top button of the denim. I would eat a granola bar for lunch and whatever my mom cooked for dinner, never breakfast. Even so, I thought I was fat. I believed the entire world thought I was fat. Why wouldn't they? I had to work at being skinny. It's not something I was just born with and I could eat whatever I wanted and stay that way. There was always something wrong with me. I'd look in the mirror and I never saw the reality of my body but rather a concocted image of myself that was usually much larger and uglier than I actually was. I look back at photos of me now and wish I could grab that kid by the shoulders and tell them "Stop hating yourself, you're enough!" But my journey to self-acceptance was only just beginning. I thought I couldn't hate myself more...

And then I got an eating disorder.

I lived in secret for most of my high school years, starving myself. I had to stay a size 2/4 and meet the societal expectations of my stereotypical small town where the popular kids could have been models, and if you didn't look the part, you were just average. How could one be okay with just average? I remember trying so hard to wrap my fingers around my forearm so they could touch on one side. I remember the first time I tried on my usual size jeans in American Eagle, only to realize they were too tight, and how my heart broke more than when my first boyfriend dumped me. I remember a boy in my class pointing out my ever-so-slight "muffin top" where my tummy hung over my jeans. I was only 115 lbs at the time. For most of high school I spent my days starving myself or purging secretly in my downstairs bathroom, and told absolutely no one. I wanted people to believe that being skinny just came easy for me. Before I realized it, I had anorexia and bulimic tendencies. If I'm being honest, I didn't care either. I believed that staying skinny would be my only salvation, the only way I would feel loved, cherished, and important.

And then I got fat.

Not just the "freshman 15" that we hear about before going to college, but a full 130 lbs difference in weight by my junior year of college. Chalk it up to never knowing how to feed myself after living off of granola bars or my mom's dinners, or maybe the fact that I no longer worked out or played sports. It could have been that I dealt with my immense feelings of loneliness and self-hatred by eating an entire bag of jalapeno cheddar kettle chips while drinking a case of Dr. Pepper. I hardly recognized myself anymore. I went to college and it was as if every restriction I placed on myself vanished and was replaced by a constant need to fill every hole of insecurity I had with food. I would mindlessly eat anything in sight. My eating disorder tendencies had turned into diagnosed binge eating disorder with bulimic tendencies. I would go to the dining hall with friends only to return to my dorm room and eat snacks once I was alone and isolated. Sometimes, when the guilt would consume me and I knew I couldn't keep doing this, I would force it all out of me one way or another in the basement single-use restroom meant for guests and visitors so my floor mates wouldn't find out. I had gained weight. I was having to buy new clothes almost every semester because the clothes I had no longer fit me. Every time I looked in my cheap floor-length mirror on my closet door, I would see myself growing into the person I was always so terrified of becoming. I would stand there, naked and crying, looking at the stretch marks up my abdomen, the lumps in my hips and upper thighs, the dimples that existed in places they never used to. Who was I? How did this happen? I felt completely lost.

And then I was queer.

As if my physical reality in my body wasn't overwhelming enough, in college I began to interact with queer and LGBTQIA+ people more and more and began to question my own sexuality. I transferred to a larger university where I became immersed in the LGBTQIA+ center on campus and almost instantly knew I had found a community I had deeply longed for. In some ways, it was the exact opposite of the community I grew up in. Everyone at the center was so accepting and rarely passed judgements, especially on the basis of appearance. It was easier to be myself, to feel that I was being genuine for once. I stopped purging and began to work to get my eating disorder under control, but as I improved in one area of my life, my confusion around my sexuality and attraction to other people intensified. I was surrounded by people who seemed so secure in who they were. Activists on campus, the regulars that hung out at the center, folks in the LGBTQIA+ alliance student organization, they all seemed to know themselves and were so confident in their queer identities. I didn't know if I'd ever get to that point.

My grade school was as cisgender and heterosexual as they come. People waited years to come out after high school, including people quite close to me. I realized I identified somewhere between bisexual and pansexual, ultimately being attracted to people from all genders and sexualities. I had never had words for this until now. I somehow thought that by admitting to being attracted to more than just cisgender men, I was being held to twice (or more) as many expectations and standards of what would be "attractive." It was a toxic thought that had no evidence other than my own assumptions, but it consumed me.

And then I was nonbinary.

Often on one's journey through sexuality, gender comes along with it. I realized that just being feminine was not enough for me. It was no longer capturing who I was as a person. Now almost done with my master's degree, I was entering spaces and feeling as if I was gaining control of the compounding identities I was developing. I was entering spaces and feeling more confident to ditch the things society was always telling me to do. I was embracing things I actually wanted. I used to walk swaying my hips to appear more feminine. I stopped doing that and developed a wider stance. I could feel the tension leave my hips and how comfortable even the simple act of walking had become. I began to wear androgynous clothes that made me feel more at peace with my gender and my body. It became less stressful to go into a store and not feel confined to just the "women's" clothing where often they were too tight, too small, and too restricting for me to ever feel comfortable. There were days where I would present as more masculine or days where I simply did not want to present as anything at all. In the back of my head I would hear how wrong this all was. I wasn't sure why that voice was there, but it scared me to present as anything other than feminine. I was terrified people would judge me, especially people from my hometown. I didn't think anyone would understand who I was or why I was presenting in this way.

And then I was lost.

I had no idea where I fit in anymore. I suppose that's the problem with communities. It often feels that if you're not entirely involved with one of them, it's difficult to find your fit. Eating disorder communities help me process an often debilitating mental and physical illness but are dominated by cisgender thin females. My fat communities help me accept my body for what it is and find self-love but only exist in social media spheres where people spend most of their time defending why they deserve to exist to fatphobic trolls. My queer communities help me process my gender and sexuality but are often dominated by cisgender or passing gay men. I often do not feel as if I fully belong in any of these communities. It's as if I am somewhere in the middle of all of them.

So where do you go when you don't feel you belong anywhere?

I ask myself this question a lot. No matter how many groups, communities, or outlets I try to find, nothing has ever truly been my home. I realized I would have to create the physical, social, and mental environments I needed and wanted for myself. I could no longer rely on other people to create and manage those spaces for me. I didn't know how to move forward when all I'd done was hold myself back out of fear and complacency. I was on the verge of the next chapter of my life and just needed to figure out how to turn the page.

And then I recovered from my eating disorder.

I left the social media groups for eating disorder recovery that were being dominated by people who did not understand that fat people can have eating disorders. For many years, I thought it would help being in those groups and building a community with people also in eating disorder recovery. What it actually did was fuel and trigger me into relapse. There were no licensed therapists or recovery specialists monitoring these groups. People would post about their weight, how skinny they felt, and other harmful messaging that would cause me to spiral out of control. When I realized this outlet for recovery was no longer serving me, and possibly never had, I decided that my "community" did not have to be this big group of people. It is my past and present therapists who have helped me learn coping skills and to distinguish between the thoughts that are mine and the thoughts that belong to my eating disorder. It is my support system of family and friends who respected me when I asked them not to talk about their diets or weight loss in front of me. It is a community of eating disorder recovery activists on social media who share their journey of self-love and acceptance every day and inspire me to do the same.

And then I accepted my fatness.

I worked tirelessly to see my fatness as just a part of me and tried to reduce the amount of judgement I had learned to put against it. I threw away my scale, deleted calorie tracking apps (yes, even Weight Watchers), and stopped following all of the "healthy diet plans" on Pinterest. I began to associate myself more with fat people or those who are fat accepting. I went to a conference where they held a session on fat-inclusive environments and it was the first time I'd been in a room where fat people were celebrated, not shamed. I thought my tears of happiness would flood the room as I left. I began to talk openly about what fatness means to me and to society with the people in my life. I disassociated with the fact that healthy means thin. I began to follow fat activists and anti-diet culture accounts on my social media. I read articles, listened to podcasts, and sought out movies and TV shows where fat people were normalized.

And then I advocated for my sexuality.

Now that I was no longer in college, I could make my queerness fit me instead of making myself fit the queer atmosphere that existed on campus. I joined a city-affiliated queer group so I could connect with other queer people in town. I joined a queer yoga class. I sought out affinity groups through my job so I could continue building community and finding support. I continued building relationships with those from college who always made me feel validated. Like many folks who identify as bisexual or pansexual, I often feel erased. I spent a lot of time justifying why I deserved to be in a queer space and to avoid being lumped into the sexuality of my partner. I created friend groups of people who never made me feel like I needed to do that.

And then I developed my gender expression.

While this is the newest venture of my identity development, it has been the most rewarding. I am constantly and consistently experimenting with my gender identity. I'm often perplexed at the nuances of gender and how it has been surprisingly more visible when I am not presenting myself as a feminine bodied person, especially to my friends and family who have known me for many years. It's hard for some to adjust when we're not meeting their expectations. When I first cut my hair off, I had so many jokes at my expense. I often laughed along, but they were never very funny and often associated me with being a lesbian (which I'm not) or butch (which I'm also not), and neither of those are a bad thing or something to be joked about. To dive deeper into these assumptions still terrifies me. Even now, I find myself very selective with the people I'm around when I express more nonbinary fashion choices and to be who I feel I really am.

And then it all comes together.

There are always setbacks to all of the progress we make in our identity development. It is continual work to always be advocating for yourself. There are people who intentionally do not want you to fit in. They do not want to see parts of you normalized. That is why sharing our stories and how we navigate the world is so important. The more it happens, the more normalized it becomes. I see a world where it's no longer taboo to discuss your fatness, your queerness, your eating-disordered past, your gender identity. It doesn't have to fit neatly into every little box, and maybe one day, we'll throw out all those boxes and let it all blend together. But life isn't like that for me right now. I still feel the pull in each and every direction. I feel the need to not like myself, to wish I was different.

And then I fight against that negative pull and remind myself of who I am: a fat, queer, recovered, nonbinary person who is deserving of love, especially from myself.

"The End of the World"

C. Adán Cabrera

I

The world was going to end on Sunday. At least that's what the preacher man said on television. The King of Everything, the Alpha and Omega Himself, would ride down from Heaven and from his Sacred White Horse strike down every Wicked Man, Woman, and Child exactly seven minutes after the sun set over Jerusalem. The cherub-cheeked old man paced in front of a bronze-colored podium, pausing only to dab at his forehead with a limp, pink handkerchief. That gave us, I figured, three full days to repent and thus avoid the divine wrath that the preacher declared to be imminent. More importantly, though, three days was also what we needed to take that long drive up north for the Boys and Bellies river rafting trip we'd booked a year in advance. We weren't much into the scene (cubs, bears, otters—a veritable zoo) but we'd spent two days full of breath-stealing skinny dips in the American River, spooning under a star-scattered sky and learning to fuck in near silence in a tent when surrounded by dozens of other campers that we'd decided to do it all over again. I saved for a year to make it happen. Yeah, we weren't together anymore, but at least we'd have one last hurrah. I'd deal with my feelings or whatever later. The trip was another chance to escape the heat. After all, July in Los Angeles was hotter-than-Satan's backside, hot enough to tempt the big J.C. to unnail a hand from his crucifix and fan himself. Point is, come Monday I'd either be broiling with the rest of the sinners or find myself back at work, pushing yet another cart of returns down the drugstore's air-conditioned aisles. The only thing I'd done thus far on my week-long vacation was drink and guess at paternity results along with Maury Povich's studio audience. That, and smoke way too much weed with Tomás at our apartment, where the dusty secondhand fan pushed the dank air around.

I was on vacation, but for Tomás it was just another Thursday. Today, at least, I decided to not let it get to me. We'd be leaving for the rafting trip in a few hours and who knows when we'd ever spend so much time together. Because, you see, Tomás was leaving. I told him we should start packing. He was dozing on the recliner, digesting a slice of leftover pizza and a handful of tortilla chips. The afternoon heat had melted off his clothes, leaving him in a pair of green briefs and a tight, black tank top. The hairy underside of his belly, the shirt's fabric stretched taut over its generous bulge: that was the part I loved the most. A half-finished bottle of beer was pinned between his hairy thighs. I imagined myself between them.

"That's this weekend?" Tomás said, yawning. He tilted back farther in his seat.

"I thought you'd remember boys and bears in any combination," I said. The recliner seemed to squeak in protest.

"Well, at least we can get out of the city for a bit," he said. "Before, you know, the Apocalypse or whatever." Tomás closed his eyes again, stretched out his arms and let them fall again with a sigh. I reached down to grab my Jack-and-lemonade. It was a little tart, but I drank it anyway.

Tomás opened one green eye. He reached for his beer but knocked it over instead, neck first. It fizzled down the recliner's leg rest and onto the carpet. "Goddamit," he muttered. He peeled off his tank top and folded it into thirds. (Behold the full chest, the nipples the color of melted caramel.) He leaned forward and pressed it onto the puddle of quickly drying beer. He tossed the wet shirt onto the kitchen floor, a foot away from the hamper.

I'd learned long ago that scolding him was useless and made a mental note to pick it up later. I took a long sip of my lemonade.

"So, when do we leave?"

"Tonight," I said. "And we'll stay 'til the world ends."

Tomás bent forward to pick up his tank top. "I'll get my backpack ready. And sorry, man. About the carpet. If they try to charge you for it when I leave, let me know..." He started to gather some things together.

"It's cool," I said. "Man." I finished my lemonade. Two sour gulps.

I turned back to the television. The preacher was still rambling on, becoming ever-more exasperated while he spoke, furiously patting his hairline, as if the sky had opened up and he could already feel the fire and brimstone raining down from Heaven itself and no one but he could see it.

II

Tomás and I had split up a few months earlier, our relationship having lasted three years. We'd met when we were both 18 and had just turned 21 when we broke up. A week before we left for the river, Tomás had announced that he had finally found a job and would move out with a friend the day after we got back. A friend had apparently promised him a part-time gig in Silverlake, on the other side of town. He explained this with confidence because all that stood between Tomás and a steady paycheck was one of those detox kits that flush out the weed in your system. I nodded and told Tomás I was happy for him, while imagining the days ahead yawning ahead of me, chasm-like. I'd moved down to LA from San Francisco to study but met Tomás just a few weeks after I arrived. So I hadn't really got used to being on my own. We'd been living together for most of that time, cramped into a studio a few blocks from campus. I dropped out after a few weeks and got the part-time gig at a local drugstore shelving returns and hoping no one I knew saw me working there.

My folks didn't know any of this, of course; every phone call had its special set of lies and I visited them often enough to keep their curiosity at bay. Telling them the truth—that I'd stopped going to class, lost my scholarship, and was supporting my live-in ex-boyfriend on a meager salary—would make me a *maje*. Loosely translated from the Salvadoran: dumb ass. Also: no more help with the rent and whole lot of guilt trips to make me move back to the Bay. But soon enough they seemed satisfied with whatever lies I'd make up. I'd worry about "graduation" later.

But back then, I knew it all. I was high on independence, living in the City of Angels, far from my family. Don't get me wrong: it's not as though San Francisco was an awful place to live. In fact, I missed home, missed my mom's homemade pupusas, missed the murals and the underground howl of the BART when I passed the 24th & Mission station. But I didn't mind surviving off microwaved hot dogs and stale Cap'n Crunch if it meant having a place of my own. Our own. I'd even scrubbed our clothes clean in the kitchen sink when we had no money for the laundromat. Miserable as it could be, at least I had Tomás. My constant companion, my microcosm of desire. And, for a time, I was all Tomás had too. I first met him as I was leaving class one afternoon that first week. This was before all those first mobile apps where you can take your pick of a number of available men around you. Tomás was wandering around campus, jotting down something in a small spiralbound notebook, and immediately caught my attention: see, there weren't too many chubby guys at the university. Not any cute ones, anyway. I'd been with a couple of guys back home whenever I'd wandered up to the Castro district, but my experience was limited. I couldn't let him get away. I walked toward him, taking out my notebook with a rainbow flag sticker on the cover. Advertising, I called it. Tomás looked up at me as I passed. Behold the dimples, the fuzzy cheeks, the mole on his eyelid, the big ears, the green eyes, the hairy, manly forearms. The generous belly.

Fast forward a week and there I was, giving him head in a humanities building bathroom. A couple of weeks later he was staying with me on the weekends, eager to escape his stepmother who constantly begged him for money. His father, who owned a few businesses back in Guatemala, had died a year before I met Tomás, leaving him a meager inheritance which was now coveted by his widow to spend on her new boyfriend or cheap perfume or whatever else she wanted the cash for. Tomás wouldn't give her a cent. That puta isn't gonna waste my papi's money, he'd say. So I'd let him stay over whenever he wanted and soon his clothes were entwined with mine in that natural, unnoticed way. Our relationship, the first for both of us, bloomed: cuddles on the recliner, drowsy in his lap, breathing in his cologne. Kisses filling the soft crevices of his cheeks. Sketches in charcoal while he took in the springtime sun. Cold mornings in bed, his arm wrapped around me, holding our warmth firmly in place. Electric-blue silhouette in the late-night talk show glow. Long, rambling poems. Tickle of toes in the moonlight.

Soon, Milton and geometry and whatever the hell else I was studying seemed less appealing than Tomás. So I dropped out and started working at the drugstore. Tomás, it turned out, had simply been wandering around campus the day I met him and was not interested in enrolling like I'd initially thought. He said he wanted to be a writer, and that school would only get in the way. He had some ideas for a novel, just needed some time to relax and work out the kinks before sitting down to write. That's all, he'd say. More of his stuff appeared in corners of the studio. Soon I was lying to my parents and then one day right after I came he asked if he could stay with me for a while so he could work on his book. He placed my spent hand on his warm, wet belly. Supporting the arts, he said, and dipped down to fill my mouth with a kiss. I couldn't say no.

Time passed. We fought; we fucked. We laughed and had angry, tearful arguments. My grandma died. Followed by my favorite tío (uncle). I cheated. So did Tomás. I made him tell me details. A clumsy threesome with a cute bear with different sized nipples we met in a chatroom, and then another with a friend of a friend who also likes chubby dudes. I hated seeing them finish so much that I couldn't bring myself to orgasm. Both times. We closed our relationship back up. But I still saw his headless profile on the apps: the sight of his birthmark above his hairy belly button shifted something inside me. I'm pretty sure he saw my torso on there, too. Because showing our face would be too direct. Neither of us said a word. And he didn't write a word. It seemed things would never change.

And then, three months ago, we broke up. I still don't know what happened. One day I woke up to find Tomás, shirtless as usual, sitting at the edge of the bed, his hairy back turned to me. Something's missing, he said. I want to break up. And that was that. No big fights, no name-calling, no litany of past favors, no din of dishes against the cheap stucco wall. All things I'd seen as a kid. I didn't respond to Tomás. What I wanted to say: if something's missing, let's find it. Please. But I just turned to face the window and stared at the light filtering in through the blinds. I hated the way his phone kept buzzing. Later that day, he said he would move out as soon as he could afford to do so. There'd be rules, but we could continue living together and doing stuff as usual, including having sex. It made sense, he said. For both of us. That was Tomás for you: the world could be ending, the stars splashing into the ocean, and he would insist on going at it one last time. For a while, it seemed things would continue like they always had. Then began the arguments about money, his stupid unwritten novel, what he called my insane jealousy, what I called his selfish ass. We seemed to keep misunderstanding each other and were irritable as fuck, but we couldn't seem to pull apart from each other either. The sex, of course, didn't help in that regard.

If anything, it got better: we consumed each other, engulfed in our mutual lust, knowing there would be a time when we would be apart. Well, at least I did. And then, Tomás announced he'd found a job and would be moving out with a friend. He didn't tell me his friend's name, and I didn't want to know. He hadn't written a word at our apartment, he explained, and was moving out to spark his creativity. We were smoking weed out of King Bong, the pipe he used only on special occasions, when he broke the news to me.

"So I'll be out of your hair soon enough," he said, blowing a cloud of smoke just above my head. "I bet you're relieved." He grinned.

I said nothing and reached for the bong, lighting the bowl again and again until there was nothing left.

III

Sobered up, we'd left at the last minute and were heading north on the 405, passing the Getty Center, when Tomás asked me to pull over. He wanted to give me head, he said, while we overlooked the Valley from Mulholland Drive. Sex was an important part of his forthcoming book and he said he wanted to do some research.

"Now?" I said into the rear-view mirror. I had been trying to switch lanes but some asshole in a red pickup truck wouldn't let me merge.

"Son of a bitch," I sighed.

"Why? For wanting to suck your dick?" Tomás snapped.

"Not you," I muttered. "That guy." I placed a hand on his warm thigh. He was wearing shorts and I pulled the hem up slightly to feel the tufts of hair on his knee. Tomás shifted in his seat and moved toward the window. I let my hand linger on the center console where it had fallen. Just then, the asshole in the red truck passed us, honking when he sped by. I flipped him off and swerved into the next lane, advancing only a few feet in the process. Taillights burned like hundreds of fading embers.

"You're so angry, all the time," Tomás said. He reached into the glove compartment and took out what we called his travel pipe before slouching back into his seat. He rolled down the window. "You exhaust me."

"Oh, c'mon, babe," I said softly.

"Please don't call me 'babe,'" he said. No pet names: a recent post-break-up rule.

"Sorry. Man," I said. The car hummed: brake, gas, brake.

"We just gotta make it to the campground before midnight," I said.

Last year we'd arrived at nearly 3am and found that the organizers hadn't set up a tent for us because they thought we weren't coming. So we'd spent that first night crammed in my peanut of a Kia, winding up with a few winks of sleep and stiff necks.

"I just wanted some inspiration," Tomás said. "For my book."

"Right," I said.

He turned away from me to face out of the window. I left him alone. He'd feel better after he smoked a couple of bowls.

Pouting Tomás—that was what I called him whenever he didn't get his way—took some weed out of his pocket and stuffed it into the pipe. He lit it, took a deep drag, and blew the smoke onto the dashboard. That was the thing with Tomás: he didn't have much money, but always managed to have marijuana. It was like the seaside miracle of fish and loaves. Five hours, several bowls, and a bag of trail mix later we were near Modesto, about an hour and a half from the campground. We had to piss, so we decided to pull into a rest stop.

It was dark and starless, and hardly anyone was there. An RV was parked in a corner along with a couple of other sedans, but that was it. Our footfalls echoed when we walked into the bathroom. Rows of steel sinks glittered under the stale fluorescent light. I was about to zip up my pants when I felt him against me, his big thing pressing into my lower back. He grabbed me by either bicep, his lips grazing my neck. He took my earlobe into his mouth. His hands found my hips, slipped into my jeans, ran down the soft part of my thighs. Tomás writhed against me, and released one of my arms so I could unbuckle his belt. I turned around, feeling him tremble as I slowly—slowly—pulled down his pants. Tomás smiled before bending to kiss me. My tongue met his, mid-air. I pulled him toward the rearmost stall, his jeans shuffling along the floor.

IV

We got there a few minutes shy of midnight. We'd called one of the organizers after the session in the rest stop stall and a gruff voice said our tent would be the one farthest from the river, last row. After we'd found the parking lot, we had to walk to the campground. It was pitch black so we used our phones to guide the way. Scurrying insects. Piles of dead tree branches. Remnants of what was once a racoon. Our tent was next to a mangled oak tree. All around us came sounds familiar from the year before: snores, the rustle of sleeping bags, a disembodied whisper, crickets.

We slipped into our tent, our backpacks heavy and our sleeping bags and pillows tucked beneath our arms. We zipped it up behind us with measured slowness. Tomás turned his phone's light back on, its thick beam illuminating the blue nylon interior. He rummaged through his backpack. A spider was suspended from the top part of the tent, falling toward the light. Tomás reached up and burned it with his lighter. He turned back to his bag. He took out his sunblock, batteries, and toilet paper and stacked it next to his saltines.

"Here it is," he said at last, pulling out a sandwich bag, the kind you put in the freezer.

It was half full of marijuana. "I thought I'd forgotten it."

"I doubt that," I said. I unrolled my sleeping bag and stretched out on top of it.

"Grouchy," he said. "I think someone needs to smoke, too."

He pulled out a small pinch of weed and thumbed it into the bowl. We smoked, passing the pipe between us until the small tent was filled with a cloud of marijuana. We were far enough from everyone that no one probably noticed, but I was paranoid all the same. I'd saved for a long time to pay for the trip and didn't want to get kicked out. Tomás, as usual, didn't seem to consider this. He turned off the light, blanketing everything in a deep darkness. I felt him stretch out on his sleeping bag, too.

My mind floated and my body buzzed. I loved feeling the cold earth against my back. Through the tent's nylon floor I counted pebbles with my toes and traced a fallen tree branch. Something rustled in the leaves. Tomás breathed evenly next to me. We were separated by a chasm no wider than a forearm. My hand inched toward him and I let it travel. I touched the hair on his arm, stroked his bicep with my fingertip. I wanted him near me, to rest my hand on his belly and feel it rise and fall until I fell asleep. I knew it was another thing I'd miss.

Tomás cleared his throat. "I'm trying to sleep."

"Sorry," I said, turning away from him. I stared at the darkness, waiting for my eyes to adjust to the lack of light. I heard his sleeping bag rustle and sensed that he had turned his back to me. A few minutes passed in silence. A tent unzipped somewhere, followed a few moments later by the dribble of a urinating camper.

"You okay, man?" he said. "Last year you couldn't stop talking about how excited you were to get on the water."

"I'm fine," I said. I sank my head deeper into my pillow, my eyes still wide open.

Tomás snickered. "Good shit, huh? That strain's called bota culo, guaranteed to knock you on your ass and outta this world. Which is good, 'cause the Second Coming, or whatever." By his tone I could tell he was way more baked than I was.

"Goodnight," I said.

V

The next morning, after a breakfast of peanut butter sandwiches (Tomás had forgotten the jelly), we put on our trunks and herded alongside the other river-rafters to the water. Like the year before, most of the other participants were white men, the gay type of Caucasian that had gentrified the Mission, my old neighborhood. You know what I mean: the invasion of the gringos in tight jeans and black-rimmed glasses atop vintage bicycles. French bulldog in tow optional. My parents, both refugees from El Salvador, never failed to complain about their beatless music or their textbook Spanish. Just speak to me in English, my mother would groan.

As we were brown and younger than most of the other men, I sensed heads turning to look at us the moment we stood on the banks. Everyone was waiting for the rafts to come down and were chatting in small groups. There were men in various states of undress all around us.

Mostly bears and chubs and cubs, yes, but also a lot of chasers, and admirers, and all those other categories of cute and available men. There was also an even mix of bellies and the buff. A few daddies and polar bears and the one black guy who turned when Tomás took off his shirt. He was never shy about being shirtless, unlike some other chubby dudes I knew. I felt stupid as I watched him struggling to buckle his orange lifejacket over his belly. I had a sick feeling it was going to be a long day.

I started applying sunblock. It wasn't yet 9am, but the sun was already heavy on my skin. The bloated rafts appeared, bobbing on the sparkling river. Boulders half-submerged bulged skyward. Like last year, we were all separated into groups of 12 and each group was assigned a raft. Tomás and I climbed in with ten other campers, wedged between an older couple on our right and a tall redheaded man to our left. The latter, Ginger as we later named him, struck up a conversation with me while we were waiting for our team leader to give us instructions.

"First time?" he asked. He stuck out a hand and introduced himself.

"Our second," I said, squinting at the sunlight on the water. I shook his hand, followed by Tomás.

"Tommy," he said.

I looked at him strangely.

"Nice to meet you," Ginger said. He paused. Smiled. Stared? "Glad we get to have some fun before it all comes crashing down!" He started applying another layer of sunblock. A small, blue-capped bird landed on the edge of the raft. It teetered for a moment on one of the boarding handles before flitting away. Tomás, who up to that point had been tying and tightening the strings on his lifejacket, piped up.

"First time rafting?" Tomás asked. The fuck? He was never friendly with strangers.

Especially if he didn't have any weed in his system that day.

Ginger: "Yep. His, too." He pointed with a long finger to a plain-faced man sitting next to him. "My friend," Ginger seemed to explain. He waved at us and said hello in a small voice. He flashed a tight smile.

The water sloshed indifferently around the boat. Just then, our team leader—a youngish woman with blonde hair tied up in a ponytail—climbed into the raft. She had purple plastic paddles tucked under either arm. "Let's get this party started!" she shouted, and started distributing small oars to all of us.

She surveyed the group. "What a strong-looking bunch of guys we have here. I'll need someone to row with me up front and help me steer. Any takers?" Everyone looked at each around, waiting for a volunteer.

"Me," Tomás said, rising from his seat. He was full of surprises today, I thought to myself. The blue-capped bird landed on the boat again, this time next to me. I shooed it away with a quick splash of water and it flitted away.

The morning was warm and the afternoon was stifling, but the combination of the clean mountain air, the teeth-chattering plunges into the river water, and the summertime heat felt great. Ginger and his friend were terrified at first of the bumps and bursts over the bright water until Tomás pretended to fall into the river, instead dragging Ginger into the current with him. The poor redhead flapped in the water like a giant bird with wet wings. He feigned being extremely cold, and when his concerned friend went to him, he pulled him into the river as well. Their heads bobbed just above the water, white streams of sunblock and sweat running down their faces. Their laughter echoed across the canyon's green and stone walls.

I'd been rowing absently the entire time, but couldn't help smiling along with them. At lunchtime, we docked on the shore alongside the three other rafts. We climbed out onto the riverbank and all of us received a paper bag that contained a bland turkey sandwich, an apple, and a can of soda. Tomás and I sat on the beach away from the other campers, watching the river race by. I chewed with great effort, feeling tired. He lit a joint. A few of the other men turned in our direction but didn't seem to mind.

Tomás drained his soda and crumpled up his paper bag.

"Race you to that boulder?" he said, pointing to a moss-covered rock in the middle of the river. "Since when do you race?" I asked. I stuffed my half-eaten sandwich in the bag.

"What's wrong now?" Tomás said. He pointed to the boulder again.

"Nothing," I said. I took a drag of the joint even though I didn't feel like smoking. I didn't feel anything. Another puff. Still nothing. I picked up a pebble and threw it into the water. "I think last year was better."

"Maybe," Tomás said, standing up from the sand, "but they have to change things up every so often. Otherwise people get bored." He bent down and picked up a stone. He blew the sand off of it before throwing it across the river. It skipped across, smacking straight into the boulder that he had pointed out earlier before it fell back into the water. He stared out at the ripples.

"Lunch is over," he added, glancing over his shoulders at the other men.

I said nothing, and dug my toes into the sand.

Tomás grabbed his lifejacket. "Let's go back," he said.

VI

Tomás paddled alongside the leader for the rest of the afternoon. I rowed in the back behind Ginger and next to a geriatric single who yapped the entire afternoon about a grandson who had spent some time in El Salvador while in the military. I'd only been there once when I was six, but he kept asking me what life was like there, nodding vigorously with every fact I invented. It was a way to pass the time.

The rafting trip was soon over. We had made it through the South Fork, our leader announced, which also signaled the end. We docked at another riverbank and were then loaded into buses that drove us back up to the campground. After a dinner of flank steak and some salty spinach, Tomás and I drank a few beers along with some of the other campers.

Someone brought out a speaker. Tomás hung out with a badly burned Ginger and a group of other campers, most of whom were thin or muscular. Either way, Tomás was definitely their type. They were passing around a joint and some other guys looked on. I tried to strike up a conversation with a Filipino couple, but they didn't seem too interested in talking. We all drifted apart until one of the leaders announced dinner was over and that we had the rest of the evening to do as we pleased, but the next morning camp would be broken down promptly at 8am. Tomás looked to be wrapping up a conversation with Ginger and one of the guys who had stared at him earlier on the shore. He caught my eye, but I turned around and started walking back toward the tent. Our tent. I was still a little buzzed. I swatted at the gnats as I made my way among the other tents, nearly tripping over a tree root and some kid's rusted toy wagon. It was dusk by the time I slipped into the tent. I fell asleep shortly after, listening to the distant laughter of the other campers, including Tomás. Someone was playing something that sounded like a Kenny G song. Of course.

I awoke to hear Tomás struggling with the tent's zipper.

"Goddamit," he whispered.

I lay perfectly still, and closed my eyes. I could hear him tugging, to no avail.

"Need help?" A different voice, vaguely familiar.

"Yeah, that'd be great," Tomás said.

The voice pulled on the zipper a few times before finally unsticking it. A warm draft nuzzled against my toes.

"Tough, huh?" the voice said, laughing. That same thunderous laugh. "See ya Monday, Tommy."

The fading crunch of soil. I sat up, rubbing my eyes. I turned on the flashlight.

"Hola," Tomás said, stepping into the tent. He zipped it up behind him effortlessly.

"Sorry, didn't mean to wake you. Damn zipper." He stretched out on top of his sleeping bag.

He smelled like weed and cigarettes and booze.

"It's cool," I said, lying back down. I turned to face him. "Have fun?"

"A blast," he said, closing his eyes.

"Who was that with you?" I said, tracing his dimples with my gaze.

"A new friend," Tomás said, turning his back to me. "We sat by the river. I was telling him about my novel. Turns out he lives in LA also. Really nice guy. Offered to help me move out when we get back."

He said nothing else, and within minutes he fell asleep. The flashlight's circle of light floated like a dusty moon on the tent's canopy. I stared at it for a long time, memorizing its imprint.

VII

The next morning, Tomás and I headed back to LA. It was 8:30 on Sunday morning. I had a headache. We drove in silence while we wound our way down the mountains. Our phones vibrated back to life. I glanced at mine: one message. Probably from my mother, I figured, and decided I would wait until we got back to check it. Tomás had also received messages. I watched him out of the corner of my eye while I drove. He held up the phone to his ear, squinting at the screen and pushing buttons to skip some. It was while he was listening to his final message that I noticed a change in his expression. He then shoved the phone in the glove compartment. Tomás sank into the car seat, pressing his forehead against the window. He said nothing for a long time. He didn't even reach for his pipe.

As we got on the 5 freeway to head back to Southern California, I asked him what was wrong.

"I didn't pass the drug test," he said flatly, still staring out the window. "Guess the kit I bought didn't work or whatever." Tomás sighed, fogging up the glass. He rubbed the glass clean with the tip of his elbow.

"I'm sorry," I said.

Tomás shook his head. He closed his eyes. I watched him take his lower lip between his teeth.

Outside, the bland freeway that crosses the fields of Central Valley was coming into view. It was 9:30. We'd be back home by 2 or 3 that afternoon. I turned on the radio. No good music was playing, so I turned the tuner to something that sounded like NPR. A woman was crying. She had apparently spent her life savings to fly her family and a poodle named Pistachio to Jerusalem to witness the Second Coming, only to wind up heart-broken and disappointed when the Savior failed to materialize as the now-missing preacher had promised. The reporter said that a small, cheering crowd had gathered at the Wailing Wall to welcome the Messiah's arrival seven minutes after sunset. But there was no White Horse, no Fire and Brimstone, no Trumpets Blaring, no Whore of Babylon drunk on Sacred Blood. The only thing that had happened was that Pistachio had temporarily got off his leash, yapping at the other pilgrims. The sun had set over Jerusalem as it always had, and as it always would. At least for now, the woman said.

The segment ended moments later, and before the host could announce the upcoming program, I turned the radio off.

So much for the Apocalypse.

"Land Acknowledgement for My Body"

Alix Sanchez

I am tired of the white person's land acknowledgement
Don't get me wrong, you should know whose land you're
    standing on
Know the history of why that fishing village is now a Target
    and a Home Goods
as you glance meaningfully in the direction of the one or two
    indigenous people in the room
To show you're hearing the words and are a very very good
    person
who listens to land acknowledgements
But I'm tired
More than that, filled up with grief and rage and sometimes
    hope
Give me more than the white person's land acknowledgement

I want a land acknowledgement for my body
So deeply and effectively colonized from birth that it took me
Thirty-five years to realize I was trans
Because I thought you were just supposed to feel deeply
    uncomfortable in a fat body
Thought that if I could get my tits high enough I could figure
    out how to like them
Thought that if I could contour my face just right I could
    finally like the softness of its jaw
Thought that if I hunched my shoulders and stuffed my belly
    into shapewear and cast my gaze to the floor I could take
    up so little space maybe I could...what...disappear?
The highest calling of womanhood
I want a land acknowledgement for my weary skin

I want a land acknowledgement for the terrain of memory
Clearcut
Razed so perfectly that I can't picture myself as a child,
Can only remember in flashes, in fits and starts
Can only smile and shrug when people try to reminisce
Stare at a blank page when asked to write about my life
    before I was grown
I want a land acknowledgement for what I can't recall

I want a land acknowledgement for my tongue
That stumbles over the language that was dangerous for my
    grandparents to speak
That my mother never learned

That I learn in pieces staring at a screen, hundreds of miles
    from home
When I finally realized I was trans, I had to google the word
    for what I am
Because I knew my people had a word but I had no one to ask
    what to call myself
Aanini is the word
We always had it, even after they tried to take it away

I wrote a land acknowledgement for myself:
"We acknowledge that the aanini before you is unceded
    indigenous territory
That their body is a motherland, seat of rebirth
a holder of memory beyond their own
Of story still unfolding
That their embodiment is not a privilege
But a sovereign right
That they belong only to the ancestors
And to themselves"

"Legacy"

Miguel M. Morales

And now in this pandemic,
in this fight for Black lives,
remember that our fat and queer
and fat and trans bodies,
when not being ignored or fetishized,
have always fought oppression.
They've served as barricades, shields,
ladders, message boards, and transportation.

Our fat bodies
stood on the front lines at Stonewall,
crossed the bridge in Selma,
went on strike in agricultural fields
and meat packing plants,
defended sacred water at Standing Rock,
protected the environment,
and advocated for our animal friends.

Our queer bodies
knocked on doors,
made phone calls,
passed out fliers,
registered people to vote,
drove people to the polls,
and defended the right to vote.

Our trans bodies
chained themselves
to the White House fence
during the AIDS crisis,
committed and were arrested
for acts of civil disobedience.

Our fat and queer
and fat and trans bodies
have been abused, assaulted,
beaten, bloodied, stabbed, and shot.

Our bodies
have been refused
housing, treatment,
legality, entry into
classrooms, work spaces,
airplanes, and places of worship.

We've marched
on Washington for LGBTQ rights,
as part of the Women's March,
with the youth of March for Our Lives,
and the Latino March on Washington.

We've marched
to state capitals,
to city halls, police stations,
and to congressional offices.

We've marched
down city streets,
across town, on campuses,
and in protests and parades.

Our fat and queer bodies
have been part of every social movement,
every fight, every attack on the weak,
every community celebration,
every birth, every death, and every breath.

This is the mighty legacy
of our beautiful fat and queer
and fat and trans bodies.

Let us rise tall in our bodies.
Let us continue to embrace and
collude with intersectional movements,
but let us not forget
to raise *our* voices,
to call on *our* allies,
to lead *our* marches
and *our* parades.

Let us fight for *our* youth.
Let us protect *our* elders.

Let us proudly carry the weight of
our fat and queer and
our fat and trans legacy.

"Mantra of the Fat Faggot No. 27: 'Develop a Skin Thicker Than the One You're in'"

Dan Vera

throw off the filthy green frog-skin of hetero-
imitation to discover the gay prince underneath.
—Harry Hay[1]

Even the revolutionary lovers called for princes.
and because you were raised an expert of the
hidden gaze you quickly understood princes
were thin and beautiful and rode at the head of
every procession. For the revolution had traded
one mythology for another just as oppressive.

---

1   From a speech delivered by Harry Hay, founding member of the
    Radical Faeries, at the first Spiritual Conference for Radical Fairies
    in Benson, Arizona, 1979.

This is how the rags of the revolution
and the books of even the deep soul
writer are all covered with gleaming
torsos that tempted and tormented
our youth because sex and terror sells
and even in freedom they are not free
of this. You may slip invisible from
view.

Develop a skin thicker than
the one you're in for every
flower needs its petals and
make friends with each of
them those layers of living
that protect what grows
within.

One day you will meet a flower faced fellow
your bodies will open wide like prairie and he
will caress your changing form and you will
wander his geographies and every touch will
be like a bee at a beloved blossom a revelation
greater than any revolution ever imagined or
foretold.

"Seven Unsated Appetites"

Aubrey Gordon, Your Fat Friend

One

"That doesn't seem right. Are you sure?"

A stranger screws up his face at the paper I have just handed him, outlining the Oregon counties that legally allow employers to discriminate against LGBTQ+ workers. He scours the state map, looking for his own county.

"So, not here?" he asks, nonplussed.

"Washington County has banned LGBT discrimination, but most counties haven't," I confirm before returning to the script. "Right now, gay and transgender Oregonians can be denied an apartment, a job, a table at a restaurant, or a room in a hotel, just because of who they are. Do you think that we should ban discrimination against gay and transgender people in Oregon?"

He looks at me again, unmoved.

"I mean, I guess so," he sighs. "As long as they don't, you know, prance around." For a moment, I imagine carousel horses. Then I wonder whether he has met gay people. I do not ask him, nor do I reveal my queer identity to him. Instead, I hand him a postcard to address to his state legislator, asking for support for the Oregon Equality Act and the Oregon Family Fairness Act. He signs.

It is 2006, and this is my first day canvassing voters in my home state on LGBTQ+ issues. I am a summer intern, working the early days of what will become a 13-year career organizing for LGBTQ+ rights, racial justice, immigrant rights, and voting rights. Knocking on strangers' doors and dialing unknown voters' phone numbers are quiet terrors to me, and ones I've decided to spend a summer pushing through. While I had canvassed before, it was never this vulnerable, this charged, this kind of frightening, heady adrenaline rush. I'd come out before, but never like this, to one stranger after another, not knowing how they would react. *I'm queer. Do you think I should be able to have what you have?*

But as a lifelong anxious person, that's just one of my worries. I worry about houses with dogs that snarl and bare their teeth. I worry about assuming a gay person is straight. I worry about getting beaten up. I worry about knocking on too many doors, or too few. I worry about being fired from an as yet unpaid position. I do not yet know that these will be the least of my worries. That the greatest disappointment will come in the long term, not the short.

After the canvass, my new colleagues and I debrief our conversations. A trans Latinx organizer shares the story of a voter who tells him that she opposes discrimination "unless it's against Mexicans." A white volunteer is delighted to report

that, in the midst of her rap to one voter, that voter unzipped
her sweatshirt to reveal a Melissa Etheridge shirt and shouted,
"Baby, I'm family!"

Two

When I visit a family member, she meets me at the front door
holding her tablet, eager to show me what's on the screen. She
invites me inside before standing beside me, holding my arm
in a half-hug while she shows me what she's found. She seems
so proud of her discovery, certain it will bring me joy, relief,
happiness. It does not.

As my eyes drift to the tablet, my heart sinks and my face
falls. The screen is filled with before and after pictures, advertisements for weight-loss surgeries. On the left, a woman my
size, slouching and exposed, in fitted workout clothing. Next
to her, that same woman, beaming and standing tall, half her
previous size.

I am before. I am always before.

These are images I have seen countless times, presented
with enthusiasm by thin people who are certain they have discovered deliverance from the hell they imagine my body to be.
My family member, like so many before her, proudly reports
back what she has learned about the differences between gastric bands and gastric bypass, sleeves, and staples. She watches
my face for a wave of the relief she imagines I will feel when I
learn that there is a way out of the body that I have—all it will
take is $23,000 to cut that body open, truss its organs, and leave
it to shrink itself.

"I saw these pictures and I thought of you. Think of how much healthier you would be. The partners you could date. I know you love clothes—you could wear whatever you want!"

She means so well. Still, it hurts. I am awash in the desolation she imagines my life to be, and the wonderland she envisions for thinner women. The "after" women are her size. Still, she bemoans her own weight.

I search the faces of the "before" women. They stare ahead, blank, stony, knowing that the bodies they have—the ones they are not meant to have—will live on in this photograph. They will forever be captured on film, looking like me.

"I'm not trying to lose weight," I explain for what feels like the hundredth time. "I've always been this size. It's just not in the cards for me."

She looks at me, pained, the way you look at a child who's given up after a first attempt at trying something new. The last time we spoke about this, her face was blank while I told her about going to fat camp, about the prescription diet pills I took that were later revealed to cause heart disease and brain damage, about the disordered patterns of eating I had so long kicked against. I did not use the word *anorexia*, knowing how she would balk, believing a behavior to be a body type. It didn't reach her then, and it won't reach her now.

"You can do it," she says earnestly. "I know you can."

What hurts most is her hope.

Three

A good friend calls, quietly despairing. He has spent the last six months organizing to defeat Proposition 8, California's prohibition of marriage for queer couples, despite being a trans immigrant of color with his own mixed feelings about marriage. He plans to marry his partner, yes. But more than that, he's been told time and time again that once we win marriage, it will be his turn. If he shows up for cisgender white gay people, we would return the favor when the time came. Many states have offered this explanation. But when the two of us talk, we name the sad truth that it often takes cisgender queers years to "come back for" trans people, if they do at all. (Wisconsin, for example, banned discrimination on the basis of sexual orientation in 1982. As of the time of writing, the state still has yet to ban discrimination on the basis of gender identity and expression beyond government employment.)

Still, he dedicates himself fully to a fight that he knows likely won't return the favor. Like most field organizers on massive campaigns, he set up his life for auto play. He planned for months of working six or seven days a week, spending 12- and 14-hour days in the field, stopping only to sleep. He did what countless organizers before him had done. He disappeared into organizing, sometimes forgetting where he ended and the campaign began. His office kept a *de rigueur* countdown calendar at his desk, reminding him of how many days it was until the election. When he hit a goal for fundraising or volunteer recruitment, he'd raise it. He doggedly pursued the sometimes pyrrhic victory of a simple majority. And according to the lion's share of pundits and news analysts, this victory was well within reach. If anyone could win marriage, it would be California.

But it didn't.

On election night, 2008, California voters elected Barack Obama, and passed Proposition 8. (At the time, white gay people used this as an excuse to put their racism on display, insisting that black homophobia had been to blame for the passage of Proposition 8, rather than the state's millions of white voters.) The community was in mourning and outrage, both from within and without.

Even those of us who'd been skeptical of marriage were angry, hurt, crushed. In 2004, roughly one third of US states passed so-called "defense of marriage acts," amending their very constitutions to exclude anyone who wasn't straight and cisgender from marriage. We didn't win one single state that year. We'd been clobbered and publicly reminded that even our families and neighbors didn't think we deserved what they had, didn't believe us when we told them what we needed.

In the intervening years, LGBTQ+ organizations had built new funding streams, created innovative new approaches to change. We had built massive volunteer networks, shored up the community. Proposition 8 was a test of all that hard work, and we anticipated proof positive that our collective work had paid off. California was supposed to be our great hope. And on this day, November 15, 2008, it feels like that hope is lost. Following the ballot measure's failure, Willow Witte and Amy Balliett organize "Join the Impact" rallies that are later credited to Cleve Jones. The rallies are flooded with people, queer and straight alike, who are incensed at the outcome of the election. The turnout for these rallies exceeds that for even some of the most high-profile campaign events.

"I saw this couple," he tells me, exasperated, voice sharp with anger. "They turned me down for a volunteer shift *last* week. They said it was going to pass. They said history was on our side."

He tells me that he watches while they applaud at rally speakers who demand to know where straight people were for this fight.

"Where was *anyone?*" he asks me over the phone. "Where *were* they?"

Four

It is May 19, 2014, and I am at the Melody Ballroom in Portland. Oregon US District Court Judge Michael McShane—one of precious few out gay people serving on the federal bench—has handed down his ruling, striking down the state's prohibition on marriage for LGBTQ+ people. "I know that many suggest we are going down a slippery slope that will have no moral boundaries. To those who truly harbor such fears, I can say only this: *Let us look less to the sky to see what might fall; rather, let us look to each other...and rise.*" The language is righteous and heartfelt, constantly quoted by Oregonians for months to come. The ruling is so beloved that Powell's Books, the nation's largest independent bookstore, prints pocket versions of the ruling. The small, beautiful booklets sell out in short order. It is a moment that mimics so many political movies, the kind of *Mr. Smith Goes to Washington* moment when reason and right seem to prevail. The kind of sudden change that so many organizers know is preceded by years, decades, and sometimes centuries of social change work.

It is the day of Judge McShane's ruling, and I am at work. My organization has coordinated faith leaders and non-religious officiants to hold free ceremonies for any LGBTQ+ couples who want to marry. Couples stream through the doors all day, some dressed for the occasion, others in work uniforms, marrying at the first opportunity after their shift for the day.

I stand just outside the doorway to the ballroom, directing queer couples and well-wishers alike. My arms are clammy and tired from carrying bouquet after bouquet of flowers brought by straight people. One hands me a bouquet and asks if she and her boyfriend can get married for free, too.

"We said we wouldn't get married until everyone could," she says proudly. It was a kind of heterosexual cultural meme, supercharged by Brad Pitt and Angelina Jolie's proclamation that they wouldn't wed until marriage equality was the law of the land. Nearly every organizer I knew was exasperated by this bizarre gesture. No one was counting how many straight people postponed their weddings. It didn't garner new support for the movement, nor did it make LGBTQ+ couples any safer or more respected. How did it help us for them to relinquish rights that were never under threat for them? Why didn't they just get married, then donate and volunteer? We'd been asking for their help for so long. Why did they only show up now, a day late and a dollar short, with a symbolic gesture we'd never requested?

Over the course of the day, my happiness for the many queer couples is overshadowed by a noxious kind of frustration—one that has been building for years. We did all this work with the active support of precious few straight people, and now the many bystanders wanted to join in the celebration. Like the

Little Red Hen, denied help by all of her barnyard compatriots, we'd planted the seeds, harvested the wheat, milled the grain, learned to bake. When straight voters had decided we weren't worthy of their institutions, we proclaimed *we'd do it ourselves*, and spent years building movements largely on our own. Now that the bread is baked, even those who've long been fed want to eat. *We won't eat until everyone can.*

Still, this is a watershed day for my LGBTQ+ community, and one of celebration. We know it is likely to be one of our biggest wins—maybe ever—and that this is the most money and influence we will ever have. And beneath this huge victory, this tectonic shift, is a sense of profound emptiness. Many of us know this wasn't the issue that needed us most. Even in the midst of a celebration, most of the organizers I know express a profound sense of emptiness. Did we just make the impossible inevitable? Or did we just miss the biggest opportunity available to us?

That evening, I vent to the former Proposition 8 organizer about the deep frustration I feel at seeing so many straight people lined up to congratulate us, when so few worked to make the victory happen. I tell him that most of the LGBTQ+ people I know are conflicted at best about winning marriage, but that straight people seemed ecstatic, many plastering new "love is love" bumper stickers on their cars, just as the fight ended. They pledged their allegiance to the victor only as the war had ended, then declared victory with a miasmic kind of relief. As though they'd been fighting, too.

"Yeah, but think about the alternative," he says. "If they think about it too much, they'll have to confront their own homophobia. And they're just not going to. Instead, they can just pretend that it was never a problem."

In the months following, I watch countless straight people disappear into the cultural amnesia of this moment. It is only years later that I realize their celebration of this moment is, at least in part, a celebration of that amnesia. We were free to get married. And they were free to forget the discomfort they'd so long used to hold us back.

Five

I am visiting my family member again. Today, mercifully, she has not mentioned weight-loss surgery. I consider this an opening, and begin to tell her about my recent trip to the grocery store. I tell her that, unbidden, a stranger lifted a melon from my grocery cart, explaining to me that it had too much sugar. She is stunned by such bad behavior. I am exhilarated by what seems like a turn in her politics, and take what feels like another opportunity. I tell her about the stranger who most recently approached me on the street to recommend a nearby weight-loss surgery clinic.

"Who would do that?" she asks incredulously. And suddenly, all that exciting opportunity melts away.

Once again, I am awash in exhaustion. In the telling of this story, it seems lost on her that this stranger has done once what she has done a dozen times: insisted unprompted that my body needs a cure, that I need correction, and that only her noblesse oblige can save me. There was no reflection, no sense of realization. But then, I hadn't confronted her behavior—just someone else's. I wondered if this work, this unpaid and unending effort to carve out space for my own dignity with thin people, would mimic the years of thankless work I'd done with straight people.

Just seconds before, I had felt the electric potential of transformation. Now, it was gone. I could see the years of a seemingly willful lack of accountability and self-reflection that would continue to come from the people in my life who were privileged in ways I was not. Like LGBTQ+ rights, winning some semblance of dignity for fat people would likely entail years of debate over whether or not *it's a choice*. "Correcting" queer and trans people's identities was falling out of favor, but "fixing" fat bodies—forever seen as failed thin ones—wasn't. Even if we manage to slow the most overt forms of anti-fatness, will thin people take the time to reflect on their own complicity? Or will it happen the way it has so many times before, with them happily sleeping in the poppy field of their own privilege?

I imagine the satisfaction of seeing this family member owning up to all the ways she's hurt me, to all the little transgressions and indignities she has brought to me. I imagine her listing an inventory of the many ways she's slighted or belittled me, hurt or harmed fat people in my presence. But I know that, on the exceedingly rare occasion that I am granted this wish, it is never what I've hoped for. When those moments finally arrive, they are often awkward and anticlimactic. They leave me feeling empty and ashamed, not gratified, and certainly not healed.

But then, what kind of conversation am I waiting for? What will accountability look like in action? Will it feel as healing as I have so long hoped? Was I looking for healing, for nourishment, or just satisfaction? My family member had presented a healing fantasy of thinness—the belief that changing my body would right anything that was amiss within me. But was my healing fantasy any more realistic, any more grounded in experience?

Was I, once again, making myself the midwife of my own disappointment?

Six

My brother and I are out to dinner. He asks me how things are, and I tell him about my most recent, frustrating moment with the family member who has so regularly pushed me toward bariatric surgery.

My brother looks at me plainly while I speak, looks through me the way he's always been able to do.

"You have a disease," he tells me. "It's the disease of wanting to be understood. And you're looking for a cure you're never going to find."

Seven

"I don't trust those chairs," my co-worker tells me.

We are at a staff retreat, spending three days planning the six months of our LGBTQ+ organizing work together. I have long dreaded staff retreats, imagining ropes courses and trust falls, the kinds of body-based experiences that only build trust for those thin and abled enough to participate fully. I imagine the weight of me crushing a colleague in a trust fall, or the embarrassment of being whisked away for a dislocated knee on a ropes course. Even in the absence of such dramatic activities, I imagine breaking a chair in front of the colleagues I like and admire most. I imagine the blood rushing to my face, its neon red elevating the moment from professional embarrassment to personal humiliation.

So I start planning our staff retreats. I do it partly because facilitation is a passion and a joy of mine. My colleagues request me as a lead for retreat planning. I love the time we spend together on staff retreats, and I take on that planning in part to show my appreciation for the team, and to showcase their dogged organizing for our LGBTQ+ communities. But I also do it because I know that whoever plans retreats gets to pick the spaces where we have them. Taking the lead on this project lets me plan our agenda, avoiding the physical trust and resiliency exercises I've so long dreaded. It lets me scout out retreat spaces, making sure that wherever we go is physically accessible, that its furniture is comfortable and sturdy, that there will be chairs that won't buckle beneath my weight. (Similarly, I regularly volunteer to coordinate flight arrangements, so that well-meaning thin colleagues won't book me into center seats, or too near strangers who might complain, leaving me stranded in some far away city at a conference.)

I do all of this silently, knowing that even in spaces dedicated to social justice, bringing up accessibility for fat people will be met with bemusement at best, and angry rejection at worst. Years earlier, a fellow young organizer dared to name anti-fatness as a system of oppression in a social justice organizing training I attended. It was surreal to watch participants' and trainers' faces as he spoke, their respect for him diminishing in real time. His remarks didn't just change the way they thought of his politics. They no longer thought him credible at all.

So I learned not to speak up about anti-fatness. I just quietly planned retreats, and hoped desperately that no one would notice my body.

I didn't count on meeting David.

David is my newest colleague, a fat trans man who came out of organizing in the Bay Area. As our retreat activities begin, he looks out over the rickety folding chairs that have been used to add seating for our growing staff team. Despite my best planning, by the time the retreat begins, only these rickety chairs are left to sit on.

"I don't trust these chairs," he tells me confidentially. "They're not made for fat kids." I laugh, both longing for this recognition and uncertain what to say, how to accept it, if I even know how. I fall awkwardly silent.

"I think I saw a bench on the front porch—want to move it inside?" he asks. "We need a place for the fatties to sit."

I help him move the bench into the living room of our rental house. For the rest of the retreat, David and I sit together. We call it the fat kid bench. In a world where describing our size is met with dismay and instant distancing—*Sweetie, no! You're not fat, you're beautiful!*—this simple act of naming our bodies is a profound one. In the years to come, as our relationship deepens from colleagues to friends, this becomes a surprisingly meaningful refrain. We are both fat, both queer, and we are learning together how to carve out space for our bodies, our dignity, our oft-misunderstood and maligned lives.

In the years ahead, I discover the gifts of more and more fat queer friendships. I breathe deeper, the corsets of thinness and straightness momentarily loosening around me. When we spend time together, for once, I am in a space that doesn't insist on the straightness and thinness I have never been able to deliver. In the unforgiving outside world, my queerness and fatness are often treated as linked phenomena, regarded as dual failures from all sides. There were refrains from straight people: *if you just lost weight*—think of all the guys you could get! And there was anti-fatness from queer people, too: the athletic lesbian community leader, for example, who regularly bemoaned what she considered too much visibility from plus size queer women. Some of us care about our health. *Why do they always show the ones who are eating themselves to death?*

In the face of all that, my friendships with fat queers and fat trans people are a salve. In a world of *shedding for the wedding* and *body after baby*, it is an immense and surprising relief to lay down the impossible dual standards of thinness and heterosexuality. These are often richer than my friendships with thin people, more thoughtful and supported than my relationships with fat straight people. We do not universally share some deep political analysis, an inherent outgrowth of living in fat bodies. This relief is much simpler than that: it is the ongoing revelation that when we are together, we can simply be, uninterrupted by a constant onslaught of diet talk and weight-loss advice, loud judgements about fat people, and the constant attempt to corral our untamed bodies and hearts into the restrictive stable of thin straightness. These are the most unvarnished forms of liberation: not a celebration, nor a heralded moment of arrival, but the quiet realization that we no longer have to pretend.

Yes, the work ahead to uproot anti-fatness, homophobia, and transphobia is exhausting in a familiar way. Its contours echo those of all the fights we've already had. Yes, we will have to fight to be left alone. Yes, we will have to fight to form our own communities, and to defend them. Yes, we will be told time and time again that we need to be corrected, our cumbersome bodies and inconvenient identities rewritten to something more understandable to the relentlessly straight, relentlessly thin world around us.

We will once again succumb to our desire to be understood. We will not be saved, but we will be one another's deliverance. We may not be treated, but we can be each other's cure.

"FATQUEERPOEM"

Miguel M. Morales

In this poem, you are as fat as you are queer. Read this poem without worrying about your rolls. Don't push this plate away, declining savory seconds. Don't wear a shirt at this fabulous pool party. You can read this poem while walking on the treadmill or dunking iced oatmeal cookies into chilled milk. This fat poem doesn't want you to suck in your queer gut. It will send a friend request to read your posts, to share its fattest selfies, and curviest poses.

This queer poem knows you photograph beautifully and hopes you're less inclined to filter your flaws or remove them altogether, though it quietly confesses doing both on occasion. This poem likes to spend time naked in sexual and nonsexual ways granting itself consent to be naked, fat, and queer all at once. This poem shares its body more freely than it did when it was younger and unsure of what it could offer, of what it could ask of and receive from others.

This fat poem bears scars, stretchmarks, blemishes, and dimples. It is layered and lopsided. Its thick stanzas twist and contort in ways surprising to even itself. Its rhythm reveals different tones and textures depending where your eyes, hands, and lips roam. This queer poem takes up the page, takes over the page. This fat poem breaks lines, breaks chairs, and breaks hearts. This poem is strong, as is its laughter, its anger, and its love. In this poem, you are as fat as you are queer. ♥

"Pop Goes Perfection"

Jonathan Hillman

In 1992, Hasbro relaunched its popular board game, *Perfection*. The goal of the game: to fit all the plastic shapes into their proper places before the time runs out, before the board pops up and they all go flying. *Perfection* quickly became a favorite among my family members—but not me. I sucked at it. The problem was, I was always trying to fit the shapes into the wrong spaces. Because why should a triangle fit only into a triangle space? Couldn't it also fit into a square space, if you turned it a certain way?

Everyone told me I was wrong.

When I was in middle school, my doctor told me I was obese. She said that my life would be difficult if I didn't change, that I wouldn't fit in, that I should follow the food schedules and fitness plans provided in the folder or else suffer a heart attack and diabetes and death. Back then, I didn't understand the game; I couldn't see how a commercialized weight-loss culture profited from my pursuit of Perfection. In the moment, I was only aware of my belt tightening, my body inflating—filled with the humiliating realization that there was something wrong with me. That I took up too much space.

Not long after, I found another piece of myself that didn't fit. Unlike my few guy friends, I had zero interest in a loveless middle school marriage with a girl. Instead, I fantasized about men—fat men. On some level, I knew my queer identity was something I couldn't change. But maybe—maybe I could follow my doctor's advice and change the other piece of myself. I'd always been bullied for my fatness. I figured if I lost weight, coming out would be easier. So, in high school, I lost 45 lbs. I practiced how I should move, how I should modify my voice to sound straight, and when I came out to my parents at 21, I embodied a new shape. I felt safer knowing my shape fit more neatly: *I'm gay, but my body is normal. I'm gay, but I'm masculine. I'm gay, but I don't take up too much space.* I spent the rest of my twenties as a slim gay man.

When I arrived at graduate school, studying writing for children and young adults, I reflected on my fat, gay youth. My creative thesis was a young adult novel featuring a fat gay protagonist (if published, it will be only the second fat, gay protagonist in the young adult canon). I focused my critical work on the same intersection. In my extended essay titled "No Fats, No Fems: Queer Male Bodies in Young Adult Literature," my research showed that even among those who identify as straight, fatness has a queering effect. In other words, fat bodies experience marginalization and microaggressions similar to those experienced by queer bodies, as fat bodies are marked as deviant or "other." I found that the words "fat" and "fag" are often used interchangeably when degrading someone's manhood. I found that boys who identify as both fat and queer are doubly marginalized, as their fatness and queerness operate in tandem to threaten the masculine paradigm. I found that the gay body ideal is fueled by internalized homophobia, that masculinity is currency among gay men, and that although size is valuable in the gay community, it is only valuable so long as it serves to masculinize the body.

For many years, I thought my fatness would preclude my acceptance into the queer community. I was painfully aware of the idealized body standard, seeing the "perfect" bodies on display at gay bars. I spent countless hours at the gym, set regular goals to lose weight, sometimes succeeding, always chasing the body type I thought would make me valuable. Of course, there is no finish line in the race for Perfection; the more weight I lost, the more clearly my imperfections showed. Even as I berated myself for my belly fat that would never burn into a six-pack, I admired and dated fat men. Finally, I asked myself: why was I holding myself to a different body standard from the one I held for others? Why was I trying to fit my pieces where they didn't belong?

The board popped up.

The pieces went flying.

Done with the game of Perfection, I began a journey to reclaim my fat identity. Unlike my attempts to achieve the perfect body, this journey was about redefining what "perfect" meant to me. I loosened my belt, let myself breathe. I changed my relationship with food and fitness to be less subtractive and more additive: rather than subtracting carbs, I added vegetables and greens. Rather than subtracting my daily calories burned, I added time walking in the sunshine. I did these things because they made me feel good. But I also knew that happy hour made me happy, that pizza was the real Perfection, and that "cheat day" wasn't cheating if you divorced the Man who owned your body. Over the course of three years, I gained 100 lbs.

Now fat and queer, I feel more at home in my body than ever. As I grow softer, I am softer on myself. I eat until I'm full, and my life is fuller. Living, really living—it doesn't fit into neat and tidy spaces. It doesn't always fit into pants with a 32-inch waist. If you're always growing, always changing, is it your body that's the problem? Or is it the pants? What if you let yourself be bigger?

"Dropping Fictions and Gaining Visibility"

Bruce Owens Grimm

Gainer. Someone who derives erotic and/or sexual pleasure from the act of eating and/or gaining weight. A gainer is always looking to grow, fantasizes about becoming bigger than they are currently. People on the gain may weigh themselves every day, count calories to make sure they are hitting their goal to get bigger, not maintain or lose weight. Contrary to how it usually works in our culture, losing weight is a gainer's nightmare.

But a broad general definition applied to a group of people never encompasses all the variations and nuances. For example, in gainer culture, there are the men who prefer to keep gaining in the realm of fantasy and pad their clothes to give the illusion of size, of fat. They can indulge in the concept of size without having to live it on a daily basis: when the urge strikes to be big, they stuff pillows or other materials under their clothes or, if they have the means, don a purchased padded suit. Some gainers don't consider the padders "real" gainers because there is not an actual physical change to the padder's body. Those who believe this think the padders have it easy, partly because they don't have to deal with fat phobia.

On the other end of the spectrum are the guys who want to be immobile. These men want to be so fat, so large, that it impedes their daily lives. They want mounds of flesh cascading down their sides until they cannot get out of bed. If they meet their goal, they may need help breathing. They may need someone to help wash and care for them. The only way they could leave their house would be to be wheeled out. This isn't rare, but it isn't the "average" gainer goal, either, and it's not my goal.

The idea of someone, anyone, trying to police what is okay in any fetish is problematic, and I'm not here to do that. I don't judge these other kinds of gainers, but these are not my personal goals.

I, too, am a gainer, and while I want to grow to a size that most civilians (the term for people who are not into the gaining scene) consider very fat or obese, I want to maintain mobility. I want to leave my house because I want the world to see how fat I am. I do not want to be a secret.

❋ ❋ ❋

Encourager. Someone who derives erotic or sexual satisfaction from participating in the growth of a gainer. They may verbally encourage a gainer by reminding them to eat, asking for updates about what they have eaten, and pushing them to eat a little more even when they are full. They may praise the gainer for growing and reward the gainer by rubbing or squeezing the gainer's belly or other areas of their bodies that have grown. They may cook or buy special foods for the gainer. They may set weight gain goals with the gainer. They may actually feed the gainer, sometimes with utensils, sometimes with their hands, and in some cases, a funnel. Encouragers can be nurturing or disciplinary, or a combination of these and other styles. The gainer wants to please the encourager, eat for them, grow for them. There is mutual satisfaction and gratification in this dynamic.

❀ ❀ ❀

Example. A barista at my neighborhood coffee shop shares my fetish. We know this about each other because there is a social media site for male gay gainers that both of us are on, and I have face and body pics on my account. He doesn't have any pictures, so when he messaged me to say hello and that he was the barista at my local coffee shop, I didn't know which barista he might be. When I went to the coffee shop later that day, I watched, eavesdropped on the conversations the baristas had with each other, in an attempt to discover some clue that would tell me which one he might be. It felt like a movie, and I wondered if I should have taken a donut, and the one who asked "Just one?" would be revealed as the mystery encourager. I had hopes for which one it would be—the cute one, as I called him when telling friends about him. When, in fact, the cute one waved at me, and patted his belly, I immediately heard Meg Ryan telling Tom Hanks in *You've Got Mail*, "I hoped it would be you."

The barista tells me on his break that he would have known I was a gainer even without seeing me on the site because I dressed in tight shirts that accentuated my belly, sometimes just barely covering it. But I look put together, not sloppy—my hair always done, my beard groomed. Because he's an encourager, the barista notices how men who are fat accidentally or don't want to be fat—who are ashamed of being fat—hide their fat, don't know how to dress their bodies. They want people to ignore their bodies. But not me.

I sit at the counter, reading, or writing, and he slides a sample of milkshake toward me as he walks by. I arch my back, pretending to stretch when really, I am showing off my belly for him, displaying the growth he is helping me achieve. He asks me if I want more to drink or to eat. I always nod, and he always smiles. When I order a latte he switches the milk from 2 percent to half and half to ensure maximum calorie density. When he can, he doesn't charge me for the extra things I eat or drink. Sometimes he gives me a discount. Often we never say a word to each other; no one else around us knows what we are doing, the fun we are having. We share these secret, erotic, experiences in public, in front of other people, and without ever touching each other.

❀ ❀ ❀

But we are both the type for whom the unspoken only satisfies for so long. We want to give voice to what is happening. We whisper questions to each other. How long have you been a gainer/encourager? Our answers are the same: for as long as either one of us can remember. He wants to know how fat I want to get. I tell him 300 lbs is my first major goal. He likes the idea of me at that size. He tells me that he thinks my frame could handle 350 lbs easily. Encouragers have always been able to imagine more than I can, but I like the idea of 350 lbs. He asks if I have ever been fed, had my belly rubbed by an encourager.

"Yes," I say to both. "But it's been a while."

"How long?"

"About six months."

"That's too long," he says. He walks away to help another customer before I can agree.

❀ ❀ ❀

Secrets never want to stay hidden, even if that's part of their initial appeal.

There is an erotic charge in the secret that the barista and I share, but the day arrives when he wants to hang out after he's finished work. I'm nervous and glad that he suggested this because although there is power in secrecy, too often that power transforms into shame.

We meet in the park at the end of the street. The illicitness is no longer enticing as I think about the history of gay men cruising parks because there was no other way to meet. He brings me cookies from the coffee shop. I eat them as we talk about horror movies, books we love. The barista wants to touch my belly, and I let him. It feels good—thrilling and relaxing at the same time—despite his hand being cold as he runs his hand along the edge of my belly, squeezing my overhang.

Then he pulls my shirt back down. "I have to stop," he says. The barista has a boyfriend. A civilian. He loves him. They might get married. He already feels unfaithful.

"I understand," I say. I ask him if he plans to tell his boyfriend about this fetish.

He shakes his head. "He wouldn't understand."

"You know this won't go away," I tell him.

"I know," he shrugs. "I have to see if I can live with that."

We spend a few hours discussing the rarity of randomly finding someone with this fetish "out in the wild" as he puts it, someone that you see on a regular basis. We discuss whether or not gaining and encouraging is something you can incorporate into your daily life. For him, it has to stay separate, a fantasy. For him, it has to stay a secret.

❁ ❁ ❁

When I first started writing, I wrote fiction. It was autobiographical, but it avoided certain topics. The parents in my stories were neglectful or absent, but not overtly abusive; abuse was left in the margins. As was queerness. These were my secrets, kept even from my writing.

As I worked on my graduate school thesis, I started introducing the supernatural into my stories. Using the paranormal was a more comfortable way to discuss the oddness of life, anything out of the heteronormative usual. Writing the supernatural was a way of admitting that I had a secret that needed to be discussed even if I wasn't fully aware that this was what I was doing.

When I started graduate school, I presented as a straight married man, who was accidentally fat. I could not discuss being gay, or being a gainer, with anyone, but those were two aspects that were fighting to not be a secret anymore. The more I actively oppressed them, the more they tried to come out in my writing.

This was most obvious in a story I wrote about a vampire. In the story, a man hears pebbles being thrown against his bedroom window one night. When he goes to the window he sees a man, recently deceased, motioning for him to join him. The men had been childhood friends, they had been in love, but the narrator chose to stay closeted and get married. He wants to go to his vampire friend, but he still can't bring himself to venture into the unknown. The friend visits every night for the next week. They repeat the same pattern. The narrator looks forward to seeing his friend, but then the visits stop. He wishes he had had the courage to join his friend, to have chosen this other life—one that includes a type of feeding.

The metaphor was clear to the people in my workshop: the narrator wishes he had embraced his queerness. Here was a part of myself made public without anyone else actually knowing it or at least without anyone openly acknowledging it. If they guessed it was about me, no one said anything. I never showed that story to my wife Darlene. When she asked if she could read it, I told her it wasn't ready.

Unlike the narrator of my vampire story, I eventually came out. I ended my marriage. I embraced my queerness. Discovering the gaining community and realizing that I was a gainer was the catalyst for those changes. I would still write fiction for the next few years.

When people ask me how I knew I was gay after being married for nine years, I always say I just knew. I leave out the part about stumbling on a video on YouTube of a man, a gainer, eating a bowl of ice cream, rubbing his belly as it grew from the ice cream he ate, and my fascination, my excitement—the feeling that something had switched over in my brain, in my very being, and I finally knew everything about myself.

When I saw that video, I knew I wanted to grow. I wanted to feel another man rub his hands over my belly, press my belly into his, I wanted to grow for him and with him. But I felt I had to hide the part of my fantasy that was about gaining. That was the part about which I felt the most shame. The part I didn't feel I could tell anyone. Not even, maybe especially, Marco, the civilian who was my first serious boyfriend.

I met him at a time when I was losing a lot of weight; I'd been 315 lbs, but when we met I was around 230 lbs. I continued to lose weight during the course of our relationship. Like the barista, I thought that gaining and encouraging wasn't that important to my sexual life. But gaining isn't just sexual: it is a way of life. To grow the way you want to, you have to always be working at it. To only leave it for when you feel horny is to be too inconsistent.

As my body shrunk, I felt less like myself, less like my body belonged to me. It made me sad and cranky. But that boyfriend was the first real love of my life and I worried that if I told him what was going on, he'd think I was weird for wanting to be fat and I would lose him. I'd feel the call to gain and would try my best to ignore it.

Friends congratulated me on my weight loss because they had no idea I had been that fat on purpose. Our culture believes that fat people have no agency in their fatness, that they are victims of it. Maybe for some people that is true, but there is no counter narrative.

* * *

During my time as a thinner person, I became more active in the literary world. I'd like to believe that this had nothing to do with being thin and more about the fact that I had found my voice as a writer and my role in the literary world as an organizer of a reading series focused on queer writers of color. But I have to admit it was easier to stand up in front of crowds and approach other writers at conferences or events with that body. When I would go to the gym or go for a run, I'd tell myself this was getting myself "TV ready." When I'd see pictures of the "rising stars" of the literary world, they were all thin. They were all praised for being good-looking. As I lost weight, I was told more often that I was handsome. If I wanted to be successful in the literary world, it seemed, I would have to maintain this standard of thinness.

I had felt invisible in the literary world when I was fat, despite working for a high-profile magazine. I published more as a thin man than I did as a fat man. There was no way to know until later that this was correlation and not causation.

During my thin time, when I was at a dinner and would push my plate away, people didn't know that I wanted to eat it all, and their leftovers too. They didn't know how uncomfortable I felt in clothes that didn't have buttons straining against my body. I could walk into any store and buy nice clothes, something I couldn't do when I was at my highest weight. There was no way for them to know the longing I felt when I'd see a fat man and wish I looked like that. This was like pretending to be straight all over again. I'd been carrying two secrets and only one had been revealed. I convinced myself that to keep my career on track, to be a desirable writer to have in a magazine or at a reading, I'd have to keep this second secret, the fetish, suppressed.

But after my break-up, I decided to gain again.

Part of it was for comfort. Part of it was that I wanted to be me. But the gaining journey is never quick. I started and stopped. I worried about my health. I worried about my career. Put on 10 lbs and most people won't notice; 30 lbs is a different story. Thirty pounds in a couple months is a very different story.

At a critical moment, Marco said he was concerned about my weight gain—so much, so fast. At first, I said what I always said: I don't mind the extra weight. But not minding and enjoying it are two different things. I knew the vampire was waving for me to join him. So, I told Marco I was a gainer. I explained what that meant, how it bothered me to keep it a secret. He didn't abandon me as a friend. He didn't suddenly take my writing less seriously. He didn't think I was the weirdest person he had met. He said to make sure I kept an eye on my health, but otherwise he supported what made me happy.

He was the only civilian I told for a while. As I continued, and continue, to gain weight, I feel more and more strongly that I want people to know that the size of my body isn't an accident. I am in control of this. Being fat is what I want.

"Large and in Charge"

Fletcher Cullinane

For most of my life, I've been the fat kid.

I'm not sure how it happened, but looking back at 12 successive yearbook photos, I can tell you when it happened. It started sometime between second and third grade, and then continued steadily through high school graduation. With every new volume, my black-and-white face with its forced smile got plumper and rounder. In most class ensembles, I was unambiguously the fat kid; I was also the "smart kid," and sometimes "the funny kid," so perhaps those minor prestiges spared me years of overt bullying and humiliation. That's not to say that the idea of being on the receiving end of negativity didn't occupy my thoughts. Quite the opposite. I was intrigued by it, and the most potent, deep-rooted memories of my fatness have always been tied to social interactions where people reacted to my size.

Probably the earliest I can remember were the nurse's physicals in grade school, which always excited me. There was a thrill in the spectacle of the weigh-in: all the boys lined up, paraded up to the great metal scale one by one, stripped off their shoes, forced to account for their bodies, judged according to their measurements. As the fat kid, I most certainly made the scale go clang. The boys ahead of me were always lighter, and then here I'd waddle up and bang! that metal bar would slam down, a surefire sign that a porker had just stepped up for inspection. The feeling of knowing those other boys' weights, knowing that I was fatter than them, and knowing that they knew I was fatter than them—it was somewhere between embarrassment and pride, if not auto-schadenfreude then surely low-key exhibitionism in action. My fatness was going on my permanent record, and was now a matter of public record among all the boys at my school.

But I soon found that I wanted more intimate interactions between those boys and the object that was my body. As it turned out, one of my closest friends also shopped the "husky boys" section of the local clothing store. Jimmy wasn't as big as me, surely, but still chunky. If I was the fattest boy in class, then he was one of the larger satellites in my orbit. We often played at his house, down in his basement, away from the observation of his mother. We would take off our shirts and compare our bodies. We would contort them, see our fat rolls bunch up, mark the differences between us. It felt so right to me. I'd draw little pictures of me and Jimmy shirtless, each belly roll carefully articulated, his slighter and less numerous than my own. I captioned them with the little nickname we called ourselves, "chubby cherubs."

In the present day, Jimmy is massive, married to a woman, and has some kids, but his Facebook picture gallery suggests that he still enjoys showing off his body. I haven't spoken to him in decades, but I've masturbated to a picture of him posing shirtless comically on a stripper pole more than a few times.

Through Jimmy I got to know another boy in the neighborhood, Kevin, who went to a different school. After we graduated eighth grade, Jimmy moved out of the neighborhood, and Kevin became my primary male friend. As with Jimmy, I formed a close tie to him, and we often hung out in his basement together, sometimes with his neighbor, Ricky. Kevin felt older than me, and I suspected he had been held back at least one year in school. He was also a few inches taller, and much thinner; Ricky was my height, as thin as Kevin but not nearly as bright as him.

By this time, I was easily 14, but still not fully sexually developed. Yes, my voice was changing, and I was growing body hair and a small mustache, but I had largely explored my body not sexually through touching my cock, but sensually through my fat. And there was a lot of fat to explore. At 5'8" and 220 lbs, the chubby cherub had evolved into a swollen seraph, and with the days of public weigh-ins long over, I was eager to have a safe audience in which to exhibit myself.

In Kevin's basement, we would listen to music with explicit lyrics, burn incense, sample alcoholic beverages—all pretty standard high school rebellions. Less standard were the times when we'd all get shirtless and show off our bodies to each other. If Jimmy and I had been mutually admiring each other's fat, and reveling in the comparisons between us, then Kevin, Ricky, and I were instead playing with the contrast between their skinny bodies and my fat body. Most memorable were the times when Kevin or Ricky would have me jump around and jiggle my fat for their amusement. I wanted their attention, their laughter, their light mockery. It felt powerful, being a fat showpiece that evoked clear expressions of engagement. Smiles. Laughter. Physical touch.

This was also the late 90s, and I haunted AOL's M4M chatrooms under my secondary, burner screenname that couldn't be traced to me and my AOL Buddy List. These chatroom spaces introduced me to erotic conversation, to "sexting" before texting even existed. Men would ask me to describe my body, and in turn they'd describe theirs for me in detail. They'd walk me through fantasy activities like stripping off my clothing piece by piece, seeking my feedback as we played along: "You like that?" one of them might instant-message me; "Oh yeah, I do," I'd message back to him. Even as I was internalizing the dialogue structures from these anonymous, virtual chats, it was those sexually charged show-off sessions at Kevin's that added the raw content for the stories I told myself as I learned how to masturbate.

Thrilled as I was by the shirtless camaraderie of my younger days, those were the rare moments out. Most of the time, I keenly felt the stigma of being fat. It was so obvious that I was one of the biggest kids in school, that I wasn't built like the sporty boys whose fathers beamed with pride as their sons became specimens of manhood, who could capably throw a baseball or dominate at shirts-versus-skins basketball. Even if some 20 years later several of those men who were once playground superstars have become just as fat as me (and maybe less successful), they still relive their glory days of once being an alpha male that dad could be proud of. Meanwhile, my own father, maybe both alarmed at my growing body and ashamed of what it said about him as a parent, forced me to enroll in several team sports, even as I sucked out loud at every single one of them. It didn't matter that I was coming home with A+ report cards if he couldn't stand toe-to-toe with the other dads on their son's small-stakes athletic accomplishments. I remember one time where, at a family dinner in public, I helped myself to an extra butter packet, slathering it onto a dinner roll, and then licking the butter knife. My father got enraged and slapped the knife right out of my hand, where it clanged against a restaurant partition loudly enough for people to notice. I think it was at that precise moment I knew I was a disappointment to him, and probably to others too.

So, I stayed ashamed of myself and my body, wore baggy clothes to hide my belly, kept my shirt on at the public pool to restrain my boytits from bouncing for the gawking eyes of the other swimmers—and especially the lifeguards who were just a few years my senior, taller, and growing lean muscle where I had been developing mounds of softened butter. While Kevin's basement was a safe space where I could be accepted for my body, high school was a place of unknown dangers. As an academic standout, I got more attention from peers than I wanted, but even if I had been a mediocre student there would have been no way of fading into the woodwork as one of the bigger boys at school. You can't hide in a corner if you can't fit in it.

The hallways, though, were relatively monitored spaces. Less so were the dark recesses of the boys' locker room. I was so afraid of having to flop and wobble through calisthenics and then shower down with unfamiliar boys that I ended up delaying my gym class requirement for two years. I was relieved when at last my school waived that requirement for students who wanted to take four full years of a creative elective. Instead of having my body on display for the high school boys, I spent that semester in art class, learning how to draw better pictures of them next to me, their lean muscles a contrast to my own stack of jelly rolls. And at home, in the safety of my basement, I imagined those popular boys forcing me to strip, inspecting my every roll and curve, making me the center of their cruel but rapt attentions. I continued to rehearse those interactions with Kevin and Ricky in a safe environment where I could run away if I ever lost control of the scenario. There was always the risk that Kevin's brother could come down and interrupt what was clearly homoerotic role play, or worse, that one of his parents would barge in and demand an explanation for why three shirtless teens were jumping around the room slapping each other's body parts.

As I moved on to college, and Kevin and Ricky didn't, they faded into the backstory of my life. At college, I was finally in a room of (mostly) my own, and free to start creating encounters with men in the world. Through the growing social network of Gay.com I began meeting other students at my school, and sometimes older men beyond the campus walls. But arranging the meet-ups often felt like an exercise in self-censorship. Would KewlBoi4U really assent to meet me if he saw my naked body? Would YoungHung1981 block me if he got the chance to inspect the goods beforehand?

This was the days before smartphones, before "selfies" existed as a concept. Taking a photo of yourself and getting it online was a production. If you wanted to fuck, you needed to know your way around a digital camera and a computer. The photos I took were always composed to make me look slimmer, and were always from the neck up; whatever fat I couldn't hide, I'd crop out in an image editing program. Along with the carefully composed profile pics, I would lie about my weight (usually shaving off 15 lbs) and my height too (becoming an aspirational 5'9"), and hope that when I showed up to meet guys they would just accept what they got. I don't remember any instance where they turned me away, but in one particularly humiliating encounter I started to remove my shirt and the guy said, "No, leave it on."

In hindsight, I see what power my fat body had over him and his erection, but in that moment, I only felt shame, regret, and self-loathing. A person with self-respect might have immediately terminated the session, put on his pants, and walked home; me, I think I probably apologized to him.

In those days, my fat was my liability. At the end of my sophomore year, I was tipping the scales at close to 225 lbs—if not higher—and I was struggling with severe depression. I was smoking a lot of weed, fogging my brain from having to process the weight of my problems. I skipped class, missed examinations, and almost failed college. I needed to escape my body, my mind, and my life. I started taking a now-discontinued weight-loss drug that contained ephedra. Even as reports were hitting the media that the drug was the source of numerous heart-related injuries, I was desperate for results. The pills boosted my energy and my mood. As I starved myself, I started going to the gym, too, fueled by the diet pills and a desire to be sexy and popular. By the end of my senior year, I had lost almost 60 lbs. I felt confident—maybe even desirable. But I wasn't "thin" thin. A decade of fatness had left flab and excess skin, and while I began to perceive myself as attractive, I also continued to feel the drive to be the center of attention, to be sized up and evaluated for my body's shortcomings in an intimate setting.

After graduating college, I found myself living alone in South Korea, making gay friends via the internet and discovering that many of them lived too far away to meet in person. But it was the mid-2000s, and not only was there higher-speed internet service all over Asia, but also affordable and reasonably functional webcams. Now the online chats that sustained my safe exploration of my expanding sexuality could take on a visual dimension. I could be on display from the comfort of my own home, and always with the safety of being able to end the chat session. These online interactions provided a sense of control and comfort even as I felt stranded far from the world I knew. The food was different, the language was challenging, and making friends was difficult without intensely social structures like school to enable them. I had also started gaining weight again, eating mounds of rice and convenience store snacks and drinking cheap beer and soju. Without my diet pills as my crutch, the only way to keep off the weight was self-discipline, one of the many virtues that a lifetime of schooling had failed to inculcate in me.

I met Sangjun somewhere online—at that point I must have been using multiple online networks. We often talked through Yahoo! Messenger, which had a video chat function. And as our conversation deepened, soon enough my clothes started coming off for him, and my body was on display at his command. Sangjun made me—or maybe I encouraged Sangjun to make me—show off my body at different angles, jerk off for him, and make me admit my body's flaws to him. Despite those flaws, or maybe precisely because of them—or maybe because of the sexual games we played, or maybe, just maybe because he actually liked me for who I was—Sangjun would talk with me almost every day, and often enough dominate me and my body through webcam. "You're so fat, sexy pig," he'd whisper with his inflected English. And in response I'd grab whatever handful of belly I could and wobble it for him, proof of my pure sexual lure.

After my work contract in Korea ended, I found myself back in the States. Now halfway across the world from Sangjun, our schedules were totally misaligned. There were no more cam sessions for me to encourage him to encourage me to get dominated by him. And over the years we lost touch gradually until he finally stopped returning my messages about five years ago, though the advent of "read receipts" in messaging services tells me he saw what I had to say and just didn't care to respond anymore.

By now it was late 2007. The AOL chatrooms had long perished, but a new generation of gay online spaces were competing for my attention. Craigslist's Men Seeking Men message boards titillated with low-barrier, high-risk meet-ups. Meanwhile, an increasingly market-segmented set of profile-based gay social sites had developed, like Manhunt (pre-Scruff studs), Adam4Adam (many men of color), and Recon (leather and kink). I even "pledged" myself as a member of BeefyFrat, a fraternity-themed social network that opened up the community of gainers and encouragers to a younger audience. Some of the casual chat friends on that site with whom I traded belly pics, mutual teasing, and encouragement would become long-time buddies with whom I still keep in touch. But the interactions these sites facilitated were distributed, individualized, and full of peril. Message that sexy guy and you may get no response; or worse, you get no response and yet see that he saw your message, viewed your profile, and thought "nope."

I still found myself often lurking on Gay.com's chatrooms, with names like "Chubby Chasers" or "Bears," sniping messages at guys who piqued my interest. But in real life, where I was around 180 lbs, I was struggling to stay in a shape that made me feel comfortable enough to talk to guys when I'd go to physical spaces like bars and clubs. I was regularly hitting the gym but also indulging in desserts and alcohol. I was presenting myself to "normals" as a playful cub who you'd surely love to cuddle, while to the freaks I was showing off my soft fat parts that were eager for a spanking, or maybe even for getting stuffed with gooey cupcakes because, hey, fat boys need rewards too, and so what if they get a little fatter in the process? There'd just be more to spank.

One day, in Gay.com's "Discipline" room, I met Eric, a fellow lurker. I liked his look. A few years my junior, a few inches taller, and, most importantly, more than a few pounds thinner, he was the perfect backdrop to project my needs onto. "Eric" probably wasn't his real name, but it was the one I was going to have to work with. Over the course of a few years, he and I exchanged some brief but unfruitful messages (and always at my initiation), the "hey"s and "how's it going"s that eventually led to mutual silence. One day, though, they led to something completely unexpected.

It was now late 2011, and I was hovering around 200 lbs, having spent much of my personal life over the past few years relaxing at home and eating with homebody boyfriends, and now I'd just moved in with a new one. But as my real life got more sedentary and structured, my online life was exploding with possibilities. Even as I had fully assimilated hook-up apps like Grindr, Scruff, and Growlr into my chat repertoire, I'd still been logging into the ailing Gay.com and popping into its chatrooms as they underwent multiple cosmetic changes—first for the better, and then for the worse, before eventually collapsing completely. Perhaps it was the impending death of the social network, the slowly dwindling participation in the chatrooms that prompted Eric to talk with me at last.

Eric was, for lack of a more precise term, a cash slave: essentially, a person who derived value from being drained of all of his valuables. I didn't know this about him when we first started exchanging messages in earnest, but it revealed itself after a few weeks. I had never even heard of the concept of financial domination (or "findom") itself. It seemed like a fetish behind a fetish, an item from the untranslated page of an unfamiliar cuisine's menu. I didn't really know what to do with this information: Eric's profile data simply identified him as more of a bottom type, and his own self-descriptions painted a more nuanced picture of a guy into serious degradation with a healthy dose of cum-hunger. Eric would do anything for men's semen. He frequented bathhouses and erotic bookstores and sucked off men for hours until he felt queasy. It didn't matter who the men were, or what they looked like, so long as they could temporarily sate his constant compulsive need to consume loads of jizz.

I had found my inroad. I told Eric how I sympathized with his constant hunger, how I would sometimes just revel in how food made me feel as it satisfied my appetite, how junk food choices that invariably made me fatter felt like a dark and joyful indulgence, how the "thin" body I had created for myself also felt like a constant prison of rules and self-denial. After all of this confessional, it surprised me when Eric—tall, lean, attractive—asked me to show him a picture of my body.

This was a moment of truth. I could send him one of the curated, meticulously cropped pictures I'd taken with my Canon PowerShot and mini-tripod with me in excellent lighting, sucking in my belly, puffing out my chest, mugging at the camera with near-Zoolander smolder. Or I could lean into the mutual honesty we'd established, show him the flawed body I'd described to him, and maybe if I embellished my size a little—a little belly-stick out here, a carefully emphasized fat roll there—I might get Eric's verbal attentions in the way I'd wanted from so many men before him. I knew what needed to be done.

"How much?" he responded to the pictures of my body and its glorious fat unhidden from view. I wasn't sure how to answer the question. How much did I weigh? Well, that was in my profile data (give or take five pounds). How much had I lost? Eric didn't exactly know all of my dieting struggles, so that didn't make sense. How much had I gained? I guess maybe in context of our chats and these pics, he thought I had been getting fatter. He wouldn't have been wrong. But I pressed him for clarification on what he was asking for.

"How much money do you want?" was his response.

I definitely didn't know how to answer this question, and countered with some of my own. "Why would I take any of your money, and why would you pay me in the first place?"

"I'd pay you because I don't want to look at your body," he typed at me. It wasn't a typo either: Eric didn't want to pay for photos of my body as pornography, but rather, he would pay for them as a kind of anti-pornography, something that would serve only to wreck his sexual desire. A boner destroyer. And that he would pay money to experience that kind of humiliation was, for him, an even deeper layer of degradation. Was I really going to do this, become a twisted parody of an online chat whore, and put a price on photos of my body that only served to disgust someone?

I don't remember how we settled on a number, but we did: each one was five dollars, delivered to me through an online payments site. I had opened the floodgates. Soon the five-buck payments were starting to grow to ten, even twenty dollars before we settled into a rough price tier system of which body parts were worth what. Sometimes I'd take money from him just because he offered. But most of the time, I gave him something in return that he didn't want but nevertheless asked me for: photos of my swelling furry manboobs that my boyfriend affectionately called my "B-cups" ($5); pics of my hairy and untoned butt whose width was slowly outpacing my skimpy briefs' ability to contain it ($10); pictures of my now-growing belly, posed expertly to show off those re-deepening fat rolls that I'd once painstakingly drawn in my chubby cherub fan art ($15); and the money shot, as it were, pictures of my cock, as it became slowly engulfed by the pad of hairy pubic fat behind it ($20). The more he encouraged me to take advantage of him, the more he became comfortable with berating me for doing it. "You're a greedy fat ass," he'd tell me. He'd challenge me to eat junk food like Twinkies, show him the evidence of my having done it, and then pay me a percentage of the calories I'd consumed in virtual cash. I couldn't tell who was dominating whom here, and the ambivalence exhilarated me.

Meanwhile, the same photos and videos I was charging Eric to be disgusted by were becoming legitimate (but free) jerk-off fuel for men I was starting to connect with globally on a new gainer-focused social network. And some of those men had also found ways to re-enact Eric's patter. If one of them also called me a greedy fat ass, was it because they independently discovered that mystical phrase, or because I carefully primed them to call me it?

The exhibitionism that the gainer site afforded me was dizzying, and the influx of money from Eric—and from some other new cash slaves I had started to court on specialty find-om sites—only fueled my greed more. In particular, Eric and I would get into intense, hours-long sessions of trading cash for photos until neither of us could count how much he had paid me, or how many calories I'd consumed. I'd wake up and check my payments account, and step on the scale and check the damage. Once I used an entire night's intake to fund a rare extravagant dinner with my boyfriend. Afterwards, as we cuddled in bed, I remember he spooned me and grasped my chest, and whispered, "I think they're C-cups now."

Eventually, the arrangement with Eric faded. I suspected he was losing control of his impulses, and outpouring that much cash into my fat body (and who knows how many other guys' bodies) just wasn't sustainable. But I did know that there were always other men beyond the horizon, and I was prepared to meet them.

By mid-2017, I was back to what has been my lifetime average of 220 lbs. I still felt that I could exercise, get "thin" again, or maybe grow muscle, but to what effect? To adhere to unrealistic, demeaning standards of what a body should look like? And with a new, involved work life starting to eat up my free time, I mostly wanted to lounge and relax. I still worried about my health (my partner did, too), and I tried to moderate my indulgences. If I had ice cream one night, then maybe I'd have a kale-rich smoothie later that week, a sort of "take a penny, leave a penny" approach to dieting. But I also felt big, sexy, and incredibly alluring, and ever-aroused by the world of fat worship and humiliation.

I had been building a repertory of scripts, conversational dialogues that could be injected into any improvisational routine. But even if I were still inexorably drawn to men who I perceived as my physical "betters," in crafting my submission to them I had also learned how to dominate, humiliate, and worship other fat boys. This intersection of control and attention was, for me, the essence of "encouragement," what the gainer community terms the act of helping someone grow bigger and fatter, into the body they want to be. And even if I felt conflicted about the long-term effects of adding any more fat to my own body, I felt less so about externalizing those desires and piling pounds onto the willing fat boys I met online. I'd even done it in person years back with men I'd met from BeefyFrat, having spent one afternoon funnel-feeding one guy, Kyle, milkshakes until he got brain freeze, and another time force-feeding a cupcake to another guy, Sam, before we jerked off together.

In 2019, I even met Sam again and made him eat donuts for me and I kept his erection afloat with intense verbal worship and humiliation. "You're a fat fuck, Sam," I'd whisper into his ear as I rubbed his sensitive nipples. As I watched his eyes roll back in ecstasy, I couldn't help feeling that even if I was nominally "in charge," most of the pleasure was directed at Sam and created around him. He was my guest star at center stage, and I was the writer, director, and stage crew all rolled into one. It didn't matter that I may have looked fatter than him—in fact, in one little game we played in which we compared our body's measurements and found his dick length smaller than mine, his belly's circumference actually was slimmer than my own—the performance we crafted was a hit.

My conversations with Kyle and Sam continued, and began to coalesce on a sexy conspiracy to fatten Cody. I'd also met Cody online, sometime around early 2014. He lived many states away, and while we imagined what might happen that one day we'd meet up, neither of us belabored the illusion that it would be a realistic feat. In those days, Cody was 200 lbs or so, just a few pounds lighter than me. Since then, we'd kept up a mostly regular dialogue, with a major theme being his inevitable weight gain. Sometimes he'd show off for me on Skype, displaying some messy food item that he intended to consume for me as I verbalized all of the humiliating words he craved for me to say. "Look at you, you bloated mass of lard," I'd growl as he shoved a slice of cheesecake into his face and rubbed his dick off-cam. But also: "You big beautiful boy, you love eating for me, don't you?" And he'd nod his head and issue a muffled "Mmmhmm" from a mouth filled with lasagne or donuts or whatever else he was hungry to display that particular day.

By early 2020, Cody had finally surmounted a plateau that had long vexed him. He was now finally at his goal weight of 250 lbs, perhaps due in part to the numerous eggnog and blended cake "gainer shakes" he chugged for me on cam over the holiday season. He had done it, had posted his new weight on his gaining profile, triggering an automatic status update that announced his weight gain to the social network at large. I watched him posting new photos of his body, showing off the fat I had helped to pile on him. I saw guys like his photo and his status update, giving him supporting comments like "You're so hot" and "Congratulations on 250!" and "Fuuuuuck, you're a fat slob." Cody responded to each of those comments with his own likes. As his many followers watched him get bigger, he had watched them watch him. He made the scale go clang and all of these men were talking about it not behind his back, but right to his face. He wouldn't have it any other way.

Throughout all of my fat-centered interactions, physical and remote, I've always treasured the intimacy that they have fostered. Even if the trappings of these encounters might look cruel or manipulative to an observer, they in fact consensually subvert the cruelties of a world of onlookers who are skilled at judging what they see but unwilling to empathize with why it exists. The world at large points a finger and says "Look at the fatty" and laughs at its shoddy attempt at humor. The smaller, safe worlds I feel I've helped to co-create don't pretend to deny our natural inclination to size up one another, but neither do they weaponize it. Rather, they celebrate that reality, and say, "Look at the fatty—and isn't he fucking gorgeous." And maybe these magic words can seem mean or sadistic, but as many fat boys might tell you, a little bit of bitter makes the chocolate so much sweeter.

"Him"

D. Nolan Jefferson

He didn't look like his picture.

In that picture, the sole image in his gallery from his sparse profile on a pre-smartphone online hook-up site, he is naked and reclining in a chair. His legs are slightly spread and reveal, well, everything. The headless picture stops at his throat revealing his torso, stomach, the tops of his thighs, and cuts him off again at the knees. He looks as if he works out, maybe not to the extent that many gay men aim for in their quest for physical perfection, but it seems he's not quite at complete carb avoidance.

His profile states he is 47 years old, six feet tall, and weighs 170 lbs. In the image, he is hirsute in a way that I find attractive and desirable and, to be honest, think to myself he could stand to throttle back on the trimming.

I shoot over a message of interest not expecting to hear back from him because the fact is people rarely respond to people who look like me. I live in a metropolitan city that is so full of queer men, there isn't really much of a gayborhood because we don't *need* one. One might currently claim Logan Circle and the area that stretches north of it towards the Trader Joe's on 14th Street as the geographical queer ground zero, and that in its heyday, it used to be Dupont—but the fact is in 21st-century Washington, D.C., we are *everywhere*.

The district is, especially if you are a gay white man with even an average or nondescript body type, probably a pretty great place to have a social life. There is no shortage of extra-curricular opportunity like softball, ultimate Frisbee, and volleyball, and other intramural team sports often connected to fundraising for queer causes usually related to supporting queer youth. There are also myriad happy hours and bars, and occasions to carouse and cruise, to caress and canoodle, should that be your goal. If you're seeking to date, or merely be in the pursuit of sex, the DMV will do right by you. This changes a bit in the district if you are a person of color and even more drastically if you are black. Despite the moniker of being the *Chocolate City*, D.C., has been subject to incredible waves of gentrification, high rents, and jobs that attract the mostly white and over-educated who want to make the world a better place by doing their part within the district's four quadrants. That is to say, the city is less black than it's been in decades, back when Parliament-Funkadelic sang about it as such, and the numbers continue to shift downwards.

The district is, especially if you are a gay white man even of some size—and identify as a bear or chub complete with your beard and beer gut—*still* probably a great place to live or just hook up, though things likely narrow for you. You see the warnings in the profiles: *masc for masc, no fats, no fems, no blacks—just a preference*, but then again, you are white and, with that, experience tremendous privilege compared to your BIPOC folks with the same physicality. I dare say the idea of fat falls on a spectrum. I don't doubt the needs and wants of . Zumba-dancing, spin class enthusiasts who fast intermittently as they seek to shed those last five pounds so their readily viewable abdominal muscles pop that much more, but then there are also those, like me, at the other end of that continuum. And for me, here in this city? Dating sucks.

Black men of all sizes are subject to this country's ugly history and are burdened with the myths regarding our sexual prowess, endowments, and physicality and that get fetishized to the point where you are reduced to your mere exoticism. Sure, you went to law school, probably on financial aid and because of quotas, and clerked on the hill, and might even be a respectable and contributing member of society, *but let me see that BBC, baby.* Adding queerness further complicates the matter because sex and sexuality, and dare I say fucking, are also tethered to queerness in a way that seems to fuel all of these dynamics and so things get even more complicated.

So, all of this to say that when he wrote back "Cute" or "Sexy" or something else in the affirmative, I assumed it was someone taking pity on me, which is what I was used to, and which had been my experience—temporal, short-term but exciting trysts that were fulfilling but brief, never having been in a long-term relationship. I had to wonder though. Maybe he wasn't just fetishizing *black* bodies, but also *fat* black bodies, because why on earth would he want me? I'm not ripped. My shared pics are shot in such a way that I work my angles but don't misconstrue for a second that I'm something that I'm not. I assumed, given the secretive, shameful way in which all of my sexual experiences were couched, that this would be another fleeting notch in my belt and, frankly, I was fine with it. Or so I thought.

We got through the perfunctory chitchat fueled by testosterone and desire, the working out of logistics of who was hosting who, STI (sexually transmitted infection) statuses, recent testing dates, what we were looking to do, and once agreed on, I invited him over. The inevitable lull that happens after you sign off can seem eternal. And in it, your pulse quickens, your heart races, and your stomach churns. You hope that if he actually shows up, because they don't always, he isn't insane; you pray he takes hygiene seriously; you hope that when he locks eyes on you, on *all* of you, as others have done in the past, if he decides in the moment to soldier through beyond the 300+ lbs before him, he doesn't show any distain. You hope that when the door opens he doesn't care at all about snorting loudly through his nose and saying that this isn't going to work out once he's looked you over, and that he's changed his mind, hurting your feelings that much more beyond your already tenderly frayed nerves.

But that afternoon when he knocked on the front door of my basement apartment and I opened it and invited him in, hyperaware of my weight, of the girth of my thick thighs and droopy, fat pecs and my stomach all neatly concealed as best I could under a cotton t-shirt, there was none of that.

He smiled.

He wore a baseball cap, a pair of gold tone Ray-Ban aviators, and beneath that he wore a genuine, sincere smile. He didn't want a glass of water (something one thinks about should they travel out for some recreational fun in lieu of being drugged), and before I could close the door, he took my head gingerly in both of his hands drawing it closer to his and began kissing me with passionate but restrained tenderness. Recalling it even now makes me go full Amélie as she, at the sight of her crush, transmogrifies into a fleeting puddle of water. In those first few moments with him, my self-consciousness about my body also dissipated. And it was clear to me that afternoon that he was there because he *wanted* to be. He liked what he saw and wasn't put off by whatever numbers might reveal on a scale, and didn't reduce me to some cut-out image in his head. And when we retreated to the bedroom and the clothes came off, we liked what we saw in the other, but I noticed, and not to any detriment, that he didn't look exactly like his picture.

To be honest, if he had posted a picture of how he accurately looked that day—and I do believe that it is indeed him in the image but from a time when he thought and felt he looked his best, his most fit, his most trim, his most delicious—I would've been more than fine with it. He is, after all, a queer white man in the district of some means and affluence. His clothes, car, mannerisms, and ease all reveal a kind of organic comfort that couldn't be just a flex for approval. This man is not interested in attention, no. No, not like we see with the sculpted, selfie-obsessed so-called Instagays of social media. I *liked* what appeared in the door of my basement apartment more than the sculpted and presumed(?) alleged(?) more desirable body underneath his Levi's and wrinkle-free button-down. I *liked* his middle-aged spread of paunch. I found it and him sexy. I couldn't believe how lucky I was, running my fingers across his chest, our foreheads touching when we were in my bed and with each other. Before, he'd only been represented by a complex series of digital encoded bits combined in such a way to create a flat visual two-dimensional file on my computer screen, but it was enough to be the linchpin of our transactional tryst.

That first time was important. It was the first time I saw myself as something more than just a fat, black, sometimes sassy, nearly always too much in my head, bitchy ole queen. And suddenly, most of my fears about being too extra, too this or that, but mostly too fat, were gone.

After he left, I sat in my tiny apartment and put on a record. Nina Simone, or Sufjan Stevens, Sam Cooke, or Stevie. I stretched out on my secondhand sofa while the music floated around the basement and wondered if he could be the one. I'm a terrible, hopeless, in-love-with-the-concept-of-love type of lover and there I was again, right back in it. I let all six seasons of *Sex and the City*, the show I'd watch one after the other before starting them all over again in sequence, swirl around in my head, conjuring up images of a knight in shining armor coupledom. I thought, given our afternoon, that maybe he wasn't like the others. I thought he was different with his affection. It started off a one-off hook-up and, in the afterglow, I went from zero to registered at Pottery Barn.

I thought about excursions we might take to the museums downtown, maybe to the Renwick, or shoulder to shoulder, hand in hand, bundled in scarves and fueled by espresso to the atrium of the National Portrait Gallery on a winter weekend morning. I thought about a life I didn't think was available to me because fat guys like me never get the guys that look like him. I was very much, all of a sudden, a Carrie.

I'd sign on to the site and wait for him.

On early mornings before work I'd sign on to that archaic site, where I'd clicked the star next to his username marking him a favorite, and eagerly wait for his name to light up. On days when I decided working from home was better than a slow day in the office, I'd do the same. Sometimes he was there and I'd chat him up and, because the site was ancient and didn't perform well on mobile platforms (he always surfed from his phone), he'd miss the cues or pings or pokes and it was all for naught. But there were also times when I'd be scrolling through the slog of office email with the site on in the background and I'd hear the chime of an incoming chat and I'd light up when it was him. The dialogue never went much further beyond "Hey handsome" or "Look who's up!" or "Could you use some company?" and I'd move heaven and earth to steal away some time to invite him over. Our engagements were regular and frequent and then they'd fall off for weeks. But he always came back. Best I could tell, he lived in the neighborhood, and I made a gentlemen's agreement with myself that if I ever saw him about at the bodega or taqueria I wouldn't acknowledge him in public. The truth is, I wasn't quite sure of who he actually was. Was he partnered? Married? Closeted? Once, I offered up my phone number—you could just text me, I said, that way we don't have to deal with the glitches of the app. He declined. This went on for months that stretched into years. It went on far longer than I wanted it to and never went anywhere besides the sex. I failed to see how I'd been reduced to concubine. And yet I never once complained about our routine. He never once shared his name with me.

I met another man on a different site but one that is just as antiquated in its implementation. We're talking late 90s Geocities, but without it, I wouldn't have met him. He taught at a high school and loved to read mysteries. Shirley Jackson was a favorite and we spent hours talking *We Have Always Lived in the Castle* on our first date, with me having just read it for the first time, and him having grown up in the same town where she lived in Vermont, enveloped in the lore of mystery about her and her work. He was excitable and spoke with his hands, and surprised me, after arriving late at the landmark that is the Dupont Circle fountain, by kissing me hello right on the mouth. Despite my confession of framing myself as a "bigger guy" and assuming this was going to be a turn-off, none of this seemed to matter. Not one bit. He sent me toothy-grinned selfies from various places in his classroom during his free period.

He checked all my boxes in that he was nerdy and liked to read and had a great smile, and our initial conversations started out with an air of naughtiness and kink as we tried to figure each other out. He was coming out of a long-term relationship, a fact that often made me feel inadequate because I've never been in one. He told me to be careful what you wish for because this latest and longest for him had been troubling and stressful. Despite my claims of being broken—what else could explain being reasonably well-adjusted, gainfully employed, and on rather good terms with my folks and yet far from achieving these things like relationships, things most people accomplish by the time they graduate college if not in high school—he called me handsome and told me to calm down and be kind to myself.

We liked French fries and movies; his students kept him up on the lingua franca of the teens and we both reminisced on what it was like to be that age and on how far we come. He wanted to take things slow. I told him it was fine. And when we sat in the window seats of cafes talking about punk rock and how in San Diego, yes, we really did put those beloved French fries in burritos or subbed them out for chips making a version of nachos that would blow his mind, the conversation seemed to inevitably worm through the muck and work its way back to his ex and, with it, the shame he thrived on making him feel.

So, when my texts to him eventually went unanswered I wasn't surprised. After all, the last few dates had much of the joy that accompanied the ones of the first few months siphoned off. The slight darkness that seemed to be a tiny kernel of a seed inside this man had not just grown, it had blossomed. The last time we saw each other, at Union Market over a shared affogato, he apologized for being so out of it and that he'd just been in a mood prompted by his ex and his subsequent out-of-the-blue voicemails. No way they were getting back together though, he said, and I don't know if I believed him, but I did feel that there was something he not just desired but that he very much needed, that I could not supply. When I went back to the site where we first crossed paths to see if maybe he was still there, to see if there was something in those first few kinky messages where I could connect the dots to where we were(n't?) now, or to see if maybe he'd shed me for being something he didn't want or need, his account was gone. When I put it all together

I realized he'd been telling me in so many words that he needed to be on the receiving end of his kink, that there was something innate within him where he thrived on degradation, shame, and humiliation. In the moment though, I couldn't really see it, so I gave it all a good long thought and, in my head, wished him the best. It took me a while to consider that it wasn't me, or me being fat, that kept whatever it was we had going, it was him. And it was a real teachable moment for me, learning to understand that there might be something other than me being fat that might cause a potential relationship to fail.

I lived for years thinking that being fat meant I didn't deserve happiness or love and I put on a brave face in order to thrive at being the funny fat friend—the quick-witted one with the quips and clapbacks in order to protect myself from not being seen as a whole person. Or to be on the offensive so that I could diffuse a situation with *Well, yeah, I know I'm fat, but I'm an overachiever with a lot of education and can you drive a manual transmission? 'Cause bitch, I can.* I sold myself on thinking that no one would ever, or could ever, find me attractive. That I had to be someone's shameful secret or fetish or the outcome of a lost bet, a jokey punchline to a gag on an episode of *Punk'd*. I put too much stock into social media, pop culture, Crossfit bodies, whiteness, and what all of things in combination were telling me over and over and over again. These facets blinded me from myself and, in many ways, from allowing me to see my own humanity. As a fat, queer black man in America, I am always, always, always thinking about how my intersecting identities make me fit into this place that was never made by or for me, despite my ancestors' role in building it. If I had a dollar for every time a usually straight, almost always white colleague or friend or acquaintance reached out to me to say they have a gay friend and would I be interested, it's always in the context of *Well*, he's *gay and* they're *gay, so they should be perfect together!* It's never taken into account, despite me blessing their hearts, that there's more to making a relationship than queerness. Miss me with those Instaguys, honey.

The last time I saw him, the him from the first half of this essay, the him I spent so much time with and the him who made me feel as if I was something more than I could ever see of myself, was at Thanksgiving. It wasn't for a hook-up and I don't think he saw me. It was at a cafe where I had thought it might be quiet because of the holiday, and had decided to steal away to get some writing in. I sat in the back with earbuds and music, sipping espresso over ice, and he strolled in and stepped into line. Even in his trademark jeans, cap, and sneakers, he looked polished. He was with an older man, someone I thought might be his father, and a young boy of maybe seven or eight years old. I took them all in and paid attention to their body language and how they interacted with one another. I don't think the child was his son, though I do think this deeply private man is just that. I'd say nephew if you asked, but in so many ways, and specifically in a way that defines him, just like the picture that's probably him, but wasn't, there's no way I'll ever know for certain.

Listen, I'm fat. I am. But I'm also a lot of other things and it wasn't until very recently that I had the wherewithal to think that if you asked friends of mine, or colleagues, what they thought of me—what's the first word that comes to mind when you mention my name—they'd likely say: Funny. Thoughtful.

Music. Writer. Librarian. Twitter. No one would say fat, even if I felt for much too long as it was the thing that defined me the most. I've learned to accept that aspect of myself and, in moving forward, care a lot less about those who might judge me on that accordingly. It's a pretty great feeling.

"The Haunted House"

Bruce Owens Grimm

You'd be a most excellent playground. A man says this to me because of a picture I posted where I'm leaning back in my desk chair, my gray t-shirt riding up as it's barely able to contain my bloated belly. I've binged on chips, cookies, and cheese (for the protein, of course) for most of the day in my studio at a writing residency. The studio gives me isolation to read, write, and eat as much as I possibly can without a roommate knocking on my door to interrupt or friends wondering why I look so bloated. Sunlight fills the room, which provides a lot of flattering natural light. I feel round and fat. I feel sexy. So I take a picture. In some ways, this feels silly, almost Victorian—to feel sexy, daring, in a picture where nothing is showing except a strip of the bottom of my belly. The real enticement, the top ridge of my belly, is hidden beneath the fabric.

I can, at times, feel attractive like I did that day, but I don't walk around my daily life feeling as if a man will see me as a potential playground. I'm not sure that I would want that anyway. Although, at this time, I do not understand why this idea makes me uncomfortable. What I do know then is that I have posted this picture and this man has reached out to me on a social media site designed for gay gainers and encouragers. In my daily, offline life, I am around non-gainers. The site where I posted that picture is a bubble where I know there will be other men who find me attractive. Sexy. Desirable. Safe. All the things I don't feel in the rest of the world. All the things I haven't felt when going into gay bars or when going on dates with men outside the gaining community. I do worry about being objectified. This is why some days I feel uncomfortable about posting pictures like that. For some men, I am only a belly. A sack of fat to masturbate to.

This is why the playground comment strikes me the wrong way when I first read it. I feel dehumanized. He leaves comments on other pictures. On one where it shows the progression of my belly growth, he says that thinking about me getting fatter makes him hard. He lives in Los Angeles. Thousands of miles from me in Chicago. There is little chance that he will ever be able to use me as his playground. He can say this and not have to worry about the follow-through. It is, as my first therapist would say, "Safe."

I say this as if I'd be rushing to him if he were in Chicago or if I were in Los Angeles. I can feel safe because there's no way for us to meet up. I don't know what he'd want from me. The easy, most obvious answer would be to ask or respond in some way that leads to more flirting, more conversation about the type of playground I could be for him.

I should feel flattered, right? It's okay to feel uncomfortable, right? He's just being flirty. I don't know if feeling awkward or wanting him to have an interest in me beyond my body is even a correct reaction. Does it make me uptight? A prude?

Confession: I have wanted to write an essay about sex. The difference between "regular" sex and "gainer" sex. The differences in how I feel after both kinds. I can see the light under the door, but there is a shadow splayed across the floor that makes me scared to open it. I know I must face my fear. Face what is lurking in that room. I have difficulty talking about sex. Sex makes me uncomfortable.

Since coming out in 2009, I have worried that I simply do not know how to be gay in the "right" way—the "right" way being an ever moving, impossible thing to define. I know to even think such a thing is a fallacy. There is no "right" way to be anything. However, when men have walked out of dates after finding out I had been married to a woman before coming out or when guys say they've had a good time on our date but never call again, or when I'm feeling alone and lonely, it is difficult not to feel that I am somehow not doing something right. All those years spent in the closet, afraid, meant that I didn't have time as a teenager, in my twenties to practice dating, having sex, forming relationships, learning how to move on when my heart is broken. So when I was in my thirties, and now in my forties, other men my age have done this, and they expect me to have done this and I have not. To come out of the closet late has, for me, felt like a perpetual game of catch-up. I've seen other men who came out late, some later than I did, seem to have no trouble with fitting right in. Perhaps, I will always feel behind. Perhaps, I will always feel haunted by coming out late.

I've had one serious relationship with a man. Marco was

not in the gainer scene. I met him after I lost 100 lbs, going from 315 lbs to 215 lbs. I was at a point where I thought if I lost weight I would have a better chance of meeting someone. I wanted a relationship. I wanted to be in love. I didn't think those things were possible if I were a gainer. I didn't tell Marco about gaining. I saw no reason to because I had planned on leaving it behind for good.

Then I lost ten more pounds and those ten more pounds seemed to make a difference. I didn't feel right in my body. It felt like there was a hollow inside me where the gainer part of me hid wrapped in cobwebs. The fat body I wanted haunted me every time we had sex. I became too uncomfortable, so I'd tell him to stop. I didn't want to have sex. When he asked me what was going on, I didn't tell him. I didn't know how to tell him how I missed my fat body. I didn't know how to tell him that without being fat, without being able to engage in gaining, I felt unable to fully connect with my body.

He must have felt it too.

*　*　*

It rained. Fat, juicy drops of water ran down the sliding glass door in the kitchen. It didn't let up all day. When Marco and I went to bed, nothing seemed out of the ordinary. By the next morning, it had stopped raining. The sun was out. There was a small puddle of water in the middle of the kitchen floor. Water didn't streak from the sink or the refrigerator. A puddle with no source. We thought maybe the seal on the sliding glass door wasn't tight enough, allowing rain water to seep in. I wiped up the water with a couple paper towels.

It was unusual, but I didn't dwell on it. The townhouse we lived in was bright, well-lit, the ceilings high. Newer construction. Nothing about it seemed like it should have been haunted. But the puddle kept appearing. Always in the same spot. Never an identifiable source.

Mysterious spots of water like this can be associated with poltergeist activity. It's also possible that poltergeist-like activity can be manifested.

I'd boarded up the hallway that contained most of my physical desire. I heard it calling out my name as I brushed my teeth in the bathroom at the top of the stairs staring into the darkness downstairs. The voice sounding as if it was down there, close and far away at the same time. I'd hear it knocking on the wall as I tried to fall asleep. These noises might have been the gaining desire I'd been hiding from trying to get my attention. And as with most noises in a haunted house, I tried to ignore it until I couldn't any longer.

Marco and I eventually broke up. I told him I was a gainer months after we ended our relationship. I felt bad for keeping it from him, and for being a gainer. "Never apologize for desire," he said.

Being a gainer isn't just about getting fat, it's also about sex. For a long time, I wanted to deny that being a gainer had some connection to my sexual life.

✾　✾　✾

We went to Dunkin' Donuts after going to a buffet. My friend, Bob, and I were spending the day together. Like any good encourager, he had suggested a stop for donuts on our way back to my apartment. He sat at a booth as I waited at the pick-up spot for my iced coffee. I didn't hear anyone walk up behind me so I wasn't expecting a hug. The man behind me wrapped his arms around me. My body tensed. It was Bob. "Are you okay being touched?" he asked as he nuzzled my neck.

"Yeah," I said. "Well, it depends on who it is."

"I'm sorry, I should have asked first." He let go and moved away.

I wish I had relaxed into his hug, into his arms. But that's not what happened. I felt tense. He felt it. I wondered how many other times I had done this; how many other men had noticed this and taken it as some kind of rejection.

Perhaps part of the reason I tensed that day was that I had not been touched in an intimate way in months. I can go months without being touched by anyone, and most of the time I won't notice until I'm touched again.

I don't always know how to react to being touched, how to trust it, how to let myself enjoy it without the ghosts of other times my body has been harmed getting in the way.

Even when I've had my belly rubbed, I've felt the skin over my fat tense. That I could explain away as being ticklish. Once I relax a little, it is enjoyable. But I start to worry if I'm making enough noise, moaning and groaning under the delight of the guy's hands, his lips brushing against my belly. I'm always worried if I'm displaying, indicating pleasure in the correct way.

Marco and other guys who were into regular sex had wanted me to tell them what I wanted them to do to me, tell them how much I wanted it, and I felt embarrassed. Afraid I would sound goofy. And so, I couldn't tell them. They were left to guess.

I still felt ashamed of what I wanted. Down the dimly lit hallway of my desire was the idea that I wanted to be fucked, but not in the traditional way. If I were to turn the handle to the door where I hid my biggest fantasy, and shine a light on it, it would look like this: I want a guy to smash a pie into my belly, feed chunks of it to me, while rubbing the filling onto my gut, both of us getting messier and messier, food all over both of us. I'd seen this in a video. Two men, a couple, feeding each other. I had to see it to know that's what I wanted.

I had the opportunity to say it, to tell an encourager, this is what I want. I took a train from Chicago to St. Louis to meet Peter. I shouldn't have been nervous or scared to tell him what I wanted to do. As an encourager, he was more prone to entertain the idea.

I didn't know when or how to bring it up. I didn't want to assume too much. We shared a bed that weekend. We kissed. He rubbed my belly. He was on top of me as we ran our hands, our tongues over each other's bodies, our sweat intermingling. We had chatted for a long time, formed a connection before we met in person. Both of us were fascinated by ghosts.

On one of our nights together, we lay in the dark of his room as Peter told me a story about a friend of his who had met a man from Chicago and had fallen in love too quickly. The friend had moved to be with this man. Then it didn't work out and he had to move back to St. Louis. The friend was now in love with Peter.

He was not happy with this turn of events. Peter didn't want this friend to be in love with him.

I could see how it could be easy to fall in love with him. There was an ease to being around him that made me want to be around him more. It was easy to sit on the couch next to him, and fall asleep in his arms. But the message he gave me by telling me that story about his friend was: Don't get attached. Don't get too close. Don't fall in love.

I wasn't sure if that was a warning for me or for himself.

At the end of the weekend, he drove me back to the train station, and we passed a Jack in the Box. I told him that I wished we had gone there because there weren't any in Chicago.

"Next time," Peter said.

"Awesome," I said. "It will be fun."

He nodded.

"Maybe next time we can also try something else." I took a moment. I took a deep breath and told him about my pie and belly fantasy.

"Wish we'd done that," he glanced at me as he drove. Smiled.

"Next time," I said.

"Next time," he said.

Don't fall in love, I reminded myself.

The thing that would keep us connected after our visit wasn't gaining, it was the supernatural. We both shared an interest in it. This had been part of my attraction to him. Months after my visit with Peter, I had a dream that ghosts trapped him in a haunted house deep in the woods where help wouldn't come quickly, if at all. I sensed he was in danger. I had to go to him, rescue him. But we were in different cities, hours apart, and the evil forces in the haunted house were somehow able to use their powers to cause enough traffic in Chicago to prevent me from getting to him.

When I woke up, I texted him, *Had a dream you were trapped in a haunted house.*

Peter: *Ooooh spooky!! I went to a haunted house last night and I'm going again tonight!!*

Me: *Really?!*

Peter: *Yeah! You're a psychic!*

Me: *Weird. Be careful. Be safe. I know it was just a dream and it might be silly to be worried, but I am a little.*

Peter: *It's definitely a weird coincidence.*

The thought of Peter going to the haunted house conjured *The Haunting of Hill House*, of the house in the book being alive, of it calling to Eleanor, wanting her to stay. I thought of the scenes in both versions of the movie adaptations where the wood walls breathe and stretch out. The house a body.

I thought of doors that slammed shut. I thought of him trapped in rooms where he couldn't escape, the sound of footsteps thundering down the hall. I worried about Peter being slowly absorbed by the dwelling. I remembered this passage from the book where Eleanor thinks, "The house was waiting now...and it was waiting for her; no one else could satisfy it." Maybe the house Peter was going to was his Hill House and he was its Eleanor.

I daydreamed about going with him, taking his hand, and protecting him as we went through the house. Another daydream that was more like a movie, an extension of the original dream, was about me coming to his rescue to free him from the house. A rather romantic scenario: one man saving the life of the other man he loves. It's a scenario that queer people rarely get to actually see in movies.

Don't fall in love. I didn't tell Peter any of this. I did ask him to let me know he was okay when he got home. Later that night he texted me, *I'm alive!*

I was glad he had made it through the house unharmed. It was strange that I dreamed about him being in a haunted house when he had planned on going to one. Maybe it shows a connection. Maybe it was purely coincidental.

I do know that my true fear is that I will be like whatever walks in Hill House, in that I am for some reason destined to walk alone. At least in a romantic sense. I know I am not alone in terms of friendships or people who care about me.

But a romantic relationship is still something I want. Even though there have been times where I had the opportunity to be in one and chose not to be because it took too much time away from my writing.

There was a guy I went on a few dates with, another encourager, Dwayne, who I enjoyed spending time with, someone I had wanted to try to find space for in my life, but that didn't work out. He accidentally conjured the ghost of my father one night.

He had asked me out on a second date. We were at dinner. It felt very formal in a very sweet, romantic way. We were at a place that had candles on the table. He had chosen the location.

"I'm glad you asked me out again," I said.

He took a moment to respond. He said that he almost didn't remember asking me out. He had been drunk when he had asked. He said he had needed to be drunk to have the courage to invite me out.

I immediately became angry. I twisted the pasta I'd ordered around and around on my fork. I considered getting up and walking out. On its own, it was irritating to hear that he had forgotten he asked me out. The other layer was that my father used to say all kinds of things, make promises to spend time together when he was drunk, and then wouldn't follow through because he'd forgotten he ever said it.

Instead of leaving, I told him that it upset me to hear this, and I told him about the other reason why it bothered me, the ghost that had shown up to the table when he said it.

He apologized. We went out one more time after that dinner, but I couldn't shake the ghost. I couldn't stop thinking that anytime he said anything meaningful to me, he would have to be drunk to say it. I'd lived life like that before and I refused to return to it.

❋ ❋ ❋

And so, where do we go from here? It seems impossible to have a satisfying ending at this point because these are still issues I'm working through. Some days I don't even think about these things at all because I'm too busy living the rest of my life. I know that I have in the past tried to change who I am to fit into some ideal of what I should be. I won't do that to find a man to date or have a long-term relationship with. He, whoever he is, will have to be comfortable with me as a writer and a gainer, as someone who is still trying to figure out how to usher out the last few ghosts that remain. I am some days still learning to be at ease that these are the things that encompass me. Maybe at the end of that journey, I will meet a man, the man I'm meant to be with, and start a new one.

"Grown"

Jonathan Hillman

185 pounds

I fall head over
    feet
for a guy who's lost
a hundred pounds
and found them again.
A guy who walks
with swagger,
who lives
Extra
Extra
Large.

With him, the world grows bigger.
With him, I want to live
more than half-
way.
Stop walking with one foot
in

and one foot out.

With him, I want to be more
than a Medium.

200 pounds

I grow into
a Large.
I run on
an ellipse:

       trying to be

    Fat.   Fit

to   but

    back   always

       cycling

220 pounds

>>There is something

Extra

>>in Extra Large

More

>>pizza to share

More

>>room to spare

Bigger

>>chest for him
>>to lay his head

Bigger

>>spoon for him
>>to lay in bed

>>My body gaining something

Extra

240 pounds

They say that to be gay
I should weigh

180   or   280

            nothing in between

slim, muscled   or   fat, hairy
Twink   or   Bear
Jock   or   Chub
Otter   or   Daddy

Masc   for   Masc

260 pounds

The scale
            tipping
My pants
            ripping
My body
            bursting
                        free

285 pounds

They say I've grown.

	My chin
No longer	a pointed blade,
Now	blending, bearded.

	My shoulders
No longer	sharply shrugged,
Now	rounding, rugged.

They say I've grown.

	My fingers
No longer	weeping willows,
Now	thickening, thunderous.

	My voice
No longer	a question mark,
Now	deepening, doubtless.

They say I've grown.

	My belly
No longer	lurching,
Now	loosening, letting go.

My body
No longer   belonging to anyone,
Now   my body is my home.

They say I've grown.

My life
No longer   half,
Now   a hundredfold.

"The Trash Heap Has Spoken"

Carmen Maria Machado

My grandmother was a mountain. When I was a girl, I'd stand
next to her vanity and watch as she strung herself with what
I thought of as her "jewels"—jangling, glittering bangles
and jade-green Lucite earrings and roped gold necklaces and
Swarovski crystal brooches shaped like elephants and tigers.
She wore leopard-print nightgowns and smelled like White
Diamonds and overflowed from the bones of her chair.

Her body was a marvel to me, a form unbound and soothing
as a Buddha. Sometimes, I would sit in her lap and peek down her
shirt, to see her mysteries. She was the biggest woman I knew.

I was a skinny kid, coltish, and freakishly fast. My anxiety
seemed to burn calories; I was always upset about something
that had happened or would happen or could happen. And
when I wasn't ascending the sticky torsos of pine trees in our
backyard or mainlining Nancy Drew/Hardy Boys crossover
novels or leaving sporadic, melodramatic entries in my diary or

researching the symptoms of leukemia on the public library's computer, I watched *Fraggle Rock*. I adored the industrious Doozers and the way the Fraggles rapaciously devoured their architecture. I was fascinated by the metafictional quirk of Doc and Sprocket acting out analogues of the Fraggles' dramas in their own lives. But there was no one I loved more than Marjory the Trash Heap.

Marjory was a voluminous mound of sentient garbage and compost and leaves, who had a cherry-red cat-eye lorgnette and a banana-peel fascinator set at a jaunty angle. From the tippy-top of her head, she only spread outward as you went down. She didn't spill from anything because there was nothing to spill from: she was boundless.

When they were feeling lost, the Fraggles braved the Gorgs' backyard to seek Marjory's wisdom. She was an all-knowing oracle who gave out dadaist advice; judicious even as she moldered. She had large, floppy trash-breasts that moved if she sang emphatically enough. And sing she did: mournful, wry, bluesy songs.

She, Marjory, was attended by two ambiguously specied, Muppetish rodents, Philo and Gunge. "My boys," she called them in her raspy Slavic accent. When the scenes with her came to a close, these supplicants howled, "The Trash Heap has spoken, nyahhh," a signal that the audience with Marjory was over. "Gunge" is a gummy, unpleasant substance, like what you might find at the bottom of an outdoor garbage can. "Philo," of course, means love.

The Little Mermaid, too, was in constant rotation when I was a child. The tape was in the VCR more often than it wasn't, and I could—and can, still—recite whole scenes from memory. I thought Ursula was magnificent: the best and most terrifying of all the Disney villains. She lured traditionally beautiful, predictably rebellious princesses into Faustian bargains and thumbed her nose at the polite mermaid society from which she had been banished. She lived in a palace made from the skeleton of an ancient leviathan and ate living, trembling shrimp from a seashell dish. She was crowned with a shock of white hair, heavy-lidded with blue eye shadow, adorned with red lips and a beauty spot. Her breasts were pushed up and spilled out, and moved every time she did. Often, she came toward the viewer, quickly, filling the frame—shimmying her bosom, splaying her tentacles obscenely, showing off her elbow dimples and double chin and large teeth.

She was lascivious and vulgar, ambitious and arrogant. When Ariel first met her, Ursula sat at her vanity performing an ostentatious act: making herself beautiful, running mousse through her hair, pinching pigment from a pod, and painting her mouth as orange-red as the surface of Mars.

Ursula the sea witch, like Marjory the Trash Heap, was also attended by two creatures, in this case eels: Flotsam and Jetsam (a pun I only understood as an adult). Here she was: a fallen, magical noble with flamboyant taste, served by the detritus of the ocean.

❀ ❀ ❀

Puberty roiled up on me like a thunderstorm, and when it passed it left behind breasts and hips and other junk besides.

Here is what the mirrors saw after that: two halves of a formal dress closing up around my teenaged body like a Venus flytrap, and then stopping because of a too-large chest. My mother cursing, yanking, muttering. The sounds of other girls trying on dresses with their mothers—rustling, zipping, crying. A row of dioramas, each playing out its own miniature tragedy. Black t-shirts and jeans that never fitted quite right, sweatshirts designed to conceal. Me, gripping with a kind of rage the parts of my body that didn't hug to my bones.

Was I actually fat, back then? I certainly thought so, but looking at photos years later—when I am actually, clinically obese, the kind that makes you bad at doctor's appointments and great at online shopping—I look ordinary. Busty—my grandmother's inheritance—but otherwise average. A little slumpy and curved inward, but that's just what it's like to be a teenage girl, isn't it? Embarrassed for existing.

In any case, I kept getting bigger. I didn't absorb Marjory and Ursula's object lessons on existing audaciously, but instead landed squarely where culture wanted me: hating my body, participating in my own oppression in grotesque ways. I clipped out advertisements for weight-loss products—despite the fact that my cousin was hospitalized with heart problems after taking the prescription diet pill Fen-Phen—and watched infomercials for electrical muscle stimulation machines; all that kept me from joining these weight-loss crazes of the late-1990s/early-2000s was my lack of a credit card. I became convinced that I could break down my fatness with violence, punching my abdomen with my fists as if I was trying to induce an abortion. I drank so much water my pee was nearly clear. I tried to stop eating, but the hunger was so terrible I broke my fast by eating all I could find in my parents' kitchen: half a bag of jumbo marshmallows. Unable to change, I became Centralia, settling into a low-grade loathing that smoldered for years.

I didn't yet see that, at least in fiction, some fat women chose power. Whether they were villains or oracles, whether it came in the form of ambition or beauty or brilliance or sexual prowess or raw, uncut strength, these women were tremendous. Maybe I didn't notice because they were discrete examples amid a deluge of terrible ones: bumbling fat cops and embarrassing fat sidekicks and desexualized fat mothers and nasty fat bullies and lazy fat punchlines.

Once, in a store, my mother and I saw a very fat woman buying peppers. My mother turned to me and said, "If I ever look like that, kill me." She said it like a spy giving a subordinate spy a direct order, in the event of capture over enemy lines. Many years later, she, my mother, had bariatric surgery and melted away. She will never look like that woman did, or the way that I do. There is no risk that I will need to follow her instructions.

The first time I saw the Venus of Willendorf—in an art-history class in my senior year of high school—I could not believe what I was seeing. Because she wasn't just plump or curvy or any of the other euphemisms I was quickly adopting; she was really, properly fat. She had voluminous breasts and a round, spilling belly and dimpled knees and tiny feet and a nearly blank face. (There are other Venuses, too. My favorite might be the Venus of Hohle Fels, made of mammoth ivory: she has a tiny head, massive breasts held up by her bear-paw hands, and an exaggerated vulva, so large it separates her legs to the width of her torso.)

There are many theories about the purpose of the Venus figurines. Some people theorize that they were the prehistoric equivalent of pornography. Others notice that their feet were often pointed, so perhaps they were meant to be stuck in the ground like pegs, for some sort of ceremony. Still another theory accounts for the blankness of their faces: that they were self-portraits, created by ancient women who had neither cameras nor mirrors.

Every day, I look for myself in other women's bodies. This is what happens when you never see yourself in television shows or catalogues or movies—you get hungry. In passers-by, I seek out a faithful replica of my own full chest: my plastic-bag stomach pooched over jeans, my milk-carton hips, and my face with its peach-pit cheekbones set in coffee grounds. In this way, I see myself in pieces, mostly, and have to assemble my body in my mind.

It isn't like my mother and the woman buying the peppers; I'm not disgusted or afraid. I just want to know what I look like to other people. And every so often, I get to see all of those pieces together, and it feels like the reverberations after an orgasm—a low, deep satisfaction.

The beautiful fat woman is across from me on the subway platform, chewing on her nail. She's trying on really nice shoes in the same store where I am trying on really nice shoes. She's catching her reflection in a window in the hatched streets of our shared city, and I can't stop looking at her. Does she resemble me, or do I just hope that because she's so beautiful? Does that make me vain, or stupid? Why does seeing a woman who might actually look like me make me want to sit down on the pavement and cry?

It isn't that I don't look in the mirror, or see myself in photographs. It's just that looking at myself in the mirror or seeing myself in photographs is like listening to a recording of my voice; with my attention turned fully to consumption, everything seems different. "I don't remember looking like that," I said once when I saw a picture of myself at a party—double-chinned and sack-shaped as Friar Tuck—as if I could remember looking like anything at all.

❀   ❀   ❀

In *Mad Max: Fury Road*, the only fat women are seen in passing with milk pumps attached to their giant breasts, like cows in a barn. In *Now and Then*, the only fat girl, Chrissy, is also the only one who doesn't get her own backstory. In the first episode of *Jessica Jones*, a nameless fat woman who looks a lot like me gets off a treadmill to shove a burger in her face, and Jessica says, wryly: "Two minutes on the treadmill, twenty minutes on a quarter pounder."

Sometimes, I imagine movies and shows I love with a fat actress instead of a thin one, but identical in every other way. I think about *Fried Green Tomatoes* with a voluptuous Ruth or a stout Idgie next to each other in the pond; *Jane the Virgin* with a fat, brilliant, neurotic Jane with two men madly in love with her; *Death Proof* with a chubby Zoe riding that car's hood; *Lucky Number Slevin* with a plump Lindsey smiling and full of secrets;

Secretary with a fat Lee bent over that desk, bathed in the copper tub, sprawled out next to James Spader as he tenderly kisses every inch of her.

Fat women and girls are matrons, cronies, jokes. They're never romantic leads, or heroes. They never get to just be. It's as if writers can't imagine fat women having sex or agency or complex lives. They're just bodies for thin people to bounce off of; funny and unserious as a whoopee cushion or unconsidered as a chair. If they're even there at all.

Almost every person I've dated or slept with, man or woman, has observed unprompted that I am the fattest woman they've ever been with. I never know what that means. Are they marveling? Struggling for answers? After a series of these confessions I found myself watching lovers more closely, not because they have reminded me that I am fat, but because they have pointed out that it is unusual for them to be in such intimate, pleasurable proximity to a fat body. I think about it as I unhook my bra, straddle my boyfriend, kiss a date in her car.

Once, I thought I saw a woman who looked like me in an amateur porn video. Her breasts hung low, and her stomach folded where mine did, and I couldn't stop watching her. She bit her lip and sucked her boyfriend's cock and rode him and bent over him and laughed and made the most delicious noises. She was beautiful. He looked at her with such reverence. They were, I think, actually in love.

The guy I was sleeping with came over for dinner. I sat him down and played the video and asked him if she looked like me.

He watched it for a few minutes, his eyes softening perceptively. Then he gently pried my hands off my laptop and folded down the screen. "Not really?" he said. "I mean, a little. But not really." His expression was inscrutable. He was a nice, kind person, and I could tell he was trying to find a nice, kind response. The problem was he didn't know what I was looking for.

"It wouldn't be bad if you said she did," I clarified. "I just want to know what I look like."

We started to kiss and lay down on my bed, but then he stopped and just held me, as if I was going somewhere.

Once during sex, a man pulled me on top of him. I resisted, worried I'd crush him. "I want to look up at you," he said. On the verge of coming, I covered my mouth, and he pulled it away and told me, "I want to hear you."

Another time, I took a guy home after a date and made him beg me to take my clothes off, just to see if I could do it. I could.

❀　❀　❀

We love to talk about fatness in the past. That is, about how it was desirable once. It proved you were wealthy or healthy or fertile, which is to say valuable, to someone.

But now, fatness is framed with deserving. Do you deserve to be treated like a person? Do you deserve respect? Do you deserve good healthcare? Do you deserve love? Clothes that fit? Stylish clothes that fit? Do you deserve to see yourself on a screen, on the page, in a photo, in a way that is not dehumanizing? Do you deserve to love yourself?

The world is getting fatter. We have never been bigger, or so obsessed with not being so. We compulsively talk about food in terms of shame and guilt; we structure entire industries around the way we think bodies ought to be. We respond to this trend—to ourselves—with denial and rage and hatred. But despite the onslaught of punishment, fatness always finds a way.

What is the value of the fat body, now? The question echoes everywhere. If you won't date it or flirt with it or dress it or fuck it or feed it or show it off or show it anywhere, then what? What are we supposed to do with all these fat people?

In 2014, the painter Fernando Botero, who has spent a career committing fat women's bodies to the canvas, told a Spanish newspaper, "I don't paint fat women. Nobody believes me but it is true. What I paint are volumes. When I paint a still life I also paint with volume, if I paint an animal it is volumetric, a landscape as well... I am interested in volume, the sensuality of form."

What is the difference between a fat woman and a voluminous one? Botero was being defensive, but he also accidentally gave us a new way to consider the body. Fat is an artifact of internal bodily processes, the result of a breakdown of chemicals that eventually push us outward. Volume is about taking up space in the world, displacing what is around us. Or, alternately, a level of loudness. Maybe the new body has nowhere to go but up.

I have an intermittent daydream in which I'm a queen straight out of an epic fantasy novel. I am draped in red silk and sit in a large baroque throne, crowned with a grandiose headdress dripping gemstones that tick tick tick like Yahtzee dice when I turn my head. My feet rest on snoozing bears. I am so fat I can only leave the throne on a palanquin, borne aloft by

20 men. I am so fat it takes the air out of the room. I am so fat no advisor tells me no. I am so fat would-be conquerors flee the room in fear. I am so fat the members of the court do their best to look like me by eating onions cooked in lard, but none can match my sweeping vista, my strength, my power. I am so fat I can take as many lovers as I please.

I am so fat that fatness becomes culturally inextricable from a firm, wise, no-nonsense attitude. I am so fat the citizens who come before me for advice or assistance feel safe in proximity to my orbit, and afterwards they go home to their families and tell their children that I am even larger and more exquisite in person. I am so fat their daughters shove pillows under their clothes during play and say "I'm the queen!" and then argue over how many monarchs are allowed during their game.

In *The Little Mermaid*, Ursula's final act was to become even bigger. She took up even more of the ocean, swelling larger than a skyscraper. She made the ocean rise. She brought sunken ships up from the floor, careened their wrecks around a whirlpool. She spoke of the waves obeying her whim, while the film's normies flopped around helplessly in the ocean. She was sorceress, queen, goddess. The beginning and the end. For a few minutes, she was everything.

But then, driven by his love for a woman he'd spent most of the film not knowing or forgetting about, Eric steered the scalpel of a broken ship's bow into the fattest roll of Ursula's torso. She died, dissolved into the ocean. Small, she was no longer a threat.

The unapologetic fat body is dangerous because, like so many other dangerous things, it suggests that there's another way—and that there has always been another way. I know what's happening, the unapologetic fat body says, taking your hand and pulling you away from the crowd. Come with me and I'll show you.

Apart from their fat bodies and dedicated attendants, what Ursula and Marjory have in common are their minds. One is calculating, ruthless, scheming; the other is irreverent, playful, wise. But they both earn devotion, respect, fear.

So the fat mind, too, is dangerous. It, too, suggests another path.

The writer Shirley Jackson had a great mind, and was also fat. She loved the pleasures of food, and "long flowing dresses in bright colors," wrote her biographer Ruth Franklin, dresses that "emphasized her bulk." A friend of Jackson's once said that she "took up literally half the sofa, but when she opened her mouth, everything changed... She was witty, brilliant, and she knew it and used it."

"But." That horrible little conjunction. A tiny, three-letter word that reduces Shirley Jackson to a contradiction—a fat woman who was also, strangely, witty and brilliant—instead of what she simply was: a brilliant, witty, fat woman. All of her qualities aligned.

Unapologetic fat women embrace the philosophy of displacement. They manifest the audacity of space-taking. They cleave the very air. This is not just fatness of the body, it is fatness of the mind. If you have a fat body, you take up room by default. If you have a fat mind, you choose to take up room.

Whenever I see a fat woman with a fat mind who is excellent in that fat way that I love, I want to be her handmaiden. I want to kiss her feet and the hem of her dress. To rub her aching shoulders. To follow after her on my knees with a dish of milk in my unworthy hands. I take second helpings, thirds. I order appetizers and desserts. I get excited about homemade pasta and pork belly and chocolate cake and dirty martinis and bowls of pickled things. Sometimes when I talk about food, people around me laugh with surprise. Subconsciously, I think, they're not expecting it; they're expecting restraint, apology. I refuse to give it to them.

For years, societal judgements about femme-style beauty hid my grandmother's lesson from me. Makeup is necessary as concealment but too much is deceptive, we are told. Jewelry and clothing exist to distract from our flaws. Our outsides must reflect our insides: ashamed. My grandmother's gaudy style drew attention to what it should have been hiding.

But now, when I paint my lips poison-red, or noose myself in pearls and rhinestones, or hook a heavy earring into the punctum of my pierced ear, I think about her. When I walk outside in sequins or faux fur, or dab perfume below my ear, I think about her. She did what she was told she did not deserve to do, and I love her for that: she sat at a vanity and looked at herself and defiantly made herself more.

It is true that when Ursula had to seduce Eric, she became young, dark-haired, slender Vanessa. Even she had to make perfunctory concessions to the world's deep-seated cultural norms. But when she sang in her boat-bedroom and skewered a wooden cherub with a hairpin and looked into her mirror, she was still Ursula—mouth open wide, laughing. And even though she had the power to be thin—literal magical power, the sort the weight-loss industry would sell its soul to her to obtain—her fat mind chose her fat body.

So when sun set on the heralded third day, she let the spell break. Not just the one that gave Ariel legs and Ursula a slender waistline, but also the one that everyone had been drifting under. She cackled and showed a boat full of aristocrats what they'd been missing. Her body split through her wedding gown, unmoored; a dam that could no longer contain the river of her.

Acknowledgements

Bruce

Putting a book together is a stressful process. There is absolutely no way I would have made it through without the understanding and support of my co-editors, Miguel M. Morales and Tiff Joshua TJ Ferentini. Thank you for your patience with me, your commitment to the project, and most of all, being super fun to work with. I couldn't imagine editing this book with anyone other than the two of you! I'm so proud of the book we've put together.

Jill, Marisol, Adrian, Sara, Naomi, Carolina, Leah, and Rosebud: thank you for all that you've done to make me feel safe and loved.

To my patrons: thank you for your support. You got me through some very tough times.

To the teachers who helped set me on my writing path and inspired me to stay there, especially Mary Grimm, Thrity Umrigar, Audrey Petty, and Deborah Miranda.

Thank you to Arielle Greenberg, Marisa Siegel, and everyone at *The Rumpus* who made it possible for me to start writing about my fatness and queerness, which led to this book.

Finally, to the fourth-grade version of me, who wanted to write a book for the Young Author's Program at school, who was told by his teacher that he was not smart enough to do so, and asked about it every day until his teacher gave in—thank you for your stubbornness and tenacity.

Miguel

I want to thank the fat queer activists of the past, who've been part of every social movement. You brought us to this moment where a book like *Fat and Queer: An Anthology of Queer and Trans Bodies and Lives* can hold space. Thank you to the fat queer activists in the present, who put themselves on the line holding it down in most trying times. Thank you to the fat queer activists of the future, who are expanding our space, our significance, our contributions, our legacy.

To my friend, Bruce Owens Grimm, who originated the *Fat & Queer* essay series, thank you for inviting me to contribute. We knew *Fat and Queer* was an anthology in the making, but would we do it? Could we do it? Thanks for taking the idea and making it real. Thank you for living openly and honestly. To my friend, Tiff Ferentini, who joined what began as an anthology but quickly became a mission, thank you for your organizational skills and keen eye. We didn't know you were our missing piece until your energy made everything work. I look forward to working with this team again. Perhaps on a sequel anthology? I'm just sayin'...

I especially want to acknowledge everyone who sent in work that was not accepted into this anthology. Your work was engaging and lovely. We had difficult choices to make. We hope you continue to be in touch with us because your voice is vital.

Thank you, Tony Valenzuela, for putting an application for

the Writers' Retreat for Emerging LGBTQ Voices in my hand. You changed my life. Thanks to Lambda Literary Foundation, Split This Rock, the Association of Writers & Writing Programs LGBTQ Writers Caucus, and any other writing organization that has welcomed me into their fold.

Jewel Gomez for liking my very first fat and queer poem. You don't know how much that lifted me and let me know I was on the right path. Crystal Boson, my fellow Texan and Kansan, thank you for being one of the first to embrace my fat poems and encourage me to write more of them. Ron Suresha for publishing my first fat and queer poems in *Hibernation, and Other Poems by Bear Bards*. Angie Manfredi for including me in *The (Other) F Word: A Celebration of the Fat & Fierce* and for having big dreams for me.

Roy G. Guzmán who invited me to co-edit *Pulse/Pulso: In Remembrance of Orlando*. With one word, you elevated me to an editor. That experience gave me the courage and drive to continue creating editing projects that lift marginalized voices and examine issues. Thank you for your continuing support. Dan Vera for always being a soft place to land, a strong but gentle presence, and for embracing, sharing, and showing emotions. Your tears and laughter and thoughtfulness teach me not only how to be a writer, but how to be a human. Everett Maroon for literally (and literarily) everything you do and for rocking those sweater vests. Ady del Valle for serving inspiration and lewks for fat queer brown bodies like mine.

Fat queer and trans writers that I know in real life who inspire me with their words, actions, and bodies: M-E Girard, Baruch

Porras-Hernandez, Rachel Wiley, and the late, but still maestro, Francisco X. Alarcón.

Fat queer and trans writers I've yet to meet in person but who also inspire me: Caleb Luna, David Bowles, Mathew Rodriguez, C. Adán Cabrera, and so many others. I'm ashamed to admit that my mind cannot remember them all, but my heart does.

The Latino Writers Collective and La Resistencia familia who taught me how to present and represent. You've given so many of our Midwest latinidad a voice, including me. Gracias.

And to my family, who accepts my queerness and my fatness and my weirdness, thank you. I love you.

Tiff

I would not be the proud, queer, trans, nonbinary writer I am today without having discovered the LGBTQ Writers Caucus community at the Association of Writers & Writing Programs (AWP), where I met Miguel M. Morales, or attended the 2014 Stories and Queer reading, where I met Bruce Owens Grimm. Back when I was still closeted, back when I was still searching for the words to define what kind of queer I was, the LGBTQ Writers Caucus—and the queer writing community I subsequently met through AWP—was my first found family. Whether in person or online, the space the LGBTQ Writers Caucus created was one where I could be my authentic, uncensored, queer self, and a platform where I could eventually exist as someone who was nonbinary, who was trans, who was fat—and where I could be proud not in spite of it, but because of it.

Through being queer, I learned to love myself.

To learn about, to love, and to accept the vessel known as my body has been something I have struggled with for my entire life. If not for Miguel and Bruce, I don't think I would be where I currently am on my journey toward self-love and acceptance. Thank you, my dearest co-editors, for not only allowing me to join you on this editorial journey, but for paving the road that I needed to finally tell the story of my fatness and my queerness, a narrative I didn't realize I needed to confront—and for creating this platform with which we could discover and unite so many amazing, beautiful, fat, queer voices. Without *Fat and Queer*, I think I'd still be wondering if I was *Enough*. Thank you.

To *Revolutionary Girl Utena*, for showing me that it was okay to want to be a prince instead of a princess.

To Julian Leslie Guarch, my dearest and queerest friend to have come out of attending AWP: thank you for your feedback on every single draft of not only the essay in this anthology, but for all my WIPs, for your consistent words of encouragement, our Sunday Discord writing sessions, and last but not least, your friendship.

To Elizabeth Eslami, the best thesis advisor I could ever ask for, and a mentor who was profound in shaping my identity as a writer today: Liz, after waking up every single day of my grad school career asking myself if I might be gay, I came out to myself and finally accepted my queerness while sitting in the audience celebrating the release of your short story collection, *Hibernate*. I'll hold that night and the feeling of relief when I came to that revelation in my heart always, as well as the moment when you came up to me after sitting in the audience of my 2016 AWP panel on writing resistance, and I burst into tears when I saw you. Whenever I begin to falter and doubt myself as a writer, or worry that I'm not "queer enough" to be a queer writer, I look back on all the guidance and mentorship you offered me, and find the strength to persist and move forward.

To every stranger, family member, or medical professional who has met me with transphobia: I get no greater joy in life than knowing that my very existence discomforts you. On the days when I find the act of my sitting down to write is fueled by spite, I'd like to thank you for kindling that flame.

And finally, to all the baby gays who read this anthology: I hope the words and stories within these pages help you find those of your own, and that you never, ever stop loving yourself for who you are.

List of Contributors

Eddy Francisco Alvarez Jr. was raised in North Hollywood, California and has lived in New Mexico, Virginia, Puerto Rico, upstate New York, and Portland, Oregon. He is a first-generation college student, and his parents are immigrants from Cuba and Mexico. He is an educator, writer, cat parent, and currently an assistant professor of Chicanx Studies at California State University, Fullerton. His academic and creative writings have been published in *TSQ, Journal of Lesbian Studies, Revista Bilingue/ Bilingual Review, Label Me Latina/o*, and the edited book, *Queer in Aztlan: Chicano Male Recollections of Consciousness and Coming Out*. He is working on a collection of essays and poems about family, fatness, and his queer childhood.

M.P. Armstrong is a disabled queer poet from Ohio, studying English and United States history at Kent State University. They enjoy traveling, board games, and brightly colored blazers. Their work has been published or is forthcoming in *Neon Mariposa Magazine, Riggwelter, Thimble Literary Magazine,* and others. Their debut chapbook about childhood in the Midwest, *Who Lives Like This for Such a Cheap Price?*, is published by Flower Press (2021). Find them online @mpawrites and at mpawrites. wixsite.com/website.

Jay Audrey is a poet, a novelist, a survivor, and a lot of other things they haven't yet discovered but are constantly trying to. They earned their degree in creative writing from Columbia College and have no idea what that's supposed to mean or show about them. Their work is about the connection between pain and joy, truth and trauma, self and other.

C. Adán Cabrera is a Salvadoran-American writer and translator based in Barcelona, Spain. Among other publication credits, Carlos's writing has appeared in *Switchback*, *The Acentos Review*, *From Macho to Mariposa: New Gay Latino Fiction*, *BorderSenses*, *Parentheses*, *Spanglish Voces*, and *Kweli*. His short story collection, *Books Can Only Take You So Far*, explores the complex intersections of race, class, and sexuality. A 2011 Lambda Literary Fellow, Carlos holds an MFA from the University of San Francisco and a bachelor's degree in English from UCLA. Born and raised in Los Angeles, Carlos is currently working on his second collection of short fiction. Visit him online at www.cadancabrera.net

Provvidenza Catalano is a fat, queer, genderful, multidisciplinary performance artist and organizer living in Los Angeles. Provvidenza's work centers on the intersections of queerness, gender, fat bodies, chronic illness, and the search for emotional fullness.

Fletcher Cullinane is a writer and editor. He has published several essays and a full-length nonfiction book under his orthonym.

Nora E. Derrington is a lecturer in English at Washburn University, where she teaches composition, creative writing, literature, and film. Their work has appeared in *Hobart*, *North Dakota Quarterly*, *The Future Fire*, the anthology *Poems for the Queer Revolution*, and elsewhere, and she reviews fantasy, horror, romance, and science fiction titles for *Publishers Weekly*. They live with their wife—the writer Izzy Wasserstein—and a collection of companion animals who insist on using her as a pillow.

Tiff Joshua TJ Ferentini is a graduate of Manhattanville College's MFA Program, a 2019 Lambda Literary Emerging Writers Fellow, and one of the co-editors of *Fat and Queer: An Anthology of Queer and Trans Bodies and Lives*. Their writing has appeared in *The Gambler*, *Off the Rocks: The LGBTQ Anthology of Newtown Writers Press*, and *Songs of My Selfie: An Anthology of Millennial Writing*. They live in New York, and can be found on Twitter and Instagram @Ferenteeny.

Ruth Gibbs is a queer, fat Texan who dreams of one day running away to live with the fairies in Scotland. The folklore and stories of world cultures inspire much of her writing, as do her two bachelor's degrees in History and Anthropology. Ruth is an animist and practitioner of folk magic, and an active member of her local pagan community. She enjoys studying witchcraft and magic in her free time. When not reading fairy tales she can be found spending time with her wife or scribbling in her collection of notebooks. This is her first published piece of poetry.

Bruce Owens Grimm's haunted queer essays have appeared in *The Rumpus, Ninth Letter, Entropy, AWP's Writer's Notebook, Iron Horse Literary Review, Older Queer Voices, Ghost City Review*, and elsewhere. He is a co-editor of *Fat and Queer: An Anthology of Queer and Trans Bodies and Lives*. Based in Chicago, he has taught his Haunted Memoir: What Ghosts Reveal About Life workshop at StoryStudio Chicago and at Arizona State University's Virginia G. Piper Center for Creative Writings Desert Nights, Rising Stars conference, which named him a 2020 Desert Nights Rising Stars Fellow. He can be found on Twitter @bruceowensgrimm.

Roy G. Guzmán was born in Tegucigalpa, Honduras, and grew up in Miami, Florida. They are a 2019 National Endowment for the Arts fellow. Their debut collection, *Catrachos*, was published by Graywolf Press in 2020. They currently live in Minneapolis, Minnesota.

Leah Harris is a mad, fat, queer, and nonbinary writer illuminating suppressed and hidden narratives from the past, present, and future.

Jonathan Hillman is a graduate of Hamline University's Writing for Children and Young Adults MFA program, where he won the Walden Pond Press Award for Excellence in Middle Grade Fiction. His debut picture book, *Big Wig*, is forthcoming from Simon & Schuster in Spring 2022. He lives near Minneapolis, Minnesota, with his two cats. He can be found on Instagram and Twitter @jhillmanbooks.

Benny Hope is a 34-year-old disabled, nonbinary trans writer, painter, and autobiographical comic artist. Their work touches on subjects such as body image, gender, mental health, disability, and sobriety. They currently live in Eugene, Oregon.

D. Nolan Jefferson is an academic librarian and writer based in Washington, D.C. His prose appears or is forthcoming in *Tahoma Literary Review*, *Red Savina Review*, *Orca Literary*, *Empty Mirror*, *Hobart Pulp*, and elsewhere. He is an AWP Intro Journal Project Award winner, a 2019 Kimbilio Fiction fellow, and enjoys tacos, collecting records, and fellow introverts.

Caleb Luna is a fat queer (of color) critical theorist, artist, and performance scholar. As a PhD candidate in performance studies at UC Berkeley, their research focuses on performances of eating, and historicizing cultural representations of fat embodiment within the ongoing settler colonization of North America. As an activist political thinker, they are interested in engaging embodied difference as a generative resource toward fatter understandings of collective freedom. You can find their writing online at *Black Girl Dangerous*, *Everyday Feminism*, and *The Body Is Not An Apology*. Their print publications include *Nepantla: An Anthology Dedicated to Queer Poets of Color* (2018); *Canadian Art* (Winter 2018); and the anthology *Queer Nightlife* (2021).

Carmen Maria Machado is the author of the bestselling memoir *In the Dream House* and the short story collection *Her Body and Other Parties*. She has been a finalist for the National Book Award and the winner of the Bard Fiction Prize, the Lambda Literary Award for Lesbian Fiction, the Lambda Literary Award for LGBTQ Nonfiction, the Brooklyn Public Library Literature Prize, the Shirley Jackson Award, and the National Book Critics Circle's John Leonard Prize. In 2018, *The New York Times* listed *Her Body and Other Parties* as a member of "The New Vanguard," one of "15 remarkable books by women that are shaping the way we read and write fiction in the 21st century."

Edward Kelsey Moore lives and writes in Chicago, where he also enjoys a career as a professional cellist. His short fiction has appeared in numerous literary magazines and has been performed on national public radio. Edward is the author of *The Supremes Sing the Happy Heartache Blues* and *The New York Times'* bestseller *The Supremes At Earl's All-You-Can-Eat*.

Miguel M. Morales grew up in Texas working as a migrant/seasonal farmworker. He is a Lambda Literary Fellow and an alum of VONA/ Voices and the Macondo Writers Workshops. Miguel's work that centers on fatness and queerness appears in *From Macho to Mariposa: New Gay Latino Fiction*, *Hibernation and Other Poems by Bear Bards*, *Imaniman: Poets Writing in the Anzaldúan Borderlands*, and *The (Other) F Word: A Celebration of the Fat & Fierce*. He is the co-editor of *Pulse/Pulso: In Remembrance of Orlando* and of *Fat and Queer: An Anthology of Queer and Trans Bodies and Lives*. Follow him on social media as @TrustMiguel.

Ninamarie Ochoa is a queer xicana born in El Paso, Texas. She completed her bachelor's degree in English at Oxford University and the University of Texas at Austin, and her master's degree in the humanities at the University of Chicago. Ninamarie finds joy in heart-to-hearts with her students, the smell of creosote when it rains, and being mimis by 9pm. Ninamarie currently lives in San Diego, California, where she teaches high school and chairs her school's English department. Her work has appeared in *Last Exit* and *MALA FOREVER*.

Nicole Oquendo is a writer and visual artist that combines these elements, along with magical practice, to craft multimodal nonfiction, poetry, and fiction, as well as translations of these forms. Their work can be found in numerous literary journals, a hybrid memoir, and six chapbooks, including their other most recent works: *Space Baby: Episodes I–III* and *The Antichrist and I*. They are also an assistant editor for Sundress Publications, and their most recently curated anthology, *Manticore: Hybrid Writing from Hybrid Identities*, is available for free on the Sundress Publications' website.

Emilia Phillips is the author of four poetry collections from the University of Akron Press, including the forthcoming *Embouchure* (2021), and four chapbooks. She is winner of a 2019 Pushcart Prize and a 2019–2020 NC Arts Council Fellowship, and her poems, lyric essays, and book reviews appear widely in literary publications including *Agni*, *American Poetry Review*, *Gulf Coast*, *The Kenyon Review*, *New England Review*, *The New York Times*, *Ploughshares*, *Poetry*, *Publishers Weekly*, and elsewhere. She's an Assistant Professor of Creative Writing at UNC Greensboro.

Hannah Propp is a queer, fat, femme author and therapist. Hannah seeks to write about futures and realities where queer and trans lives, fat bodies, and femme expression are allowed to manifest to the fullest extent of their magic. "Fat Queer Freaks" and "To All the Fat Queers on the First Day of School" are Hannah's first published pieces of short fiction and poetry. With a degree in Literature from SUNY Purchase College and a Masters in Social Work from the University of New England, Hannah has pursued these two paths with a foundational belief in the power of stories. Though raised in rural Vermont, Hannah now lives in Brooklyn, NY, with her spouse and elderly adopted cat, Professor.

Samantha Puc is a culture critic and essayist whose work focuses on LGBTQ and fat representation in pop culture. Her work has been featured in *Bitch, them., CBR, The Beat, The Mary Sue*, and elsewhere. Samantha is also the co-creator and editor-in-chief of *Fatventure Mag*, an outdoors zine for fat folx who are into being active, but not into toxic weight-loss culture.

Alyssah Roth is an anxious, fat, brown, Jew(ish) dyke born and raised on the border. She currently lives in Durham, where she works as a writing tutor and adjunct at a community college. Aside from a passion for writing, Alyssah loves food and cooking, particularly as a way to stay connected to home. Though an earth sign and a Texan desert rat, Alyssah always gravitates to water, which is where you will find her in the midst of the hot and humid southern summer, probably with a beer and her quarantine pod.

Alix Sanchez is a member of the Little Shell band of Ojibwe. Raised in the high desert of Montana, and transplanted to Portland, Oregon to flourish, they are a fierce, fat, two-spirit femme, parent, and poet. They write at the intersections of fatness, urban indigeneity, and femme identity. They have been published in *Plumplandia, PQ Monthly*, and most recently in *Survivance: Indigenous Poesis vol. 2*.

Haley Sherif is a creative nonfiction writer living in Boston, MA with her amazing girlfriend, C. Haley's writing has been featured on *The Rumpus, Hobart Pulp*, and elsewhere. You can find her on YouTube unboxing subscriptions and talking about books.

LJ Sitler lives in Maryland with their two cats and multiple hobbies and half-finished projects. They originally hail from Pennsylvania and have a passion for traveling. Professionally, they work in international education and seek to improve inclusion in the industry. They graduated from Susquehanna University in 2014 with a Bachelor of Arts in Creative Writing.

K.M. Steigleder is an advocate and activist focusing on fat-liberation, eating disorder recovery, and queerness. K.M. is a professional in higher education, working to create inclusive and equitable spaces for the marginalized. In K.M.'s free time, they can be found reading, watching a period or historical drama, enjoying time with their partner, or playing with their dog, Sidney, and kitty, Shamus. Connect with them at @km_ess to keep the conversation going!

Jerome Stueart is an artist and writer living in Columbus, Ohio. He has written stories and essays that have appeared in *The Magazine of Fantasy and Science Fiction*, *Fantasy*, *Lightspeed*, *Geist*, and other magazines.

Dan Vera is a first-generation, borderlands born Queer-Tejano Latinx writer, editor, and literary historian of Cuban/Caribbean ancestry. The recipient of the Oscar Wilde Award for Poetry and the Letras Latinas/Red Hen Poetry Prize, he's the co-editor of *Imaniman: Poets Writing in the Anzaldúan Borderlands* and author of two books of poetry. His work has been featured by the Poetry Foundation and the National Endowment for the Arts and in college and university curricula, various journals, and anthologies. A CantoMundo and Macondo Writing Fellow, Vera has been a featured reader around the country, including the Dodge Poetry Festival, the Poetry Foundation, and New York City's Poets House. The long-time chair of Split This Rock Poetry, he serves on the board of the AWP.

Sherre Vernon is a seeker of a mystical grammar and a recipient of the Parent-Writer Fellowship at the Martha's Vineyard Institute of Creative Writing. She has two award-winning chapbooks: *Green Ink Wings* (fiction) and *The Name is Perilous* (poetry). Readers describe Sherre's work as heartbreaking, richly layered, lyrical, and intelligent. To read more of her work visit www.sherrevernon.com/publications and tag her into conversation @sherrevernon.

Aubrey Gordon has been writing as **Your Fat Friend** since 2016, tackling the realities of moving through the world as an undeniably fat person. Her work has reached millions of readers and has been translated into 19 languages. She is a columnist with *SELF Magazine*, where she writes about health, weight stigma, and fatness. Her work has also been featured in *Health* magazine, *Vox*, and *Gay Mag*, among others. She lives in Oregon, where she writes and organizes. Connect with her at www.yourfatfriend. com, and as @yrfatfriend on Instagram, Twitter, and Facebook.